MW00997604

THE SIXTH DOCTOR SOURCEBOOK

CREDITS

LINE DEVELOPER: Gareth Ryder-Hanrahan

WRITING: Alasdair Stewart

EDITING: Andrew Kenrick

COVER: Paul Bourne

GRAPHIC DESIGN AND LAYOUT: Paul Bourne

CREATIVE DIRECTOR: Dominic McDowall

ART DIRECTOR: Jon Hodgson

SPECIAL THANKS: Georgie Britton and the BBC Team for all their help.

"My Sixth Is Accompanied By Two Alike"

The Sixth Doctor Sourcebook is published by Cubicle 7 Entertainment Ltd (UK reg. no.6036414).

Find out more about us and our games at www.cubicle7.co.uk

CONTENTS

INTRODUCTION 4

CHAPTER ONE: AND NOT A MOMENT TOO SOON! 5
The 1980s 8
Adventure Seeds 10

CHAPTER TWO: THE SIXTH DOCTOR AND COMPANIONS 13
The Sixth Doctor 14
Perpugilliam 'Peri' Brown 15
Melanie Bush 15
The Sixth Doctor's TARDIS 16
New Traits 17
New Time Lord Tricks 18

CHAPTER THREE: THE SIXTH DOCTOR'S ADVENTURES 19
The Twin Dilemma 20
Attack of the Cybermen 26
Vengeance on Varos 37
The Mark of the Rani 48
The Two Doctors 58
Timelash 69
Revelation of the Daleks 82

CHAPTER FOUR: THE TRIAL OF A TIME LORD 94
The Valeyard and the Justice Station 95
The Many Origins of the Valeyard 102
Campaign Seed 105
The Mysterious Planet 109
Mindwarp 120
Terror of the Vervoids 132
The Ultimate Foe 143

APPENDIX: THE SIXTH DOCTOR AND THE TIME WAR 154

INDEX 158

INTRODUCTION

'I am a living peril to the universe!'

Flamboyant, arrogant and at first a little frightening, the Sixth Doctor exploded into life following his predecessor's heroic sacrifice on Androzani. His extraordinary dress sense and self-confidence carried him through a rough regeneration, and an even rougher first adventure before he was up and off at a sprint, heading out into the universe to see what he could do.

The Sixth Doctor encountered the Daleks and foiled one of their most evil plans, met an old enemy turned ally and battled the Cybermen of Mondas and helped his second incarnation and Jamie McCrimmon defeat a Sontaran plan to create a working time machine. He clashed with the reptilian Sil twice, returned to Karfel to help solve a problem from his third incarnation and, ultimately fought for his life in a Gallifreyan court against the one enemy he never expected to face: himself.

In this book you'll find details of the Sixth Doctor, his companions, his friends and enemies and all his adventures. So climb aboard the TARDIS, and, although it's tempting, don't make fun of his clothes. Because the Sixth Doctor has an incredible journey ahead of him and you're coming along for the ride.

HOW TO USE THIS BOOK

This book is designed to be a guide to the Sixth Doctor and his era as well as showing you how to incorporate his era into your own adventures.

Chapter One: And Not a Moment Too Soon! describes how to do just that – what makes a Sixth Doctor adventure different from those experienced by his other incarnations. **Chapter Two: The Sixth Doctor and Companions** is packed with character sheets and information on the Doctor and his companions, Peri Brown and Melanie Bush, as well as new traits and tricks for a Time Lord to pull off. **Chapter Three: The Sixth Doctor's Adventures** describes his adventures, while **Chapter 4: The Trial of a Time Lord** takes a look at the series of linked adventures that ended the Sixth Doctor's era, including advice for how to run the trial as a mini-campaign, as well as the seeds for a new campaign.

Each one of these adventures is broken down into the following sections:

- **Synopsis:** Where did the TARDIS materialise? Who was the Doctor with? Who did they meet? What did they discover and how did they solve the problem? This section details each adventure as experienced by the Sixth Doctor and his companions so you can use the events in your own adventures.

- **Running the Adventure:** Here, we discuss each adventure and look at the challenges in how to run it. These sections highlight challenges, big events, pitfalls and alternatives to let you temper the Sixth Doctor's adventures to your own approach.

- **Characters, Monsters and Gadgets:** details the people,creatures and things that the Sixth Doctor meets so you can use them in your own adventures.

- **Further Adventures:** Don't want to run the adventure as it is here? No problem! Three further adventures are seeded in this section, taking characters, ideas or events from the original and building them into a sequel.

Finally, the **Appendix: The Sixth Doctor and the Time War**, discusses how to use the Sixth Doctor's adventures to foreshadow what is to come, as well as presenting some more adventure seeds.

CHAPTER ONE
AND NOT A MOMENT TOO SOON!

"Ahhh... a noble brow. Clear gaze. At least it will be given a few hours sleep. A firm mouth. A face beaming with a vast intelligence. My dear child what on Earth are you complaining about? It's the most extraordinary improvement."

Running Sixth Doctor adventures, or even using the Sixth Doctor as an NPC in an adventure of your own, can be tricky. He's not just unlikeable, he's actively a little frightening in his first few appearances and that can make things very difficult for you, to say nothing of the characters that have to deal with him.

When you look at his adventures though, you start to understand why the Sixth Doctor was like he was. He was a man facing a darkening universe, and one where no one, not even his own companions, could be entirely trusted. Some of his bluster was armour, an attempt to protect himself and his friends from the dreadful consequences if he failed. Some of it, it being the Sixth Doctor, was just bluster.

"REST IS FOR THE WEARY, SLEEP IS FOR THE DEAD. I FEEL LIKE A HUNGRY MAN *EAGER* FOR THE FEAST!"

The Fifth Doctor died as he was born; with a combination of polite bravery and sadness. However, polite is the last word you could use to describe his brash, over-confident successor. The Sixth Doctor's regeneration was traumatic to say the least, the spectrox toxaemia sustained on Androzani causing massive damage to his body. As a result, the Sixth Doctor didn't so much enter the world kicking and screaming as he did loudly and repeatedly proclaiming his relief at being born at all.

This appeared, for some time, as a combination of cruelty and arrogance and it was only after a series of disastrous mood swings that the Sixth Doctor settled down. Even then, Peri took a long time to finally trust him and his mordant sense of humour and ruthless streak could still be disturbing. It was only towards the end of his life, with Mel and Glitz, that he softened, beginning to accept not only his place in the universe but that of others.

Not only that but he learnt a salient point: that his own people were at least as bad as any of the evils he'd faced. His trial was an incredibly traumatic experience for a Doctor who had been born out of the fires of Androzani. He was forced to confront not only the corruption of the Time Lords but the possibility that his whole life had done more harm than good and, terrifyingly, that Peri had lost her life as a result. Whilst he was ultimately vindicated, it's interesting how much more kindly he treated Mel. Whilst we never see how they meet, there's none of the posturing that marked his early life with Peri. Instead, the Doctor is a sadder, more cautious figure, ready to leave at the first sign of danger rather than running headlong towards it. Whilst he ultimately returns to his troublemaking ways, it's interesting to see the changes he undergoes.

It's particularly interesting when you realise that ***Terror of the Vervoids*** shows us the aftermath of the trial, during the trial. This is a Doctor whose confidence and arrogance are tempered by how close he comes to losing a companion, the clear implication that he never returns to visit her and the burden of responsibility he feels for her replacement. That emotional journey is a fascinating one and means you can use the Sixth Doctor in very nearly any way you want to. The brash, occasionally violent figure of the first couple of adventures would be a fantastic foil for another Time Lord or could even be a well-meaning, friendly adversary. The quieter, more reticent man of his later years could serve very well as a mentor to a younger Time Lord or group of time travellers, someone who could provide advice or aid when needed, but doesn't feel comfortable doing so without being asked.

Alternatively, a Sixth Doctor haunted – or indeed taken over by the Valeyard – after his trial would be a terrifying opponent. Balancing intelligence and flamboyance with malice and cruelty, he could work as a dark mentor figure, a man quite happy throwing his younger charges at awful events to 'toughen them up' for what's coming.

Similarly, the Sixth Doctor could work as a fascinating authority figure for a Gallifrey-based or Gallifrey-heavy campaign. Whilst the manic, barely under control figure of his first adventure would be a disaster, the considered, often cunning operator of his later adventures would be a real asset to both a character group and Gallifrey.

When playing the Sixth Doctor, the three key elements are: flamboyance, his companions and the alien. The flamboyance is expressed by everything from his coat to how he talks to people. The Sixth Doctor is a man who makes a statement walking into a room, and then makes that statement another couple of times just in case nobody heard him. His confidence walks hand in hand with that, and is shown in every single one of his adventures. There are few incarnations of the Doctor more willing to stare down an enemy, and even fewer more willing to take incredibly dangerous risks. After all, it's the Sixth Doctor who pretends to defect halfway through the events on Thoros Beta and the Sixth Doctor who, when offered the Gallifreyan presidency a third time, turns it down. This is a man with nothing left to prove, and, weirdly, he insists on keeping proving that fact.

"CIRCULAR LOGIC WILL ONLY MAKE YOU DIZZY, DOCTOR."

If the Sixth Doctor's brief life is defined by change, then one of the few constants are his companions. Peri Brown and Melanie Bush met the Sixth Doctor at drastically different times but their effect on him was remarkably similar.

Peri is one of the great unsung heroines of the TARDIS crew, if nothing else because she'd barely arrived when the Fifth Doctor not only died but was reborn as a very different man. Still reeling from the true nature of the universe being revealed to her, Peri found herself facing down a Doctor with wild mood swings, who even attacked her at one point. Whilst he eventually stabilised, the traumatic nature of Peri's early days in the TARDIS would be enough to drive anyone to ask to go home. The Doctor didn't exactly make matters easy for her either, constantly belittling her or making assumptions on her behalf.

For all that though, Peri didn't just stay, she flourished. She encountered Daleks, Cybermen, Sontarans, a carnivorous Androgum, Sil and the end of Earth itself and whilst she was never unafraid she never backed down. Even her final, nightmarish trip to Thoros Beta showed just how tough she was. Apparently abandoned by the Doctor, she worked with Yrcanos, contacted the rebels and ultimately led a rebellion that freed the Warrior King and the Thoros Alphans and helped ensure Crozier's conscious transferral machine would never be perfected. No wonder she ended up a Krontep Warrior Queen.

Playing Peri at the start of her time in the TARDIS is very different to playing her towards the end. Early on, she's the constant target of the Sixth Doctor's verbal fury but she never backs down, as time goes on, starts giving just as good as she gets. By the time they arrive on Ravolox, Peri's a seasoned, traveller, a woman fully capable of looking after herself in even the harshest situations and, often, bringing the Doctor down to Earth too. She's compassionate, painfully honest and more than a little sarcastic and those qualities only increase as time goes by.

Just as Peri meets the Sixth Doctor at the start of his life, Mel meets him towards the end. He's a very different man by then too, and Mel's one of the reasons why. There's no battle for intellectual superiority as there was with Peri; she's an equal the first time we meet her. Mel's boundless enthusiasm, complete honesty and love of physical exercise are all immediate, visceral things and they're a neat contrast to the Doctor. Like Peri, she keeps him grounded but, where Peri slows the Doctor down, Mel continually speeds him up. The caution and reticence he feels post trial is continually blown away by Mel running headlong into danger, just like, deep down he wants to. They both help him grow, and heal, but do so in entirely different ways. Or, to put it another way, Peri stops him getting into too much trouble and Mel stops him getting into too little.

THE 1980S

The Sixth Doctor doesn't spend a lot of time on Earth, but the concerns of the time period, and the sense of the alien that was common during that decade, are present in all his adventures. Each one is flamboyant, the villains' schemes all exponentially larger than they arguably need to be. That's your first hook into how to run adventures in this time period; go big and stay there. A villain wants to escape the solar system? He blows up the sun to propel his ship out. Earth being choked by a Vervoid? The characters have to help UNIT deploy solar mirrors across the entire moon to overload it with sunlight, whilst simultaneously fighting off the Cybermen Expeditionary Force still stationed there. These adventures are crammed full of massive ideas and if you're not running headlong at all of them you're missing some real fun. Throw everything in, all the time and never let your characters draw breath.

At the same time, don't give them anything to rely on. The trial finishes with the revelation that the Time Lord High Council have committed an all but unforgivable act and they're far from the only ones.

The good work done by Tranquil Repose and the food factories is powered by Davros, not one but two hijackers are waiting for their chance aboard the Hyperion III and not even the Doctor's old friends can be relied upon to be happy to see him. This is a universe where danger is around every corner, double cross piled on triple cross until the only thing you know for sure is what side you're on. Have NPCs betray them, then cross back over (evening, Mr Glitz) and don't be afraid to question the Doctor's loyalty either.

Even the Doctor's legacy is under threat. As well as the Valeyard and the apparent death of the Second Doctor this set of adventures also features a return to Karfel and the discovery that the Third Doctor inadvertently enabled the creation of the Borad. The Doctor causes damage as well as heals it, and that's something that will become central once you get to the trial. Keep him as a mercurial, alien figure and don't be afraid to have situations make him look bad in the short term for the long-term pay-off.

Be prepared to go to extremes. Look at the death of Peri, an event that affects the Sixth Doctor so profoundly that even after it's confirmed her death was an illusion, he's so cautious that he actively wants to avoid an adventure. That sense of mortality, somewhere out in the dark, waiting is something that runs through the entirety of the Sixth Doctor's adventures. People die badly and often as a result of the Doctor's actions. He kills two people – the Cyber Controller and Shockeye directly – which is about as shocking a difference from the Tenth Doctor's 'Man Who Never Would' approach as you can get. This is a dark time, and getting darker and the Doctor reacts to that both through his actions and his jet black sense of humour. Use this to focus on his unpredictable nature. The Doctor is consumed with guilt for killing the Vervoids one minute and quipping as people die around him the next. He's feeling the turn of the universe but, at this time in his life, he's maybe also hearing the sound of the drums.

Finally, balancing the growing darkness is the sort of cheerful excess that suits the Sixth Doctor down to the ground. The faded glory of the Hyperion III is a great example of this, as is Lytton planning a £10 million heist just to get to the Cybermen. Best of all, you have the Borad creating a stable time corridor and never using it for anything other than the occasional execution and Sil enabling the death of people on Varos just to get a better price for the Zeiton-7.

This is a time of massive growth and innovation to the point where some people are growing bored of it and use both that sensation, and the dangerous boredom that goes with it to give the Sixth Doctor's adventures a unique, epic and on occasion unsettling feel. This is a time where everything's possible and nothing's forbidden. Make your villains huge and their plots colossal, make the actions the Doctor needs to take all but impossible and most of all make everything as stylish as possible. This is an era that wears its hearts on its multi-coloured sleeves, and so should you.

THE CALM BEFORE THE STORM

This is discussed in much more detail in the Appendix: The Sixth Doctor and the Time War, but there's a lot of interesting recurrent events during his era. He deals with not one but two illegal time machines, major military operations from the Daleks, Cybermen and Sontarans, and the Time Lords' unthinkable actions. If you chose to, you could tie those events together very strongly to create a very different kind of campaign, one focused on the opening shots of the Time War taking place in an era before anyone has really noticed them.

ADVENTURE SEEDS

VAULT OF THE DALEKS

The TARDIS arrives aboard the HMS *Fort*, a secret British aircraft carrier. Co-run by the Royal Navy and UNIT, the *Fort* is en route to the South Pole to investigate the lack of radio contact from a UNIT Science team stationed there. The TARDIS crew are welcomed aboard but the *Fort* soon runs into trouble. The Science Team has discovered a sealed vault, partially exposed by the ice and clearly of alien design. When they open it, they discover thousands of Daleks inside, all dormant. As the crew of the *Fort* clash over whether to destroy the Daleks or use them, the Doctor and his companions must work out why the vault's there and what the Daleks' real plan is.

Notable Characters

Captain Tobias Garske, the commander of the *Fort*, who has orders to retrieve the Science Team and bring them home at any cost.

Professor Nathan Hood, the head of the Science Team and the first Scientific Advisor UNIT has had since the departure of the Doctor. Hood's desperate to make a name for himself and views the Daleks as an opportunity to do just that.

Professor Hannah Bracewell, the deputy head of the Science Team and adopted granddaughter of the late Professor Bracewell. She recognises the Ironsides for what they are and is torn between assisting Hood in bringing them home and helping Commander Crossley bury them forever.

Commander Elaina Crossley, the first female UNIT field commander, Crossley is career military and lost her mother to a Dalek attack. She has no truck with aliens of any kind and resents the Doctor for not being able to save her mother.

Dalek Kine, a caretaker left behind to look after the vault. Kine has been awake for thousands of years, has been programmed to have a slightly more palatable voice and is quite mad.

Things to Do

Helping the *Fort* out of an ice floe, hacking the door to the vault, accessing the vault's computers, confronting Kine, deactivating the vault Daleks, reasoning with Hood, persuading Bracewell to help, winning over Crossley.

Action Scenes

Bailing out flooded compartments and rescuing crew members on the *Fort*, chase through the vault with Daleks activating the whole time, snowmobile/ Dalek chase, fighting off the Daleks attempting to board the *Fort*, covering the scientists trying to send the mass deactivation signal.

Problems

The Dalek vault is a honey trap designed to lure in anyone with the equipment to detect it. The Daleks held inside are an expendable force consisting of failed mutants, dissidents and lunatics who will do anything they can to prove their worth. Kine is psychic and can hypnotise people into doing what he wants. The Daleks are planning to take the *Fort* and use it as a staging post to destroy the planet.

EVERYTHING, OR NEAREST OFFER

The Doctor is asked to attend the first meeting of the Third Zone Worlds' Senate on behalf of Gallifrey. When he gets there, he's not only surprised to find an Androgum representative but no sign of Sil. That changes halfway through the meeting when the Mentor makes his grand entrance, accompanied by Lord Kiv, apparently now in Yrcanos' body.

Sil announces the GMC are planning to buy the sector outright and evict each race from their 'property'. Now, the Doctor must find a way to stop the takeover, defend the first world to be cleared, Androgum, from Sil's Slab henchmen and try and put Yrcanos back in his own body.

Notable Characters

Loosene, the Androgum delegate and the first Androgum to voluntarily undergo Dastari's TA process. She's completely at peace with her Androgum nature and uses her career to sate her love of combat and sensation. She's a controversial figure but much more trustworthy than she first appears.

Mykan Dastari, the son of the late Dastari and the Camera Station representative, Mikan wants to fulfil his father's work and make the Third Zone into a hotbed of scientific innovation. He's secretly in league with Sil, but can be persuaded to change sides.

Sil, the Mentor representative, is as ruthless as ever, riding the wave of success from his 'Slab' androids all the way up to a senior position in the business. However, Sil has a secret, one that he's banking this huge action will distract people from. Somewhere in the Third Zone is the legendary world of Azure, the largest precious stone in the universe. The core of a gas giant that was burned away by a supernova, Azure is a sapphire 1500 kilometres wide. Its value is immeasurable and this one Sil wants all for himself

Lord Kiv, who is not in fact Lord Kiv. He's Yrcanos, being fed the sort of information that Lord Kiv would know via a mental implant. Lord Kiv died following Yrcanos' rescue of Peri and escaped with her back to Krontep. Sil tracked him down and, using illegal technology to blot out Krontep's sun, forced the warlord to pretend to be Kiv in order to close the deal. If he succeeds, then Sil will let Krontep live. If he fails, it freezes.

Peri, who made it off Krontep before the sun was cloaked and is intent on saving her husband and ending Sil once and for all. Whilst she survived, she's still furious at the Doctor and when she sees him at the talks, will be openly hostile.

Things to Do

Free the delegates from the Slab team sent to 'guard' them, break out of Camera Station, deactivate the Slabs keeping the staff in place, persuade Dastari to change sides, track down Azure, realise Lord Kiv isn't who he says he is, reunite with Peri.

Action Scenes

Chase through Camera Station followed by the Slabs, escape from the GMC pursuit fleet sent after the TARDIS, race through the streets of Androgum to find the Slab control point before the eviction is complete, hold off the Slabs whilst the control point is shut down, stop Peri from assassinating Sil and attacking the Doctor, spacewalk out to the ships projecting the cloak over Krontep's sun and disable them before the radiation eats through the character's spacesuits

Problems

Sil has booby trapped Yrcanos' earpiece to kill him if he tries to rebel. Yrcanos may not be able to help himself.

DARKNESS AT THE EDGE OF TIME

The TARDIS materialises on a Gallifreyan Hospital TARDIS. The Doctor is astonished, even more so when he realises it's the far future. The crew of the Hospital TARDIS explain that they're a volunteer group who left Gallifrey centuries before the Time War to study the end of time and provide comfort to the people trapped there. But there's something strange going on.

Several of the crew seem to have the same memories, the ship is most definitely not bigger on the inside, one of the patients, an Androgum man, is desperate to warn the Doctor about what's about to happen, and, outside the ship, the final stars in the universe are about to go out. What no one realises yet is what's waiting in the darkness for when they do.

Notable Characters

The Matron, head of the ship and a combination of Priest, Scientist and Doctor. She's a concerned, compassionate woman apparently in her late fifties. In reality, she's an Auton carrying the consciousness of a long-dead Time Lady. Most of her crew are too and whilst they're aware, none of them want to admit it to the only remaining Time Lord crewmember, Ratchen, for fear of how he'll react.

Ratchen, a young male nurse heading the principle treatment team. Ratchen is on his third life but remains young and rash, constantly rushing towards danger. He suspects there's something wrong with his crew, and is becoming increasingly disturbed.

Shockbrow (the descendent of Shockeye from ***The Two Doctors***) has dreamt of the Doctor his whole life, as have his entire family. For generations they've waited for their chance to thank the man who began the Androgum Revolution and have approached every Time Lord they could to try and find the Doctor. Now, at last, Shockbrow has met him and has a message: the Doctor's life is in terrible danger.

The Patient in Room 12.5 is swathed from head to foot in bandages. In reality, he's the Valeyard, who was severely injured when the Matrix exploded and only escaped through the connection it still has to the Reave Father's onboard Matrix. He used his copy of the Key of Rassilon to open a door to the material universe and stumbled aboard the hospital ship via the Reave Father's Matrix (which is still connected to the Gallifreyan one) and was severely injured.

He was saved by the hospital ship and has been recuperating ever since, waiting to be strong enough to summon the Doctor. He was able to plant a Stattenheim remote on the Doctor's TARDIS and summoned it here to try and steal his remaining lives once again.

The Reave Father, an ancient weapon mill designed to fight in the first Time War. The Matrix aboard it has long since decayed and now all it has is one word – 'Reave' – and the order to clean its weapon forges. Only now, it's convinced the universe is its forge and it must be wiped clean.

The Reaved are creatures with nowhere else to go, the ghosts of lost timelines and neverweres, the last of their species. The lucky ones find a new purpose in life and work out how to carry on. The unlucky ones find themselves at the end of their tether and on the outskirts of the known universe. There, the Reave Father comes to them and make them an offer; live forever, eat forever, help put the universe out of its misery. No one ever says no and now the Reaved number in the trillions, waiting to do the last thing they can do; consume the remains of the universe and make creation ready for the next one.

Things to Do

Exploring the TARDIS, helping treat the patients, helping repair damage following a meteorite strike, exploring the surrounding area, talking down Ratchen, discovering Shockbrow, breaking him out, discovering the Valeyard, trying to find the deactivation switch for the Autons, working out how to keep them alive without them trying to kill the characters, researching the Reaved, negotiating with the Reave Father, working out how to stop them.

Action Scenes

Rescuing patients from a meteorite strike, fighting off Shockbrow, confronting the Valeyard, chasing him to the Reave Father, fighting off the Reaved, entering the Reave Father's internal Matrix, defeating the Valeyard.

Problems

The Valeyard is strong enough to psychically control the Autons, ordering them to attack the characters and each other.

CHAPTER TWO
THE SIXTH DOCTOR AND COMPANIONS

THE SIXTH DOCTOR

ATTRIBUTES

Attribute	Score
AWARENESS	4
COORDINATION	3
INGENUITY	7
PRESENCE	5
RESOLVE	4
STRENGTH	3

SKILLS

Skill	Score	Skill	Score
ATHLETICS	3	MEDICINE	3
CONVINCE	4	SCIENCE	5
CRAFT	2	SUBTERFUGE	4
FIGHTING	3	SURVIVAL	2
KNOWLEDGE	4	TECHNOLOGY	4
MARKSMAN	2	TRANSPORT	4

BIODATA

PERSONAL GOAL

To exceed the successes of his predecessors and be recognised for his greatness.

PERSONALITY

The Sixth Doctor is brash, arrogant, endlessly confrontational and completely convinced of his own genius. He's also, beneath it, a profoundly compassionate man desperate to do right by the people closest to him. Initially a little forgetful due to his regeneration, he soon grows into a natural figure of authority, albeit one with a truly black sense of humour.

BACKGROUND

The Sixth Doctor and his companion Peri Brown (and, later, Mel Bush) travel the universe, exploring, meeting new people, visiting new places and getting involved in trouble at the first opportunity they can.

TRAITS

Adversary (The Valeyard)
Argumentative
Artron Battery
Bio-rhythmic Control
Boffin
Brave
Code of Conduct
Distinctive
Eccentric
Feel the Turn of the Universe
Hypnosis (Minor)
Impulsive
Indomitable
Insatiable Curiosity
Loud (Minor Bad)
Psychic
Random Regenerator
Resourceful Pockets
Sesquipedalian (Minor Bad)
Technically Adept
Temporal Amnesia
Time Lord (Experienced x5)
Time Traveller (All)
Tough
Vortex

Time Lord 10

PERPUGILLIAM 'PERI' BROWN

STORY POINTS  12

ATTRIBUTES

AWARENESS	3
COORDINATION	3
INGENUITY	3
PRESENCE	4
RESOLVE	4
STRENGTH	2

SKILLS

Skill	Value	Skill	Value
ATHLETICS	3	MEDICINE	1
CONVINCE	2	SCIENCE	3
CRAFT	2	SUBTERFUGE	2
FIGHTING	2	SURVIVAL	4
KNOWLEDGE (Botany)	4	TECHNOLOGY	2
MARKSMAN	1	TRANSPORT	2

TRAITS

Attractive
Brave
Charming
Empathic
Lucky
Screamer!
Unadventurous

STUFF

None

5

BIODATA

PERSONAL GOAL
Exploration and Fun

PERSONALITY
Cheerful and good natured, long suffering with regard to the Doctor and when, called upon to be, brave and resolute.

BACKGROUND
Peri met the Fifth Doctor on Earth and asked to travel with him. After his death on Androzani, she became extremely frightened by his successor. The Sixth Doctor was erratic, aggressive and even violent, a stark contrast to the gentle, cricket-loving figure she'd first asked to travel with. For a while she thought seriously about leaving, especially as she was the butt of his jokes so often, but if she wasn't there, who would save him? Now things have settled down but Peri still approaches the universe, and the Doctor, with caution.

MELANIE BUSH

STORY POINTS  12

ATTRIBUTES

AWARENESS	4
COORDINATION	5
INGENUITY	5
PRESENCE	3
RESOLVE	5
STRENGTH	3

SKILLS

Skill	Value	Skill	Value
ATHLETICS	5	MEDICINE	1
CONVINCE	2	SCIENCE	3
CRAFT	2	SUBTERFUGE	0
FIGHTING	1	SURVIVAL	2
KNOWLEDGE	3	TECHNOLOGY	4
MARKSMAN	0	TRANSPORT	2

TRAITS

Brave
Code of Conduct
Impulsive
Indomitable
Insatiable Curiosity
Quick Reflexes
Positive Outlook
Photographic Memory
Screamer!
Technically Adept

STUFF

None

5

BIODATA

PERSONAL GOAL
Adventure and exploration.

PERSONALITY
Relentlessly cheery and positive, plucky and determined and honest to a fault.

BACKGROUND
A computer programmer from the village of Pease Pottage, Mel and the Sixth Doctor met at some point in the Sixth Doctor's future. Still reeling from the events of the trial and the revelation of the Valeyard's existence, the Doctor was far more cautious than before. Mel refused to let him retreat into his shell and her unfailing enthusiasm and honesty eventually helped him recover. Although as far as she was concerned, the carrot juice had a lot to do with it too.

THE SIXTH DOCTOR'S TARDIS

The Sixth Doctor is aggressively proud of his TARDIS and less than pleased with how his predecessors treated her. He's very much a new broom when it comes to his ship, constantly tinkering with her and trying out improvements or trying to fix old problems. He even manages to fix the Chameleon Circuit at one point, although it doesn't last.

This propensity for meddling and poking around inside the TARDIS can come in very useful for adventures – perhaps the Doctor trips a circuit the TARDIS would really rather not have activated and begins to act up, locking everyone inside. Alternatively, given what the Valeyard reveals about the Time Lords' surveillance techniques, the TARDIS could get progressively more erratic, or refuse to go to certain places as the surveillance tech begins to be used against the Doctor. You could even have it land in a specific set of places over and over in an attempt to spell out a warning to him. Much like the Sixth Doctor himself, the Sixth Doctor's TARDIS is brand new, energetic and more than a little unpredictable. Use that to keep your characters' lives interesting.

The Sixth Doctor's TARDIS is tempered and experienced, much like the Doctor himself. However, it also shares his need for things to change and improve, as well as his instability. This TARDIS is prone to mechanical problems much as it's always been, but they're more likely to come from the Doctor's own tinkering or the extremes he pushes it to. Nonetheless, this TARDIS is as unstable as its owner.

THE SIXTH DOCTOR'S TARDIS

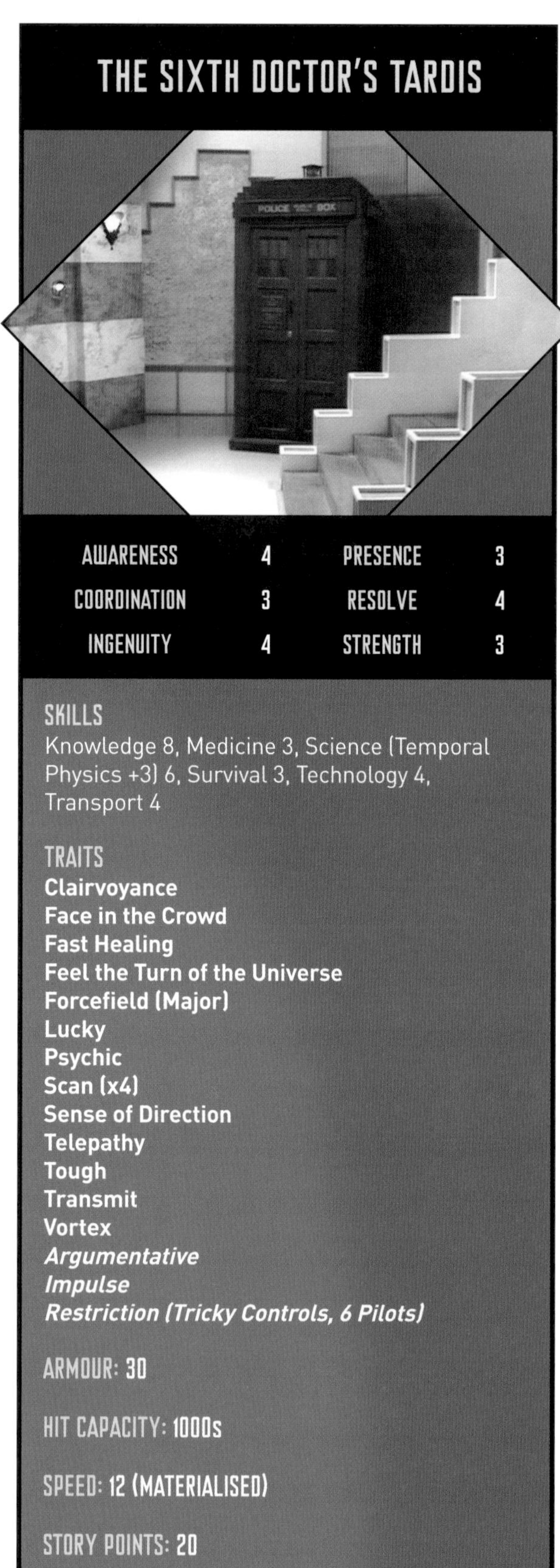

AWARENESS	4	PRESENCE	3
COORDINATION	3	RESOLVE	4
INGENUITY	4	STRENGTH	3

SKILLS
Knowledge 8, Medicine 3, Science (Temporal Physics +3) 6, Survival 3, Technology 4, Transport 4

TRAITS
Clairvoyance
Face in the Crowd
Fast Healing
Feel the Turn of the Universe
Forcefield (Major)
Lucky
Psychic
Scan (x4)
Sense of Direction
Telepathy
Tough
Transmit
Vortex
Argumentative
Impulse
Restriction (Tricky Controls, 6 Pilots)

ARMOUR: 30

HIT CAPACITY: 1000s

SPEED: 12 (MATERIALISED)

STORY POINTS: 20

WHY DOES THE TARDIS REVERT TO LOOKING LIKE A POLICE BOX?

Excellent question. ***The Doctor's Wife*** (see **The Eleventh Doctor Sourcebook**) heavily implies that the TARDIS chose her form and has decided that blue is most definitely her colour. That makes a lot of sense, especially given the fact the Doctor fixes the Chameleon Circuit but it's reverted back by the next adventure. Of course that also opens up the possibility of the Doctor and the TARDIS engage in a tug of war over what it should like. Perhaps when the Doctor and companions step out of the TARDIS it's taken a new form and then reverts to a police box the moment they're out of sight. Which raises the question: how do you train a rebellious TARDIS? Or perhaps, how do you train a rebellious TARDIS safely?

NEW TRAITS

DEAD TARDIS (MAJOR BAD)

The Time Lord has lost their TARDIS, through accident or violence. The shocking loss of their symbiotic partner removes two from each of their attributes and they lose Feel The Turn of the Universe as a trait.

HAVE I BEEN HERE BEFORE? (MAJOR GOOD)

Sometimes you get somewhere before you arrive when you travel in time. The character has an innate sense of familiarity when they arrive somewhere for the first time, even though in its past they've already visited. +2 to Ingenuity the first time they arrive on a new planet or point in history.

POSITIVE OUTLOOK (MINOR GOOD)

The character is relentlessly positive, upbeat and cheerful. So much so in fact that they gain a +1 to Convince rolls and Convince rolls against them are at a -1 Difficulty.

RUTHLESS (MINOR/MAJOR BAD)

As a Minor Bad Trait, any attempt to Convince the character to do something that wasn't in their plan or isn't immediately in their interests is at -1. As a Major Bad Trait, it's at -2.

SYMBIOTIC NUCLEI (MINOR GOOD)

The character has travelled with a Time Lord for long enough that they've picked up trace elements of the nuclei that the Time Lord and TARDIS share. This is far more easily detectable than Artron radiation and will mark the character out as being the companion of a Time Lord. On the plus side, it will also mean that the translation circuit in any TARDIS will work for them.

NO IMPRIMATUR (MAJOR BAD)

The Time Lord has had their Imprimatur removed or never developed it. This may be due to their relative youth, damage sustained in the Time War or its surgical removal (Ingenuity + Medicine, Difficulty 30). Regardless, the Time Lord cannot connect with their TARDIS and must find another way to ensure safe travel or, worse, another time machine. They can develop more over time (the Nuclei reform every regeneration at least) or they can receive a transfusion from another Time Lord (Ingenuity + Medicine, Difficulty 23)

TIME LORD MENTOR (MAJOR GOOD)

One, or in fact, all the characters have attracted the attention of a Time Lord, either as students, colleagues or those funny little hairless ape things from Earth that just seem to get everywhere these days. The Mentor will turn up when they feel like it, drag the characters off on adventures and make a general nuisance of themselves. Which, let's face it, is something every Time Lord we've ever met excels at. In the game, this can be played in one of two ways. Either sit down with the GM beforehand to work out exactly what sort of character the Mentor is going to be or choose the trait and wait for them to show up. Either way, the Mentor should be a massive gravitational force in any game they appear in, dragging everything towards them, including the plot.

NEW TIME LORD TRICKS

CLOSE RESPIRATORY PASSAGES

The Time Lord makes an Awareness + Medicine Roll (Difficulty 12) to close their air passages when they're sprayed with gas or other anti-respiratory weapons. They can operate at full attributes for two turns after this before having to make a Resolve + Athletics roll (Difficulty 10), increasing the difficulty by one per turn, until they can open their airways again. If they fail at any point, they take 1 level of attribute damage to every attribute and must immediately re-roll.

TRANCE (SPECIAL GOOD)

Prerequisite: Psychic, Time Lord

Trance is a Special Trait, requiring the character to already have the Time Lord and Psychic Traits. Trance costs 2 points. The Time Lord must either pay a story point or Roll Resolve + Survival (Difficulty 16) to enter a trance in which they can see the current location of their past self relative to their position in time. Once located, the Time Lord sees and hears everything their previous incarnation does but at wildly variable levels. Sounds become cacophonous, images distorted.

The Time Lord must roll Resolve + Survival (Difficulty 15), increasing by 3 every turn to remain. Once they fail, they are catapulted back into their own body. They may also achieve this trance using a Story Point, burning further Story Points to gain more information and remain in their past longer.

COMPLETELY IMPOSSIBLE ESCAPE

Once a game, the Time Lord can burn every single one of their remaining Story Points to escape certain doom. There has to be just a little ambiguity (ideally the other characters can't witness them die but can see the ship, vehicle or so on they're in explode) for it to work but if there is, then the Time Lord sits out several turns and gets to make a dramatic reappearance, completely unscathed.

MENTAL CAGE

A Time Lord at the end of their lives, as Azmael was, has one last trick up their sleeve. If their mind is taken over or controlled, they make a Resolve + Subterfuge roll (Difficulty 20) and throw their mental defences around the intruder, locking them in their mind, with the difficulty of breaking that hold increasing for every number they reach above the target. This allows the intruder's physical body to be destroyed but also triggers the Time Lord's regeneration instinct. Without the energy to regenerate, this triggers the Time Lord's final death.

TIME LORDS, SYMBIOTIC NUCLEI AND THE RASSILON IMPRIMATUR

The bond between a Time Lord and a TARDIS exists on a genetic level and alters the Time Lord profoundly. Most of the benefits they receive are covered by the Time Lord trait in the **Doctor Who: Adventures in Time and Space** Core Rulebook, including regeneration, psychic abilities and the rest. This also means the Time Lord can survive in the Vortex unprotected without being completely torn apart, for D6 minutes x their Resolve.

Most importantly, the Imprimatur maps the Time Lord's existence onto the vortex itself, giving them a level of protection no other creature enjoys. Earlier incarnations can be taken out of their time stream and the Time Lord will be weakened but not actually die.

Also, any timenapped incarnation will have a Blinovitch Limitation field around them so strong it's almost impossible to harm them (this is an RTD field of Strength 2, covered in detail in **The Time Traveller's Companion**). This allows the Time Lord to survive long enough to hopefully track down and retrieve their earlier incarnation.

CHAPTER THREE
THE SIXTH DOCTOR'S ADVENTURES

THE TWIN DILEMMA

'Because you have been chosen. It shall be your humble privilege to minister unto my needs. They will be... very simple – but nothing must be allowed to interfere with my period of contemplation.'

SYNOPSIS

Titan III and Jaconda, 2310

The Sylvest twins, mathematical geniuses, were interrupted by the arrival of Professor Edgeworth. Edgeworth tricked the boys, placing Amnesia discs on their wrists and teleporting them to a waiting freighter, manned by Jacondan aliens. Edgeworth consulted his master, Mestor, and was instructed to take the children to the asteroid Titan III.

In the TARDIS, the Doctor was recovering from his recent regeneration. Whilst he thought his previous incarnation was "effete", Peri was less than pleased with the change, especially when the Doctor had what seemed to be a panic attack of sorts. Recovering, the Doctor was adamant it wouldn't happen again but, soon after, he violently attacked Peri and she only fought him off when she showed him his reflection. Once he recovered, the Doctor was initially dismissive of Peri's claims until he saw just how terrified she was of him. Consumed with guilt, he vowed to become a hermit and live in contemplation, aided by Peri, of course, as his assistant.

The place he chose to become a hermit? Titan III.

At the same time, Professor Sylvest, the boy's father arrived home and found his children missing. Detecting evidence of an alien abduction, he contacted the Special Incidents Room and the alarm was raised. Commander Lang was dispatched at the head of a pursuit wing and tracked down the boys aboard the XV773, a freighter reported destroyed months previously. Before they could react, the ship engaged its warp drive.

The Doctor and Peri arrived on Titan III with the Doctor still intent on becoming a hermit. Only the crash of Lang's pursuit wing distracted him, and even then Peri had to convince him to save Lang, the one survivor, from his injuries. When he did so, the pilot promptly woke up, drew a gun on the Doctor, accused him of murdering his crew and then passed out.

Disturbed, both by this and by the discovery of a dome on the asteroid, the Doctor and Peri set off to investigate and were captured by the Jacondans. They were taken to meet Edgeworth, who the Doctor recognised as Azmael, one of his old tutors. The older man didn't return the favour at first, but on realising who the Doctor was, apologised for what he had to do. The Doctor tried to reason with him but Azmael left with the twins, locking the Doctor into what he thought was an inescapable cell. Unknown to him, one of the Jacondans also set the dome's self-destruct countdown.

The Doctor and Peri narrowly escaped death, the Doctor using a Tissue Revitaliser as an emergency time machine. On arriving back at the TARDIS, and explaining the situation to a very confused Lang, the Doctor decided to travel to Jaconda to find out just what was going on with his old friend.

On Jaconda itself, Azmael arrived and was ordered by Mestor, his Gastropod master, to put the boys to work straight away. He did this, even as the Doctor, Peri and Lang arrived and found the world a barren wasteland rather than the paradise the Doctor remembered. Exploring the nearby tunnels that led to the Master of Jaconda's palace, they found a mural detailing a Jacondan myth about the hideous, slug-like creature sent to ravage the world by the angry Sun God. He'd finally relented and sent a drought to kill them off but, as the slime trails on the surface proved, the Gastropods were both something much more than myth and very, very hungry.

Peri was captured, and only spared because Mestor found her "pleasing". The Doctor and Lang met up with Azmael who revealed the plan Mestor was forcing him to carry out. The planetary drought could be assuaged by moving two of the smaller worlds in the system into its orbit. Azmael had planned to shift the two worlds a day out of time phase with Jaconda, meaning they could occupy the same physical space, but the Doctor pointed out the problem with his plan: moving the worlds would have a disastrous effect on the Jacondan sun, causing it to go supernova. The Doctor examined the Gastropod eggs Mestor had had Azmael stockpile and realised the truth; they were designed to survive massive amounts of heat and hard vacuum. Mestor was going to use the supernova to send his children all over the galaxy.

The Doctor and Azmael prepared to face Mestor, whilst Lang led the twins, and a rescued Peri, to safety in the TARDIS. The two Time Lords went to battle one last time against the Gastropod, only to discover, too late, that Mestor could transfer his consciousness from one body to another. He possessed Azmael who had just enough strength left to hold him in place whilst the Doctor killed his own body. With Mestor's physical identity gone, Azmael triggered his own regeneration sequence. However with no further lives left, he simply died, leaving his old friend alone and sacrificing himself to release the people of Jaconda from Mestor's reign.

With the situation resolved, and the Doctor now fully stabilised, he and Peri prepared to leave. To their surprise, Lang opted to stay, stating he thought he could make a difference. The Doctor agreed and, whilst insulting him, also gave him Azmael's ring as a seal of approval. Lang settled into his new world and the TARDIS departed.

CONTINUITY

- The TARDIS wardrobe is seen, along with the Second Doctor's suspenders, trousers and coat; the Third Doctor's velvet jacket and checked cape; and outfits belonging to both Peri and Tegan.
- The Doctor can no longer remember how to get to the Eye of Orion (see ***The Five Doctors***, in **The Fifth Doctor Sourcebook**).

RUNNING THE ADVENTURE

The Twin Dilemma neatly embodies everything about the Sixth Doctor's era. The stories are huge, featuring vital events we only ever see off screen, the Doctor himself is a mercurial to actively dangerous presence in the story and the level of violence is noticeably higher than previous runs. All of which – if handled badly – has the potential to make a shrill, belligerent, violent campaign with few redeeming features.

But looked at another way, this becomes an era where the main character runs headlong into every bad situation, the plots neatly echo the vast machinations of the Time War and the increased level of violence, again, foreshadows what's coming. It's not a perfect system, but the sixth incarnation isn't a perfect Doctor and that level of unpredictability can also serve as a means of keeping your players in line if the Doctor is an NPC. Plus, as you'll see, this story is a treasure trove for a Gamemaster in a hurry.

Keep the pace up, keep the Doctor at the centre of it and make sure the sheer scale of the story is communicated. Jaconda is a world that's been laid waste twice, is being run by a Time Lord desperate to make amends for his dreadful choices and is about to be destroyed in the most destructive egg laying in galactic history. This is a huge, sweeping story. Run it that way and your characters can't help but be carried along.

THE JACONDANS

The Jacondans are an unusual, and beautiful, race, resembling humanoid owls. Native to Jaconda, a paradise world renowned for its beauty, they occupy a curious niche in the galaxy. On the one hand, they lack offensive capabilities so completely that Azmael had to steal a freighter for them to complete the kidnapping. On the other, they had no problem destroying an entire SIR pursuit wing.

The answer to this apparent contradiction may lie in the history of their world. The story of the Sun God, and the slug-like creature he inflicted on them, is clearly a coded origin for Mestor and the Gastropods and the ease with which the Gastropods took control of Jaconda on both occasions is startling. The reason for this is the same reason why Jacondans are uniquely peaceful when not possessed and completely ruthless when they are: parallel evolution. They have evolved to act as a Servitor race for the Gastropods, and any psychic roll from a Gastropod has an automatic +3 bonus as a result. This cultural pacifism may also go some way towards explaining why Azmael, a Time Lord, was the Master of Jaconda prior to being ousted by Mestor. Although another explanation is offered under Further Adventures...

THE JACONDANS

AWARENESS	2	PRESENCE	2
COORDINATION	3	RESOLVE	2
INGENUITY	3	STRENGTH	3

TRAITS
Alien
Alien Appearance
Enslaved

TECH LEVEL: 5 STORY POINTS: 2-4

THE GASTROPODS

The Gastropods' origin is shrouded in Jacondan myth, with a story revolving around the Queen offending the Sun God, who promptly sent a half humanoid/ half slug creature to punish her. The creature's appetite was colossal and it devastated the planet. In penance, the Sun God sent a drought that ultimately killed the creature. Jaconda recovered and the story of the Gastropods passed into myth. However, the Gastropods were very real, and far from defeated. When Mestor made his grab for power he did so with a vast army (albeit in egg form) behind him, and a plan. A plan it took two Time Lords to defeat.

The Gastropods have thick torsos that extend all the way down to their feet and a short neck. Their heads are round, with a recessed mouth and folded jowls and topped with two antennae.

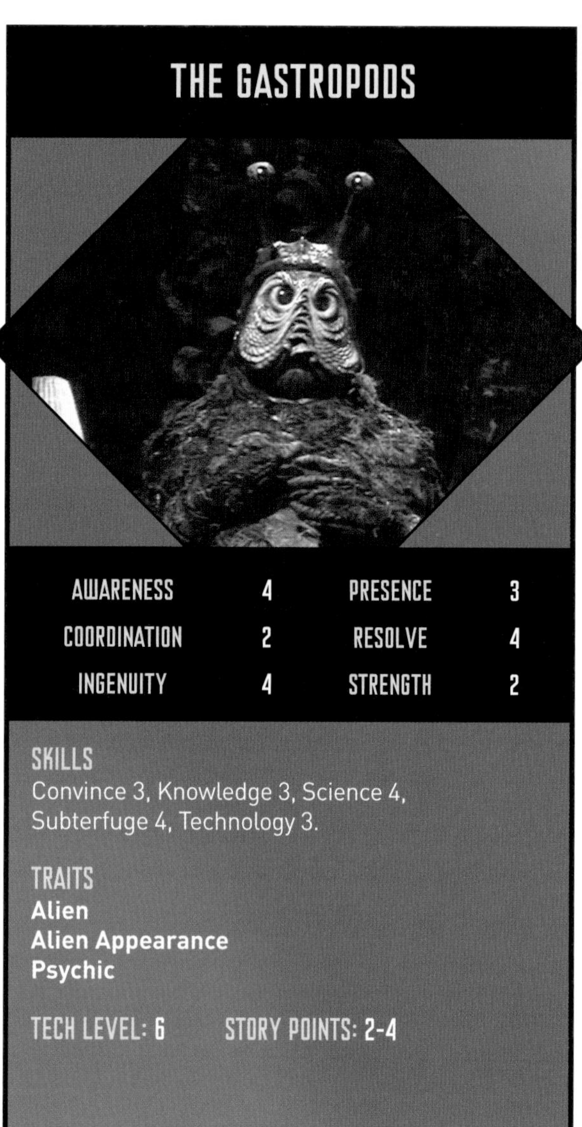

THE GASTROPODS

AWARENESS	4	PRESENCE	3
COORDINATION	2	RESOLVE	4
INGENUITY	4	STRENGTH	2

SKILLS
Convince 3, Knowledge 3, Science 4, Subterfuge 4, Technology 3.

TRAITS
Alien
Alien Appearance
Psychic

TECH LEVEL: 6 STORY POINTS: 2-4

They are extremely patient, extremely knowledgeable and endlessly hungry, as evidenced by their twin devastations of Jaconda and Mestor's plan to expand out into the universe.

NEW TRAIT: SLIME TRAIL (SPECIAL)

The Gastropods excrete a thick, slimy trail when they move. This trail will kill any vegetable matter and leech any nutrients from the soil around it. It hardens to rock like density in two Action Rounds. Any character caught in the trail after that will find themselves trapped in what is functionally concrete. An Awareness + Marksman (Difficulty 10) roll with a TL5 or higher weapon is needed to cut themselves free without injury. Alternatively, they can use a knife, but the Difficulty rises to 12.

THE SPECIAL INCIDENT ROOM

It's not entirely clear what else is going on at this time in Earth's history, and that's a particular problem for a GM wanting to work with the Special Incident Room. They're clearly part of a larger organization for a start, which could be anything from the Terran Navy to the Space Security Service from the 1st Doctor's era, or even UNIT or Torchwood.

What is clear is that they're an organisation with real, rapidly deployable space resources, investigative officers trained in ship and hand-to-hand combat and have a remit that takes them outside the solar system if needed. Focus on that, and play with their ties to other organisations however you see fit.

COMMANDER HUGO LANG

'I feel like I could make a difference here.'

Hugo Lang was a perfect example of the unusual role SIR officers play in the future. He was the first point of contact for Professor Sylvest's kidnapping report and was deployed as the head of the pursuit wing sent after the Professor's twins. Initially seeming to be little more than an office worker, Lang's comfort in the front line, to say nothing of his abilities in combat, proved just how versatile the SIR could be.

Even when his crew were wiped out and he was saved by an extremely unstable Doctor, Lang stayed on mission. His dedication, to say nothing of his refusal to back down, proved instrumental in dragging the Sixth Doctor out of the post-regeneration malaise he was suffering and Lang was a vital part of the eventual liberation of Jaconda. He remained there, to the Doctor's mild surprise, after the fall of Mestor.

COMMANDER HUGO LANG

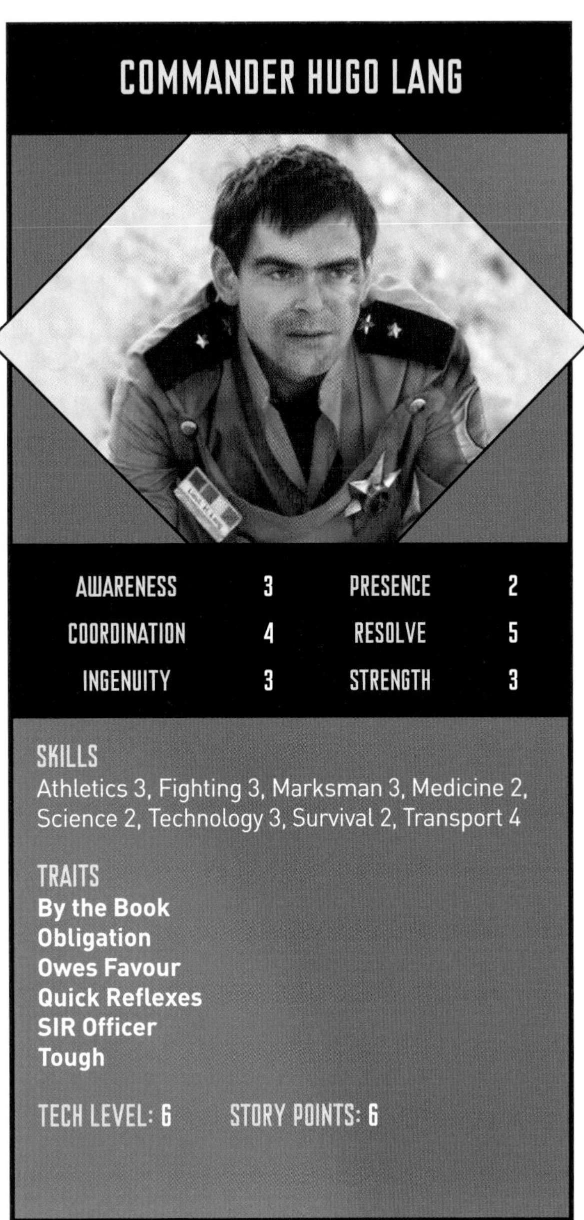

AWARENESS	3	PRESENCE	2
COORDINATION	4	RESOLVE	5
INGENUITY	3	STRENGTH	3

SKILLS
Athletics 3, Fighting 3, Marksman 3, Medicine 2, Science 2, Technology 3, Survival 2, Transport 4

TRAITS
By the Book
Obligation
Owes Favour
Quick Reflexes
SIR Officer
Tough

TECH LEVEL: 6 STORY POINTS: 6

PROFESSOR EDGEWORTH/AZMAEL

Azmael is an unusual, troubling figure. After all, how exactly does a Time Lord, and a well-respected one at that, end up as Master of Jaconda? It's not an especially friendly sounding term and, Mestor's control aside, Azmael did some pretty terrible things before redeeming himself. However, as we'll see later, there's a possible explanation for his actions and also every opportunity for the characters to meet him at an earlier, happier time.

PROFESSOR EDGEWORTH/AZMAEL

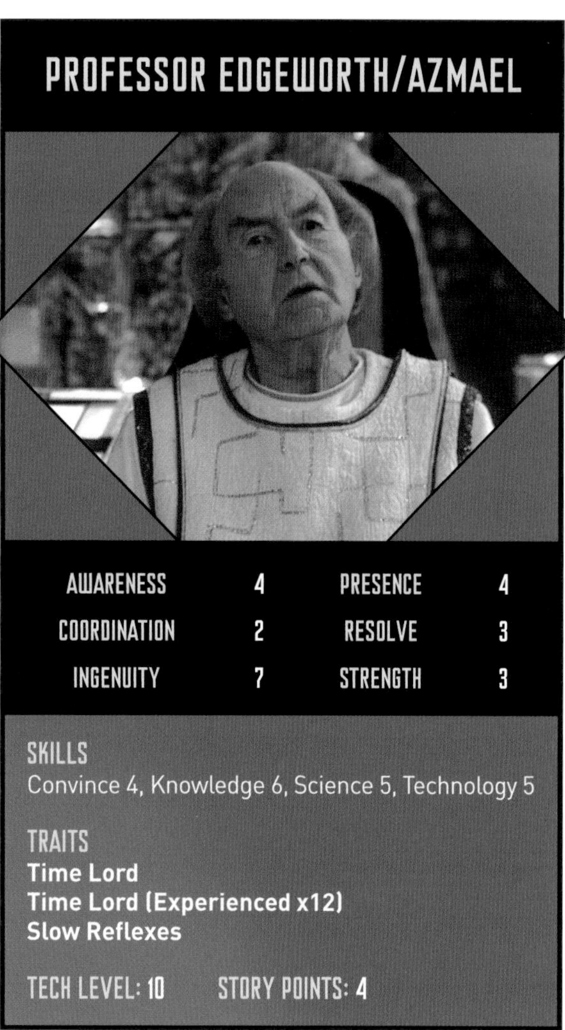

AWARENESS	4	PRESENCE	4
COORDINATION	2	RESOLVE	3
INGENUITY	7	STRENGTH	3

SKILLS
Convince 4, Knowledge 6, Science 5, Technology 5

TRAITS
Time Lord
Time Lord (Experienced x12)
Slow Reflexes

TECH LEVEL: 10 STORY POINTS: 4

NEW TRAIT: SIR OFFICER

SIR officers are constantly on call, and constantly called upon to react to numerous different situations. Lang's a perfect example of this, going from an office clerk to pursuit wing leader to sole survivor and ground combat expert. SIR work harder, and go further, than almost everyone else in the system and their skill package reflects that. The skill packages costs 10 Character Points and any player choosing this trait receives the following training: Athletics 3, Fighting 3, Marksman 2, Medicine 2, Survival 2, Technology 3, Transport 3.

However, due to the terms of service in the organization they also have to agree to serve a full, eight year tour and remain on call after that. As a result, they take Obligation and Owes Favour as Major Bad traits.

Although if they're travelling in time those eight years don't have to be served all at once.

TECHNOLOGY

Deep Healing Ray (Minor Gadget)
The Deep Healing Ray is a small, innocuous device, which, as is often the case with such things, is immensely useful. Nicknamed 'the handheld hospital' by SIR officers, it's a small, pistol-shaped device that, when triggered, will repair everything bar fatal wounds.

It's a Difficulty 7 Ingenuity + Medicine roll with 2/4/6 points of damage recovered depending on the success.

Traits: Heal, One Shot.
Cost: 1 Story Point

Tissue Revitaliser (Major Gadget)
Derived from Transmat technology, the Tissue Revitaliser is arguably the most extreme cosmetics and beauty technology developed by humanity. The Revitaliser uses a standard transmat to disassemble the atoms of the user but, instead of sending them anywhere, it 'washes' them in a tachyon field.

This scrubs the cells of any short term impurities (anything more extreme would require a far stronger, far more illegal tachyon field) and helps the user feel more awake.

As the Doctor demonstrated, it's also possible to use the device as a short range transmit with a successful Ingenuity + Science roll (Difficulty 10). Failing will still project you outwards from the machine, but at a randomly determined location and arrival time.

Traits: Scan, Transmit, Restriction.
Cost: 2 Story Points

Amnesia Discs (Minor Gadget)
Amnesia Discs are one of the more controversial uses of biological technology Humanity have employed. Small, flat, green discs with the middle cut out, they're essentially injection devices. Once placed on the skin of a target, provided they're placed over a vein, the discs open to unleash millions of nanomachines into the subject's blood. These are powered by the very motion through the veins that propels them to their target and are programmed to block every memory aside from essential skills.

The discs continue to dispense the nanomachines for as long as they're in contact with the skin and last up to a week. A mild electric shock will release them from the skin without any damage and the Nanomachines will die off within an Earth day of this taking place.

Traits: Scan, Restriction
Cost: 1 Story Point

FURTHER ADVENTURES

- **The Rise of Jaconda:** The Doctor arrives on Jaconda, two years after the events of the story, to check in on Lang. He's delighted to see the planet is almost back to its former beauty, and even more delighted to see a statue to his old friend Azmael being unveiled in the new, above ground, Master's Palace. But why are there so many earthquakes? What do the Church of the Holy Gastropod want? And why is Lang plagued with terrible dreams about Mestor?

- **The Fall of Jaconda:** A Torchwood Archive team are working on Jaconda, cataloguing the various myths surrounding the Gastropods and attempting to work out where they came from. When one team member discovers a previously hidden painting, showing the Gastropods being led to the surface of Jaconda by the Sun God, a man with a bright head of yellow hair and a garish cloak, things get a little awkward. They get worse when the Doctor arrives and is put on trial for the attempted genocide of the Jacondan race. Then, a note is delivered to the courtroom by the Doctor of the future, explaining what he has to do to prove his innocence and things get downright dangerous. Racing against time, and with the reluctant help of the Torchwood team, the Doctor must infiltrate an old Time Lord weapon, hidden in the Jacondan sun, and confront the reality that, as a hero of the Time War, not everything that wore his face was him...

- **The Third Titan:** The TARDIS arrives on Titan III, where to the Doctor's surprise, he finds a memorial to Azmael. The old Time Lord asked to be buried there, and the Doctor stops and pays his respects to his old friend. As he enters the tomb though, a holographic message appears from the younger Azmael, the man he knew. It says;

"Doctor, there is no time. Something awful is coming, a war that will sweep space and time up in its wake and change the universe forever. There is a way we can stop it, you and I, but we must act quickly. First go to Jaconda and find m-" And the message cuts out. When the Doctor travels to Jaconda's past, he finds Azmael apparently unaware of what he said and busy working with a group of visiting dignitaries, all of whom seem to have a special interest in Titan III. But why? What does the asteroid conceal? Why is it almost exclusively metal? And why is something inside it singing?

ATTACK OF THE CYBERMEN

'When you become as we are, you will serve the Cyber Race well.'

SYNOPSIS

London, 1985

In the London sewers, two workmen were surveying an old section of tunnel when something attacked and killed both of them. Meanwhile, the Doctor was tinkering with the TARDIS' Chameleon Circuit, trying to get it to work again. Peri was concerned he still seemed a little unstable but he assured her all was well and that he'd decided they both needed a holiday after the desolation of Jaconda. The TARDIS lurched suddenly, and time slowed down, before he could explain where they were going.

Meanwhile in London, 1985, Lytton, Griffiths, Payne and Russell, a group of gangsters, were planning a high end raid that would net them £10 million in diamonds. Russell, the explosives specialist, was dispatched to pick up the plastic explosive needed for the job and waited for the others to go before calling in the request. The four men were clearly tense, Russell more than most. When the raid began, they made their way to the bank through the same sewers the two workmen had died in and, unseen by the others, Lytton activated a strange transmitter.

The Doctor got the TARDIS back under control and finished repairing the Chameleon Circuit. He showed Peri Halley's Comet and explained they were heading for Earth in 1985. She became worried they'd crash into it and pointed out the comet was traditionally a herald of doom but the Doctor dismissed her concerns, even as they picked up Lytton's signal. He landed the TARDIS nearby and was delighted to see it change shape into an ornamental stove, and, even better, return to IM Foreman's junkyard on Totter's Lane. He and Peri set off to look for the transmitter and, when the Doctor realised it was being routed through a second point, returned to the TARDIS and moved it into the sewers. This time it took the form of an organ but before they could travel anywhere, they were accosted by two sinister, silent policemen.

Meanwhile, on Telos, the adopted homeworld of the Cybermen, Stratton and Bates, two human prisoners, staged a desperate, violent escape. They were trying to recover the time machine they had arrived in, but needed three men and a Cyberman head in order to complete their plan. Stratton didn't grab the head of the Cyberman Bates decapitated in time and the two were reluctantly forced to attack another Cyberman.

In the sewers, Payne had fallen behind his colleagues and was beaten to death. Unaware of this, Lytton and the others came to a dead end and found a shadowy figure (actually a Cyberman) approaching them. Russell fled in terror, whilst Griffiths shot the creature before Lytton could disarm him and surrender to the Cybermen. In the meantime the Doctor and Peri had knocked out the policemen and begun searching the sewers for the real transmitter. They ran into Russell who revealed that he was an undercover police officer investigating Lytton. The Doctor recognised the name and, troubled by the implications of him being involved decided to return to the TARDIS. Unknown to him, the Cybermen had already arrived there and attacked. Russell was killed and the Cyberleader ordered his troops to kill Peri before the Doctor used the TARDIS self-destruct system to force them to bargain. Horrified to find the Cyber Controller was still alive, the Doctor agreed to take the Cybermen to Telos in return for Peri's life. En route, he explained to Peri, and a very confused Griffiths, that the Cybermen invaded Telos because the native inhabitants, the Cryons, lived at extremely cold temperatures and specialised in cryogenic technology, something the Cybermen needed to keep their troops in cryogenic stasis.

When they arrived on Telos, the TARDIS not only landed in the depths of the Cybermen's tombs but had decided to become an ornamental gate. Almost the moment they arrived, the group were attacked by a badly damaged Cyberman, one of many in the tombs. Lytton, Griffiths and Peri escaped and were separated: Peri was almost killed by another Cyberman before being rescued by a Cryon; Lytton and Griffiths were picked up by a different Cryon and Lytton admitted he'd been working for them all along. The Cryon paid Griffiths in diamonds, common on Telos, and Lytton told him all he had to do is help Lytton capture the time vessel. The two men tracked down Bates and Stratton and gain their help in attempting to get to the ship. They also discovered that the two former prisoners were failed cyber-conversion subjects, their arms and legs replaced by prosthetics.

The Doctor, still imprisoned by the Cybermen, was thrown into a cold storage room with Flast, the former leader of the Cryons. She explained that the timeship was going to be used to stop Mondas, the original Cyberman homeworld, from being destroyed by using it to divert Halley's Comet into Earth. When Mondas attacks, in 1986, Earth would be unable to repel them, Mondas will not be destroyed and time will change forever. The Doctor, initially, was outraged that the Time Lords had done nothing to prevent this happening and then realised... they had. They had diverted the TARDIS, manipulating him into becoming involved, knowing he would deal with the situation. He was still coming to terms with this when Flast explained that the room was actually filled with vastial, an explosive that was completely dormant at the temperatures that the Cryons survived at, but would become devastatingly explosive once it was heated. The Doctor used a small amount to deal with the guard, left Flast his sonic lance to heat up the remainder and left. Not long after, the Cybermen, suspecting she'd helped him escape, threw her out into the much warmer corridor. Her blood boiled almost instantly and she was killed.

Lytton, Griffiths, Stratton and Bates approached the time machine but Lytton was captured by the Cybermen. The other three pressed on, and were just outside the room where it was being kept when they were ambushed and killed. Lytton was brought before the Cyber Controller who demanded to be told what he was planning. Lytton refused to talk, even after the Controller had two Cybermen crush his hands, and the Controller ordered that he be converted into a Cyberman.

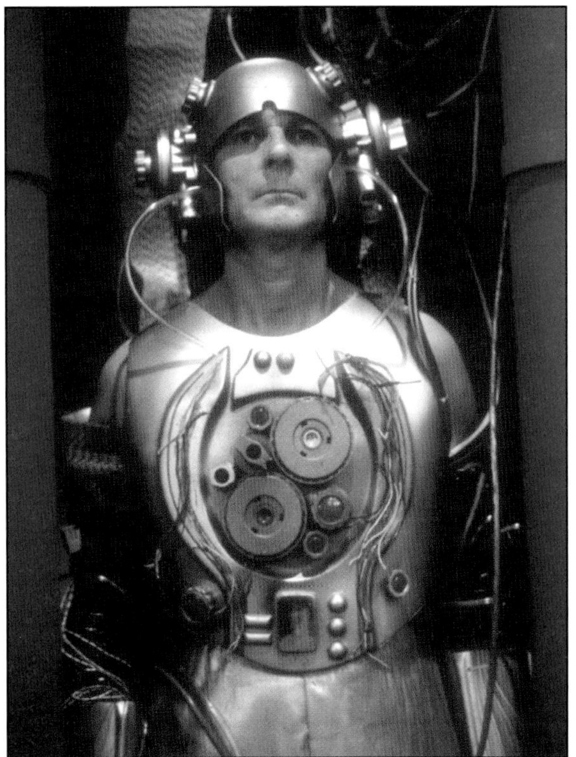

The Doctor got back to the TARDIS and the Cryons followed, bringing Peri with them and explaining that Lytton had been working with them all along. Realising he'd misjudged the former mercenary, the Doctor decided to save him. However, he arrived too late and a partially converted Lytton begged the Doctor to kill him. The Cyber Controller, Leader and their forces arrived and were killed in the ensuing gunfire, the Doctor himself killing the Cyber Controller. He and Peri left just as the sonic lance that Flast had concealed in the vastial heated it enough to explode, destroying Cyber Control and the tombs.

CONTINUITY

- The Doctor revisits IM Foreman's junkyard on Totter Lane, the setting for the First Doctor's adventures.
- We've met Lytton before, in ***Resurrection of the Daleks*** (see **The Fifth Doctor Sourcebook**), but there he was working for the Daleks.
- The Cybermen's plan is to thwart the events that unfolded in ***The Tenth Planet*** (see **The First Doctor Sourcebook**).

RUNNING THE ADVENTURE

If ***The Twin Dilemma*** is a measured, if slightly frantic, setting out of the stall, then this is the Sixth Doctor's first full-on action movie. Running this adventure successfully revolves around three basic concepts, and if you can get those right, it'll be great fun.

First off: pace. Nothing is wasted in this story. From the moment we see the Doctor tinkering with the Chameleon Circuit to the closing explosion, each seemingly unconnected event is incident heavy and action packed. Don't be afraid to push your group along if you're running this, maybe have Lytton have a few more 'policemen' he can use to cordon the area off, or make direct contact. Or, of course, have the Time Lords drop the TARDIS right in front of Lytton's crew at one point...

Also, everyone gets in on the action this time, whether they want to or not. Even Peri holds a gun on one of the policemen and the story finishes with the Doctor shooting the Cyber Controller! Throw in the multiple cyber decapitations and the horrible deaths of most of the cast and you've got a scenario with a really hard edge to it. You can either push that (and the story certainly shows you how) or tone it down a little dependent on your group. Either way, the action should be fast paced and have some real consequences to it. This is a grim adventure, with a surprising death toll, and there's a lot to be said for toning that down. Similarly, there's a lot to be said for keeping the dark, serious tone it lends the adventure. The choice is yours, but there's certainly room for both approaches.

Finally, scale. This is a story where a £10 million diamond heist is a cover for a means of getting someone's attention. Think big, act big, go for huge scale especially with the Telos locations. Have an extended chase through the tombs, throw in an extra encounter where the group have to talk down a demented Cyberman. Alternatively, have the group start as prisoners and give them the timeship at the end of the adventure. A group of human POWs careening through time certainly sounds like exactly the sort of people who'd need the Time Lord Mentor trait from the previous chapter doesn't it? Or, failing that, they would make supremely useful 'agents' of the Time Lords themselves.

THE CRYONS

The Cryons are a slight, delicate race of humanoids native to the planet Telos. They evolved in the extremely low temperatures beneath the planet's surface and as a result can only survive within a narrow, low temperature range. If they move outside this, their blood boils and they die in seconds.

Despite, or perhaps because, of this restriction, the Cryons have thrived, perfecting cryogenic technology to ensure they and their environment are always at the right temperature. Their tremendous technical aptitude, to say nothing of their weakness making them appear easy targets, led to the Cybermen invading Telos and attempting to wipe them out.

Although they believed they succeeded, the surviving Cryons instead took to the lower levels of the Cybermen Tombs, sabotaging them and slowly but surely diminishing their enemy's numbers.

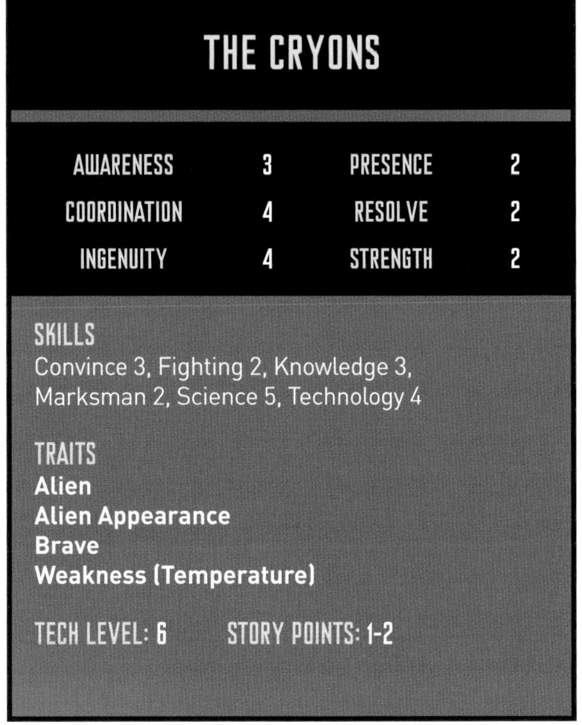

THE CRYONS

AWARENESS	3	PRESENCE	2
COORDINATION	4	RESOLVE	2
INGENUITY	4	STRENGTH	2

SKILLS
Convince 3, Fighting 2, Knowledge 3, Marksman 2, Science 5, Technology 4

TRAITS
Alien
Alien Appearance
Brave
Weakness (Temperature)

TECH LEVEL: 6 STORY POINTS: 1-2

FLAST

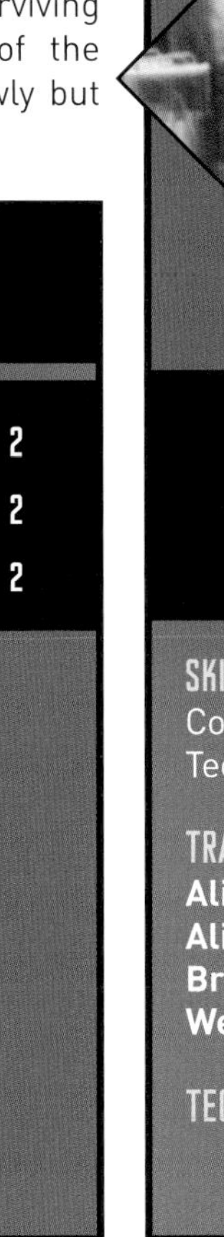

AWARENESS	4	PRESENCE	3
COORDINATION	4	RESOLVE	4
INGENUITY	4	STRENGTH	2

SKILLS
Convince 5, Fighting 2, Knowledge 4, Science 5, Technology 4

TRAITS
Alien
Alien Appearance
Brave
Weakness (Temperature)

TECH LEVEL: 6 STORY POINTS: 6

FLAST

The Cryon leader was imprisoned almost as soon as the Cybermen took over and, like her people, found it almost impossible to fight back directly. The Cybermen were relentless, almost impossible to kill and legion and the Cryons were faced with a choice between retreat or annihilation. Flast found a third way; she chose to conceal the true nature of vastial, a hugely explosive mineral, from the Cybermen and stockpiled it.

As her people fled to the lowest levels and sabotaged as many Cybermen as they could, she let herself be caught and waited for the right moment to detonate the vastial. That came when the Doctor arrived and she sacrificed her life to help rid her world of the Cybermen.

THE CYBERMEN

The Cybermen originated on the planet Mondas, which was itself the twin of Earth. Propelled out of our solar system centuries previously, Mondas was the basis for the Cyberman Empire, which took in countless worlds and, in 1986, would return to attempt to conquer Earth. The invasion was a disaster, seen off by a combination of the Doctor and a newly formed UNIT, but the Cybermen proved tenacious even in defeat. Small cells remained active on Earth and planned for both the future and the past. If they could get their hands on a time machine, then Mondas could be saved...

The Cybermen at this time of their development are humanoid aliens wearing loose-fitting silver body suits, boots, gauntlets and helmets. They have a breathing system carried in a harness on their chest and move slowly and deliberately, but without the distinctive 'stomping' march of later models. They're also more hierarchical, each Cyberman unit being led by a Cyberleader and those in turn reporting to a Cyber Controller. In the event of a Leader's death, his consciousness is downloaded into one of his soldiers.

THE CYBERMEN

AWARENESS	2	PRESENCE	3
COORDINATION	3	RESOLVE	3
INGENUITY	2	STRENGTH	7

SKILLS
Convince 2, Fighting 3, Marksman 3, Science 2, Technology 4.

TRAITS
Armour (10)
Cyborg
Fear Factor (3)
Slow (Minor)
Technically Adept
Weakness - Gold (Major)

WEAPONS: Particle Blaster 4/L/L

TECH LEVEL: 6 STORY POINTS: 3

CYBER CONTROLLER

AWARENESS	3	PRESENCE	4
COORDINATION	3	RESOLVE	5
INGENUITY	6	STRENGTH	8

With an enlarged cranium and increased intelligence, the Cyber Controller is a mysterious figure. The Doctor has encountered him in several previous lives and apparently seen him die every time, yet the Cyber Controller always seems to return and always seems to remember the Doctor when he does.

SKILLS
Athletics 6, Convince 4, Craft 3, Fighting 5, Knowledge 5, Marksman 3, Medicine 4, Science 5, Subterfuge 2, Survival 3, Technology 5, Transport 4.

TRAITS
Armour (10)
Cyborg
Fast Healing
Fear Factor (3)
Slow (Minor)
Technically Adept
Weakness - Gold (Major)

WEAPONS: Particle Blaster 4/L/L

TECH LEVEL: 6 STORY POINTS: 6

EXCELLENT?

This era's Cybermen aren't quite as free of emotion as they like to think, often clenching a fist and declaring 'EXCELLENT' when something goes well. Use mannerisms and gestures like this as a means of distinguishing them from the Lumic-era Cybermen and as a really simple cue to let your players know who they're talking to.

CYBERLEADER

AWARENESS	2	PRESENCE	3
COORDINATION	3	RESOLVE	5
INGENUITY	4	STRENGTH	8

Cyberleaders are field commanders programmed to carry out the will of the Cyber Controller in their absence. Stronger than their subordinates, they're notable for their dark-coloured helmet guards or darker-coloured helmets.

SKILLS
Convince 3, Fighting 3, Marksman 3, Science 2, Technology 4.

TRAITS
Armour (10)
Cyborg
Fear Factor (3)
Slow (Minor)
Technically Adept
Weakness - Gold (Major)

WEAPONS: Particle Blaster 4/L/L

TECH LEVEL: 6 **STORY POINTS:** 6

BLACK CYBERMEN

Black Cybermen are designed for stealth operations and combat in dark environments. Initially developed by the Cyber Legion the Doctor encountered in Attack of the Cybermen, they didn't prove successful and were phased out.

NEW TRAIT: FAILED CYBER CONVERSION (SPECIAL)

Failed Cyber Conversion is a Special Good Trait that costs 2 Character Points. The character has been through, and failed, the process of Cyber Conversion. This means they've retained their memories, features and torso but have had their limbs replaced with Cyberman prosthetics. These are indistinguishable from normal, provided they're concealed, and offer the following effects:

+3 to Strength	-1 to Coordination
-2 to Awareness	+1 to Presence

Also the character must make a Resolve + Knowledge (Difficulty 12) test once a session to cope with the psychological effects of the change, or receive a -2 penalty on every action unless engaged in combat as he struggles with the horror.

GUSTAVE LYTTON

A mercenary born on the satellite Riften 5 orbiting the world Vita 15, Lytton grew up in a culture of mercenaries, combat and brutal commerce. A naturally gifted soldier, he embraced the spartan lifestyle of his people and made his way out into the universe to make his fortune. When the Doctor first met him, he was doing this by leading a snatch squad sent to retrieve the Dalek leader, Davros. Inevitably, carnage ensued and Lytton was one of the few survivors, stranded on Earth in 1984.

To say that he adapted would be an understatement. Inside a year, Lytton was a major underworld player, so much so that he'd registered as a threat to the undercover branch of the Metropolitan police. In reality, he had been approached by the Cryons to assist with the removal of the Cybermen from Telos and was using the bank raid as cover to make contact with, and infiltrate, the Cybermen ranks. Ruthless, pragmatic and extremely dangerous, Lytton is one of the only human soldiers who could stand a chance against the Cybermen.

GUSTAVE LYTTON

AWARENESS	4	PRESENCE	4
COORDINATION	5	RESOLVE	5
INGENUITY	3	STRENGTH	3

SKILLS
Athletics 4, Convince 4, Craft 2, Fighting 4, Knowledge 4, Marksman 5, Medicine 2, Subterfuge 4, Survival 3, Technology 3, Transport 4.

TRAITS
Indomitable
Owes Favour
Selfish
Tough
Voice of Authority

TECH LEVEL: 6 **STORY POINTS:** 6

RUSSELL

AWARENESS	4	PRESENCE	2
COORDINATION	4	RESOLVE	4
INGENUITY	3	STRENGTH	3

Russell doesn't look particularly intimidating, but that's the idea. A veteran undercover police officer, he fits seamlessly into the underworld, can mix with any crowd and has a reputation that precedes him wherever he goes. Russell will get the job done, or die trying, and he's the perfect man to infiltrate Lytton's gang as a result.

SKILLS

Athletics 3, Convince 4, Fighting 2, Marksman 5, Knowledge 4.

TRAITS

Dark Secret
Face in the Crowd

TECH LEVEL: 5 STORY POINTS: 2

RUSSELL'S OTHER BOSS

You always have the option of making Russell a Torchwood officer. It makes a lot of sense, after all he's basically unfazed by the Cybermen, or the Doctor for that matter, and Lytton would certainly register on their radar. That of course opens up a whole new plot line about what role Torchwood played in stopping the invasion, maybe with a cameo or two from earlier (or later) Doctors.

GRIFFITHS

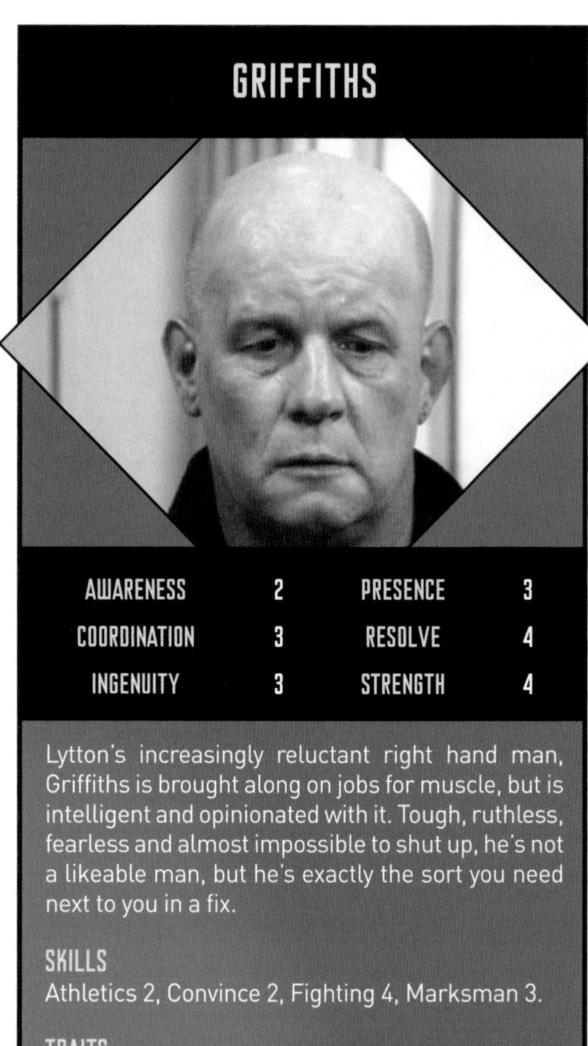

AWARENESS	2	PRESENCE	3
COORDINATION	3	RESOLVE	4
INGENUITY	3	STRENGTH	4

Lytton's increasingly reluctant right hand man, Griffiths is brought along on jobs for muscle, but is intelligent and opinionated with it. Tough, ruthless, fearless and almost impossible to shut up, he's not a likeable man, but he's exactly the sort you need next to you in a fix.

SKILLS

Athletics 2, Convince 2, Fighting 4, Marksman 3.

TRAITS

Tough
Argumentative

TECH LEVEL: 5 STORY POINTS: 2

BATES AND STRATTON

Two of the three-man time ship crew, Bates and Stratton have been on Telos for too long. They survived the horrific conversion process and their will to live was so strong that they couldn't be turned. Now, they're on one of the work gangs dotting the planet, condemned to a brief life without any hope of anything other than the Cyberman tyranny. But they have a plan to get home and all they need to make it work is luck and timing.

Bates: The Mission Commander, Bates is a man used to make the hard decisions. The hardest one of all was to survive, something which, somehow, his crew have managed. Abrasive, ruthless and desperate, Bates wants off Telos and he'll kill anyone who gets in his way, including Stratton.

Stratton: The other surviving member of the time ship crew couldn't be more different to his CO. Stratton is brittle, so terrified and exhausted that he's come out the other side of both and now just wants to live. They've taken almost everything from him and no one, not even Bates, will take anything else.

BATES

AWARENESS	3	PRESENCE	4
COORDINATION	2	RESOLVE	4
INGENUITY	3	STRENGTH	7

SKILLS
Athletics 4, Fighting 4, Subterfuge 4, Transport 5.

TRAITS
Argumentative
Armour (5)
Failed Cyber Conversion
Indomitable

TECH LEVEL: 6 STORY POINTS: 2

STRATTON

AWARENESS	2	PRESENCE	2
COORDINATION	3	RESOLVE	2
INGENUITY	3	STRENGTH	7

SKILLS
Athletics 2, Fighting 3, Transport 5.

TRAITS
Armour (5)
Cowardly
Failed Cyber Conversion
Lucky

TECH LEVEL: 6 STORY POINTS: 2

PAYNE

AWARENESS	2	PRESENCE	3
COORDINATION	3	RESOLVE	2
INGENUITY	3	STRENGTH	4

The newest member of Lytton's team, and he never lets Payne forget it. A former workman, Payne is muscle and he's quite happy to do whatever he needs to do to whoever Lytton wants it done to. As long as he gets paid...

Skills
Athletics 2, Fighting 3

TRAITS
Selfish
Tough

TECH LEVEL: 5 STORY POINTS: 2

TELOS AND BEYOND

The Cyberman homeworld presents a problem, both in this adventure and in general. Mondas is elsewhere when this story takes place, and destroyed when the invasion fails the following year but there's nothing to say all the Mondasian Cybermen were destroyed or that they and the faction based on Telos get on. Throw in the Cybermen from the alternate universe and you've got a very large, clanky, grumpy party. That's even before you take into account whether or not the Cryons succeed in taking their world back. So how do you deal with it? What happens when the Doctor leaves and how does that effect any future adventures you want to have on Telos? Here are four ideas:

Free Telos: The planet is liberated from the Cybermen and returns to a utopian state under the full control of the Cryons (or maybe not so utopian: see Further Adventures, below).

Telos In Two: Telos is retaken by the Cybermen who are now made up of three factions: the survivors of Telos, the survivors of Mondas and the shattered remnants of the Lumic Cybermen who survived their defeats at Torchwood Tower, in 19th century London and 21st century London. The Cryons are driven further underground as the three Cyber factions war, knowing full well that unless someone (perhaps someone with a blue police box...) does something, the Cybermen will eventually unite and become all-but unstoppable.

The Telos Node: The Cyber Wars are at their height, countless millions of Cyberman, Mites, Mats and Shades on countless worlds efficiently and brutally dispatching their enemies. The key to their success is the Cyberiad Tactical Grid, a vast, solar system-sized computer that changes tactics in real time, fighting the war on every front at once.

At the centre of the Grid is the world that used to be Telos. Now, it's a processing centre for Cybermen communications, the last few Cryons still fighting a hopeless war. Without it, the wars will grind to a halt, possibly long enough for the tide to turn, but any mission to destroy it faces near certain failure. Which is, of course, why the TARDIS 'accidentally' arrives there just as the commando unit sent to do it begin their assault.

The Telos Memorial: Everything detailed above happens and, when the Cyberman are finally defeated and the Silver Devastation is left behind, Telos is repaired and moved to the edge of the solar system. There, survivors and veterans from the Cyber Wars work as volunteers to tend a planet-sized graveyard which conceals one of the largest arsenals in the galaxy's history, because the Cybermen are never quite defeated and the races that have come to the Telos Memorial have vowed to be ready when they rise again.

WHY TOTTER'S LANE?

The TARDIS does seem remarkably fond of IM Foreman's Yard in Totter's Lane doesn't it? Several Doctors have spent time there and over the year there've been several explanations offered as to why this is the TARDIS' favourite spot on Earth. Here are a few:

Favourite Place: The yard on Totter's Lane is the first place the TARDIS travelled with the Doctor and it's imprinted on it to some extent. Just like humans have favourite places, the TARDIS' favourite place is Totter's Lane and it will go there by choice, or if it's hurt or damaged, whenever it can.

Anchor Point: The TARDIS and the Doctor both ran from Gallifrey when they met each other (although who stole who is a matter of debate). Totter's Lane is the first place the Doctor went that wasn't the stuffy world he'd fled from, and the first place his battered old Type 40 had been in countless years. It's where they imprinted on one another, and where the relationship between a Time Lord and his TARDIS was forged. As a result, the area exerts a tremendous pull on the TARDIS even now, and unless a specific location in London is programmed in, it will always go there.

Time Lord Outpost: We've seen, time and again, that the Time Lords take far more of an interest in their errant, occasional, President than they want to admit. Perhaps Totter's Lane is a Time Lord 'safe house', a place a TARDIS can be easily concealed whilst certain work is done...

TIMEY-WHAT NOW?

Bates and Strattons' time ship is an odd element of this adventure as the Doctor never really finds anything out about it other than what it's going to be used for. That's a shame as this is clearly a reliable, human-controlled time machine, something which gives every appearance of being historically very important, not to mention dangerous. Here are three possible explanations for it and how you could fold them into adventures:

52nd Century Blues: Stratton, Bates and their dead colleague were the crew of a commercial time-ship similar to the one the Doctor encountered in ***The Girl in the Fireplace*** (see **The Tenth Doctor Sourcebook**). However, where that craft could only open time windows, the time-ship could travel through them. It was hired by a media company to produce a documentary about the Cyber-era on Telos, but was detected, dragged through and the crew captured. The time window it opened is still active, and the characters can, if they have the skills, fly the ship back through. At which point they'll have to talk down a very twitchy 52nd century military and become overnight celebrities. That may not be a good thing, especially if a Cybermat or mite or two hitched a ride across.

Action Archaeologists: Stratton and Bates were part of the first Torchwood archive crew to pilot the Lorenzo, the part-TARDIS, part-spacecraft that Jack Harkness had been growing in the Torchwood hub. The ship, whilst not quite a TARDIS, is still immensely powerful and the three men were ordered to destroy it if the mission went awry. However, the Lorenzo decided it wanted to live and crash landed, leading to the situation we see in *Attack of the Cybermen* and a possibly mad, partially TARDIS time machine on the loose immediately after it...

The Legacy Device: The time machine is from the 52nd century and Statten is a distant relative of Henry van Statten, whom the Ninth Doctor met in ***Dalek*** (see **The Ninth Doctor Sourcebook**). The last of his family, Statten put the machine together to create the Van Statten Brain Trust, a collection of his relatives from the previous centuries that would form the greatest business mind in human history. The only problem is, the Cyberman head in Van Statten's collection has been passed down to the other family members and, unbeknownst to any of them, it wasn't quite dead. The head awoke, interfaced with the ship, knocked it off course and began the course of events that would lead to the Doctor being brought to Telos.

TOMORROW, WHEN THE WAR BEGAN

Mondas will appear in Earth's solar system and launch a massive Cyberman invasion in 1986. It's not quite a fixed point in time (The Doctor hates those, remember) but its close. As a result, the revelation in this story of the coming attack may well mess with your characters a little bit. They'll want to do something, warn people, see if they can join the fight. Here's what could happen, depending on when your characters are from:

Before the 20th Century: Any group of companions from before the 20th Century are going to be both massively concerned by the coming invasion and, weirdly, take it in their stride. After all, they're travelling the universe in a time machine driven by an alien and once you get past that everything else is never quite as strange...

1986: Any group from 1986 or thereabouts are going to be desperately concerned and want to warn people or do something. Technically the Doctor shouldn't cross his own timeline but that's (almost) never stopped him before. Have him take them to Earth during the invasion, help out a very surprised, and young, Brigadier or have a chance to see a family member again.

Alternatively, there's nothing to stop the Doctor stopping by in 1986 and sweeping them up in the wake of the invasion. After all, lots of cleaning up to do and who wants to stick around for that?

After 1986: This is arguably the most interesting option, especially if the characters don't remember the invasion. Having them return to witness it or be invited to a UNIT memorial service for those lost in the attack would make for a fascinating, troubling adventure that could explore the ability humanity has to heal from its wounds, the Doctor's presence in Earth history and how some things can't be changed. Not to mention the Cybermen left alive after the battle and the attention it will have attracted from other nearby races.

TECHNOLOGY

Sonic Lance

A much more basic tool than the Sonic Screwdriver, the Sonic Lance is still a versatile piece of equipment. It can be used to cut wires and metal as well as weld them for short periods of time. The only issue with the tool is its tendency to heat up rapidly if left on for long periods of time.

Traits: Restriction (Gets Hot), Weld.
Cost: 1 Story Point

Vastial

Vastial is a naturally occurring mineral on Telos that's completely inert at the temperatures the Cryons need in order to live. However, once it reaches 15 degrees celsius it becomes immensely and instantly explosive. Ten grams of vastial does 4/**L**/L damage, increasing to L/**L**/L for 15 grams and the explosion radius increasing by five feet for every 5 grams added after that.

FURTHER ADVENTURES

- **Deep Freeze:** The Doctor is invited back to Telos in 1995 for the ten year anniversary of the attack. The planet is covered in ice once again, the Cryons having used the experimental world engines the Cybermen were working on to move the world even further out from its sun. They plan on taking the world between solar systems, turning it into a generation ship that would travel the cosmos and offer sanctuary to the victims of the Cybermen. It's a laudable ideal, but when hostages are taken during the service, the characters find out a small group of Cryons have become obsessed with the Cyberman ideal of artificial enhancement and have adopted it. Now, these creatures, not quite Cyberman, not quite Cryon, want to join the Cyberiad and they plan on taking the entire planet with them.

- **A Murder of Comets:** It's 1993 and, somehow, Halley's comet is back. The TARDIS arrives in the solar system just in time to see it hurtle past, far too quickly, smash into Earth. The crew look on in horror as another comet flies past, and another. And another. Each one is Halley's Comet from a slightly different time stream. Each one is being targeted through a time window set up using the timeship. The characters must infiltrate the ship, reason with or defeat the crew and stabilise the time window to before the attack, before the Cyber Fleet reaches Earth and history is locked onto a different course.

- **Waifs and Strays:** The TARDIS is hit, mid-Vortex, by the timeship. Aboard are other work camp escapees and, in a specially cooled level, a pair of Cryons. They claim that the Cybermen have returned to Telos and are systematically eradicating every multi-celled lifeform there. They beg for the Doctor's help, but there's something wrong aboard the timeship. The ghostly form of Lytton walks the halls, the Cryons can't remember their names and in the lowest level, something which used to be a Cyber-Planner begins extending its mind into the TARDIS, hoping to be much, much more.

VENGEANCE ON VAROS

'It's all right for you, Peri. You've only got one life. You'll age here in the TARDIS and then die. But me, I shall go on regenerating until all my lives are spent.'

SYNOPSIS

Varos, 23rd Century

Jondar, one of the few to rebel against the planet's regime, was being tortured. He was chained to a wall, with a laser being played over his bare chest. Arak and Etta, two other Varosians were watching the TV broadcast of this. They discussed the food rationing, Jondar's fate and a punch-in vote that had been called by the Governor for later that night.

In the TARDIS, the Doctor was busy repairing the control console. Peri was relieved he hadn't added to the catalogue of disasters (three electrical fires, a power failure, a near collision with an asteroid, getting lost in the TARDIS corridors twice, wiping the memory of the flight computer, jettisoning three quarters of the storage hold and burning, somehow, her cold supper). He assured her everything was fine now, and almost straight away the TARDIS came to a halt in open space. The ship had lost all power. They were stranded. The Doctor could do nothing.

Back on Varos, Sil, the Mentor representative of the Galatron Mining corporation, was preparing to restart negotiations with the Varosian Governor over the price of Zeiton-7 ore. Zeiton-7 was only found on Varos and the Governor wanted a price for it that could let him feed his people and pay them fairly. Sil wanted nothing of the sort. The talks ended in stalemate once again because, unknown to the Governor, his Chief Officer was working for Sil. Their plan was simple; refuse to budge and eventually the Governor would remove himself from the situation.

The Governor would have to ask the people to vote for whether or not they should hold out for a fairer price, and, if they won, the negotiations would continue. If they lost, the Governor would not only have to agree but also undergo Human Cell Disintegration Bombardment, a barbaric disassembling of the body, as punishment for his loss. The Governor, defeated on the motion, barely survived and was clearly in desperate physical pain. Anxious to help buy him time, Bax, a guard, suggested that the Governor execute Jondar sooner. He agreed to do so.

In the TARDIS, the Doctor was sulking. He bemoaned the fact that Peri would simply grow old and die on the powerless ship whereas he would have to live through every single regeneration he had remaining before he could do so. She found the TARDIS manual in an effort to motivate him but instead it led to him revealing he knew exactly what was wrong; the TARDIS had exhausted its supply of Zeiton-7, a rare mineral that allowed the TARDIS to generate orbital energy which in turn allowed it to move. The Doctor realised that they were just close enough to Varos to reach it with the last dregs of power and set off.

On Varos, Areta, Jondar's wife, was visited by Quillam, the disfigured and masked officer in charge of the Cell Mutator, a device that took your innermost fear and turns you into it on the genetic level. He was accompanied by Rondel, a guard, former colleague and friend of Jondar's. Areta begged him for help but he seemed unsympathetic.

Meanwhile, Maldak, the guard assigned to watch over Jondar's death, was told to put his anti-hallucination mask on. When the TARDIS appeared, he fired on it to no effect and, thinking that the Doctor and Peri were hallucinations, was confused long enough for the Doctor to disarm and subdue him. With seconds to go before Jondar's death and with the events being transmitted all over Varos, they used the laser meant to kill him to free him and, cut off from the TARDIS, frantically searched for another means of escape. Along the way they met up with Rondel and Areta, and were forced to flee again when Rondel was killed by the pursuing guards.

Jondar revealed they were in the Punishment Dome, a huge complex designed to showcase creative and horrific torture that was broadcast to the masses. There was no way through aside from the Purple Zone, which the Doctor decided to enter. They were initially terrified by what seemed to be an immense fly but the Doctor, realising that it was an optical illusion, led them past it. The escape seemed to be going well until Jondar, Areta and Peri were captured. The Doctor fled but found himself in a corridor that seemed to be a desert. He refused to believe it but the punishing heat took more and more out of him until he collapsed and, seemingly, died.

Peri was brought to the Control Centre and was horrified to see the Doctor's body being taken to an acid bath. She was questioned by the Governor, Chief Officer and Sil, whose translation equipment kept malfunctioning (something the Governor admitted was his only amusement) and she told them about who she was. In the Corpse Disposal Room, the Doctor suddenly sat up and walked over to the two attendants to explain what had happened. One was so startled he fell into the acid and the other, blaming the Doctor, struggled with him. The fight only ended when the first man, desperately trying to pull himself out of the acid, inadvertently pulled his friend in. The Doctor made his escape.

Unfortunately, he ran directly into Quillam, who apprehended him. Reunited with Peri and the others, the Doctor was told that he and Jondar would be executed "the old fashioned way" whilst Peri and Areta would be put through the Cell Mutator. The Doctor and Jondar were led to an old fashioned gallows, where the Doctor questioned both the Governor and Sil, pointing out how badly he was extorting the Governor and all of Varos. Sil's guards rushed the gallows, trying to force the execution, and the Governor's men weren't able to hold them back. The execution was carried out, the trapdoors beneath the two men opened and...

Nothing happened. Their nooses hadn't been secured so they simply fell harmlessly to the ground. The Governor admitted it was a ruse to see what the Doctor knew and the Doctor demanded that they be taken to Areta and Peri. The Chief Officer claimed it was too late and the Doctor and Jondar overpowered nearby guards and tried to use their weapons to intimidate the officer. It didn't work and the Doctor was forced to shoot the entire Cell Mutator control console. Inside, Peri and Areta had begun to change, feathers and claws forming on their body, but the process had been stopped just in time and they emerged unscathed. The Doctor and Jondar led them in another escape attempt. Once again, this wasn't successful as a dazed Peri was easily recaptured and brought back to the control centre.

There, both she and the Governor were put in the Cell Bombardment Unit. All seemed lost until Maldak, the guard the Doctor and Peri had met when they first arrived, turned the device off and led the Governor and Peri through the ventilation ducts towards the Doctor.The Doctor, Jondar and Areta fought their way to the End Zone of the dome where they faced ghosts of themselves, lava, instantly fatal poisonous plants and cannibals. They barely escaped when the Chief Officer and Quillam cornered them. The two men were killed by a trap using the poisonous plants and, finally, the Doctor, Peri, Jondar and Areta were reunited.

Back in the control room, it was revealed that the Galatron Mining Corporation were now siding with the Varosians, as a second source of Zeiton-7 had been discovered and they were desperate to secure their own supply. They ordered Sil to pay whatever was asked for it and, when the Governor asked for twice the amount Sil had previously refused he raged at being outmanouvered but, reluctantly, agreed.

The Governor thanked the Doctor and Peri for their help and gifted them with as much Zeiton-7 as they needed. As they left, he addressed the planet, telling the startled Varosians that the torture and executions were over and things would be better. Arak and Etta looked on in disbelief as, unnoticed, the TARDIS departed the planet.

CONTINUITY

- Peri finds the TARDIS instruction manual, which the Doctor has disagreed with on several occasions (see ***The Pirate Planet*** in **The Fourth Doctor Sourcebook**), and which the Doctor subsequently throws into a supernova (see ***Amy's Choice*** in **The Eleventh Doctor Sourcebook**). Tegan agreed with the Doctor's assessment in ***Four to Doomsday*** (see ***The Fifth Doctor Sourcebook***).

RUNNING THE ADVENTURE

This is a tough adventure to run well, because there are three things going on at the same time and two of them are pretty difficult to handle.

The first, and easiest, is the traditional "When I Say Run, Run!"adventure with the characters being pursued by the Governor and Sil's forces through the never-ending, always hideous, amusements of the Punishment Dome. This is essentially a Dungeon Crawl for Doctor Who, complete with traps, monsters and secret passages. Go crazy with this approach because the more you put in, the more incidents the characters have to deal with and the more fun everyone will have.

The second, and noticeably harder one, explores the strong undercurrent of horror this adventure has. The characters are being tortured and killed for ratings, their lives and deaths turned into nothing more than ratings spikes. None of the deaths are easy or pleasant either. Balancing the urgency, and horror, of this element of the adventure is extremely difficult as if you go one way you lose this element altogether and if you go the other, the adventure becomes horrific in a way you don't want it to. Avoid this by keeping the pace going, focusing on the action element of the pursuit and use the horror, and there's plenty of it, for added spice.

The third element is the hardest one to land properly, because, fundamentally, this is a political adventure at heart. Getting the conflict between the Governor, the Chief Officer and Sil across is absolutely vital to making this work. Play up the factions, get players to pick sides – especially if they've encountered different factions independently after being split up.

One way to add even more danger and urgency is to separate the characters. Have some of them captured, others run off into the Punishment Dome and Sil suggest they prove themselves by guiding their friends through the maze. Use the Cell Mutator and Cell Bombardment systems as a threat for when they make mistakes and turn it into a game show, rather than a game. Remember: sidestep left, forward, sidestep right...

VAROS

History of Varos

Varos has a very odd history, one that the Doctor mentions in passing. The planet is the former home of an asylum for the criminally insane which, over the centuries, saw the inmates replaced by their sane descendants. However, the power structure was kept in place, with the guards becoming the nobility and the inmates becoming the workforce.

This is one of the oddest, and saddest, histories of anywhere the Doctor has travelled and it bears examination. Varos, when the Doctor visits it, is one part leper colony, one part mining outpost and one part asylum. The Punishment Dome alone shows just how off beam they are as a culture. Varos is almost feral, a colony where great strides have been made in positive and negative directions. Its simultaneously small and vibrant, massive and subdued, the last descendants of the original crew rattling around in an impersonal asylum that's part wild by itself. Keep your characters on their toes, throw something new at them around every corner and keep the action and danger at a constant high. Life on Varos can be cheap. Make sure your characters remember that.

The Punishment Dome

The Doctor visits three specific sections of the Punishment Dome: the Green Zone, the Purple Zone and the End Zone. The Purple and Green Zones both feature illusions, whilst the End Zone looks derelict and run down, as though it's been left to the prisoners driven mad by living in there. If you're running an adventure in the Punishment Dome, you don't have to stick to these sections. Varosian society has been refining the Punishment Dome for generations so any kind of hideous trap you can think of is in there somewhere, and all on camera. If you don't want to lay out the Punishment Dome with any kind of logic, here's a random table for it:

1-2	White Zone (Medical)
3-4	Green Zone (Illusions)
5-6	Purple Zone (Traps)
7-8	Black Zone (Gravity)
9-10	Blue Zone (Environment)
11-12	Red/End Zone (Extreme)

White Zone: Clean, white, brightly lit walls, the smell of disinfectant. These corridors are roamed by Guards following the orders of Mr Quillam, looking for new people to put through the Mutator. The survivors of the Mutator are also all here, left to fight amongst themselves for scraps.

Green Zone: Illusions of increasing severity, starting with simple magnification and building up to holograms of the characters that attempt to lead them into traps. Awareness + Knowledge (Difficulty 12) to notice the first time, increasing by one every time.

Purple Zone: Traps, ranging from simple tripwires and pitfalls – Awareness + Survival (Difficulty 15) – to pressure senses triggering spikes, falls and spring-loaded floor panels – Awareness + Survival (Difficulty 12)

Black Zone: Gravity cycles constantly, ranging from zero – Coordination + Athletics (Difficulty 12) to move – to sudden changes in axis and severity – Coordination + Athletics (Difficulty 16 +1 for every increase of a G).

Blue Zone: Constant changes in temperature and humidity. Corridors can flood at random, the internal micro-climate can lead to snow and hurricane-force winds and the Dome's own electrical systems are used to generate localised lightning.

Red Zone: Poisonous vines, cannibals, faults, short circuits and all of the above for good measure.

TORTURE AS TELEVISION

The Human Cell Disintegration Bombardment

Varos' barbaric 'entertainments' had precisely one thing in their favour; they were even handed. The Governor's votes were often linked to a 'Yes/No' voting system installed in viewers' homes. If they majority of votes counted went against the Governor, he or she would undergo Human Cell Disintegration Bombardment (or HCDR for short).

This process was exactly as barbaric as it sounds, a low level Transmat field that separated the subject's molecules slowly rather than the usual rapid process and held them in suspension. The subject was literally dismembered alive and the systemic shock was so huge no one survived more than four 'treatments'.

HCDR EXPOSURE	STRENGTH + SURVIVAL DIFFICULTY	DAMAGE IF UNSUCCESSFUL
1st Exposure	9	-1 Strength
2nd Exposure	14	-1 Resolve
3rd Exposure	19	-1 Strength and Resolve
4th Exposure	24	-2 Strength, Resolve and Awareness
5th Exposure	29	-3 Strength, Resolve and Awareness

Any character surviving past a fifth exposure is going to be a celebrity, and chances are, someone the Varosian government will want to execute in a very creative way, meaning they'll be allowed to rest back up and exploited a little more before their death which, of course, gives them time to plot an escape.

The Cell Mutator

Quillam's mutant child, as the guards makes sure never to call it within earshot, is loosely similar to the HCDR. However, where that's rigged up to a chair, the Cell Mutator is connected to a surgical suite. Patients are wheeled in, linked to the machine and then, their own fear destroys them. The Cell Mutator is an unusually cruel device because it reads the minds of its victims and isolates the thing they fear the most. It then uses that as a template to rewrite their DNA. It does this firstly by washing their genetic structure of all waste material, forcibly turning cells back into stem cells as it goes and then sending them new information. The process is agonising, time-consuming and almost always leads to death by the end of the five round process. The unlucky ones survive.

Like the HCDR, the Cell Mutator is a horrifying device that should be used sparingly. Unlike the HCDR however, the Cell Mutator is not a death sentence. The few that survive it have found themselves changed completely, though rarely for the better.

As a result, any character going through the Cell Mutator should make the tests on the following table. If they fail at any point, they take the damage listed. Once that damage has caused three attributes to drop to 0, or the process has reached the 5th round, it's completed. Prior to this adventure, it would be a good idea to discuss the characters' worst fears with them and, in doing so, get a roadmap for where the Cell Mutator will take them. Alternatively, an Ingenuity + Technology Roll Difficulty 14 will allow the Cell Mutator to be programmed to revert its victims to 'factory settings'. However, the process will again take five rounds and the tests will, again, need to be made, at -1 difficulty.

CELL MUTATOR	STRENGTH + SURVIVAL DIFFICULTY	DAMAGE IF UNSUCCESSFUL
1st Round	13	-1 all attributes
2nd Round	15	-2 all attributes
3rd Round	17	-3 all attributes
4th Round	20	-4 all attributes
5th Round	23	-5 all attributes

THE GALATRON MINING CORPORATION (GMC) AND THE AGE OF THE TIME-SPACE SHIPS

We don't know much about the Galatron Mining Corporation other than they were based on Thoros Beta. That not only explains Sil, but suggests a lot about how the company conducts itself. Clearly more concerned with getting caught using underhanded tactics, they're a cautious, secretive organisation but we do know one vital thing about them; they mine Zeiton-7 to help fuel time-space ships. That in itself is pretty interesting and leads to a possible way you could take the GMC if you wanted to use them in adventures not set on Thoros Beta.

Chronos Stations

The Chronos Stations are scattered across the galaxy in secure, out of the way areas. They are radio dark, small, 5-10 person space stations with food, water, accommodation and, crucially, Zeiton-7 aboard. They act as confidential refuelling stations for time machines, allowing time travellers to fill up on Zeiton-7 and pay for it without having to meet anyone who could do nasty things to their timestream. They don't advertise them because their thinking is future executives of the Corporation will know where the stations are and disseminate that information to their time machines. They also don't tell anyone that the stations have a massively advanced passive scanning array that can identify every part in a ship, strip it down virtually and rebuild it in a file that can simply be fed into a production line.

The GMC are banking on the future, literally. And it's starting to pay off.

The GMC are using the information they're gathering from the ships using the Chronos Stations to expand. They're starting to get an idea not only of how the future is going to be, but their role in it, the executives upstream sending information downstream with the ships and using the Chronos Stations as 'dead letter' drops. The end result is a corporation looking after its own interested in two separate time periods and becoming a real temporal force to be reckoned with.

The Curious Case of Zeiton-7

The Time Lords are, by all accounts, the smartest race that has ever lived. They bent time to their will, moved through it with equal parts caution and wild abandon and their entire culture was powered by the insane, brilliant concept of harnessing the energy of black holes.

They strode across the universe like Titans and, even in the dark days of the Time War, were regarded as gods by the races who did know they were there.

All of which begs the question: why would one of the smartest, oldest races in creation rely on a mineral that could only be found in a very small amount of places to power their time machines? Well, there are a number of possible answers to that;

- **Zeiton-7, Everywhere:** Zeiton-7 used to be one of the most common minerals in the universe but the Time Lords and, eventually, other time-faring races, used so much of it that only Varos and a small amount of other places are left.

- **The Breadcrumb Effect:** Zeiton-7 doesn't need to be used by timeships. It's an effective fuel, certainly, but countless other minerals can do the job. The one thing Zeiton-7 has that makes it unique is a temporal half-life, a gradual but constant release of Artron energy that's triggered the moment it's activated in a time engine.

  This leaves a trail of 'breadcrumb' particles through time that allows the Time Lords to monitor all temporal traffic.

- **Temporal Mosaic:** The very first Time Lords had a grand design, a means of altering time on the pico-second level that would pay off millennia after they were dead. They deliberately designed the first few time-machines using Zeiton-7 because the Artron decay that it causes would alter time, over time, to create exactly what they wanted. The only problem is, no one knows what that is any more...

- **Occasional Refills:** It's entirely possible a time machine need only refuel with Zeiton-7 once in its operational life. After all, we never see the Doctor fuel up with it again (and perhaps those rods that are being punched through the TARDIS corridors in ***Journey to the Centre of the TARDIS*** – see **The Eleventh Doctor Sourcebook** – are the Zeiton-7 rods).

  As a result, Zeiton-7 is still a vital part of the ship but the Doctor isn't constantly tapping the gauge worriedly, checking on levels.

- **The Motherlode:** Varos is made entirely out of Zeiton-7, meaning the supply is functionally infinite.

THE MENTORS

The Mentors are a race of small, aquatic aliens. They have skin tone ranging from black to green and yellow and a large, bony crest on top of their skulls. Their bodies taper down to a tail which allows them to move through water with tremendous ease, but means they must be carried everywhere on land.

The Mentors are an infamously driven race and the ones that have made their way out into the galaxy have made real marks in their chosen fields. Completely ruthless when called upon to be, the Mentors also delight in using their unusual appearance to throw off colleagues and 'opponents' in the never ending business wars they find themselves drawn to.

THE MENTORS

AWARENESS	4	PRESENCE	2
COORDINATION	2	RESOLVE	5
INGENUITY	5	STRENGTH	2

SKILLS
Convince 5, Knowledge 4, Science 4, Subterfuge 5, Technology 4

TRAITS
Alien
Alien Appearance
Environmental - Water
Selfish
Size - Tiny
Slow

TECH LEVEL: 6 STORY POINTS: 1-3

SIL

Sil is a business warrior, a man who prides himself in winning every negotiation he's part of. It's not because of loyalty – Sil's loyalty is as wide as his paycheck and no wider – but it's because Sil is the best negotiator in the galaxy and every single chance he has to prove it is a chance he welcomes. He's never killed anyone personally – he has people for that – but his actions have been directly responsible for the death or suffering of millions of people. None of that matters. All that does is the slick, oily joy of the contract being signed, the deal being agreed. The smell of victory, for Sil, is one of old paper and leather briefcases, air conditioned climate controlled rooms and the sweat of fear on his opponent's brows. He loves winning and he's very very good at it.

THE GOVERNOR

The unnamed Governor of Varos is a complicated man. On the one hand, he's presided over the creation of torture and murder as entertainment, recreating bread and circuses to distract his populace from their miserable lives and the awful price the GMC were prepared to pay for their hard work.

On the other, the Governor is a man who did what he had to do to stop a colony of the descendants of the criminally insane from tearing each other apart.

The fact that he went through the Cell Dismemberment three times is testament to his determination and fortitude, as is his willingness to realise the Doctor is actually there to help. A complicated man, certainly, but a good one in the right circumstances.

SIL

AWARENESS	4	PRESENCE	3
COORDINATION	3	RESOLVE	5
INGENUITY	5	STRENGTH	2

SKILLS
Convince 2, Fighting 3, Subterfuge 5, Technology 4.

TRAITS
Alien
Alien Appearance
Cowardly
Environmental - Water
Keen Senses
Selfish
Size - Tiny
Slow

TECH LEVEL: 6 STORY POINTS: 4

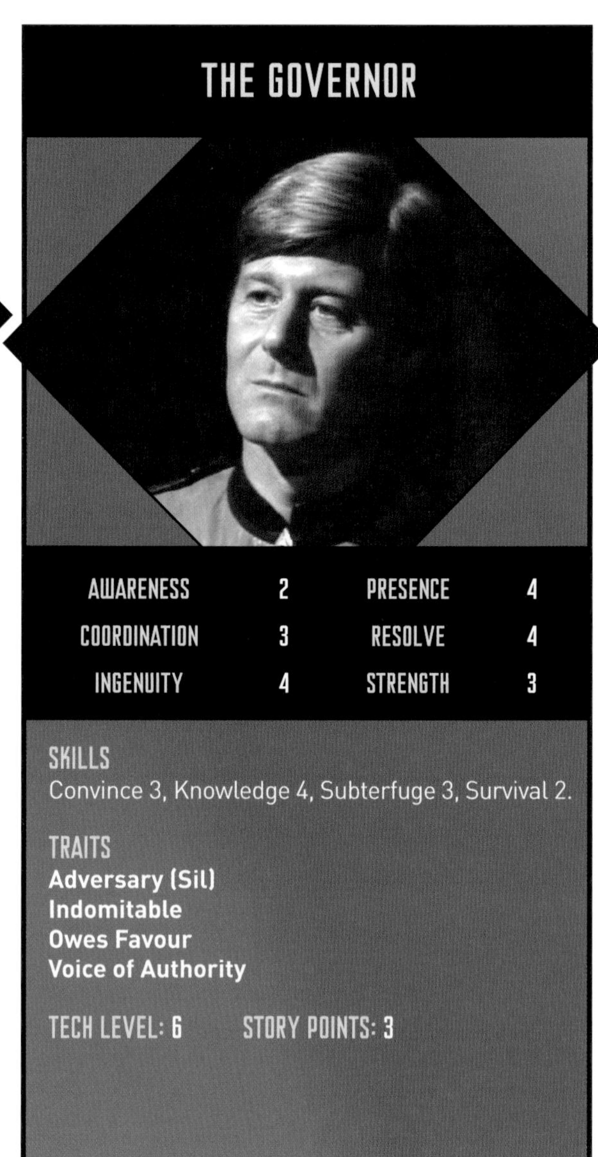

THE GOVERNOR

AWARENESS	2	PRESENCE	4
COORDINATION	3	RESOLVE	4
INGENUITY	4	STRENGTH	3

SKILLS
Convince 3, Knowledge 4, Subterfuge 3, Survival 2.

TRAITS
Adversary (Sil)
Indomitable
Owes Favour
Voice of Authority

TECH LEVEL: 6 STORY POINTS: 3

THE CHIEF OFFICER

Sil's right hand man on Varos, even though no one but the pair of them know it. The Chief Officer is an obsequious, overly polite thug. He's a man who has no problem making countless millions of other lives miserable as long as he gets paid. A career politician, and the perfect person for Sil to have working the angles for him.

THE CHIEF OFFICER

AWARENESS	2	PRESENCE	4
COORDINATION	3	RESOLVE	3
INGENUITY	2	STRENGTH	4

SKILLS
Athletics 2, Convince 4, Fighting 2, Marksman 2, Subterfuge 3.

TRAITS
Dark Secret
Tough

TECH LEVEL: 6 STORY POINTS: 2

QUILLAM

The disfigured Chief of Programming on Varos loves his work. Quillam is halfway between a TV scheduler, a psychologist and Doctor Frankenstein; a man fascinated by the machine he's developed that makes your inner ugliness your outer form. Polite, calm and sociopathic, he may be the most dangerous man on the planet.

QUILLAM

AWARENESS	2	PRESENCE	3
COORDINATION	3	RESOLVE	3
INGENUITY	5	STRENGTH	4

SKILLS
Athletics 3, Convince 4, Fighting 3, Knowledge 4, Medicine 4, Science 4, Technology 4.

TRAITS
Boffin
Distinctive
Insatiable Curiosity

WEAPONS: Guard sidearm 1/3/L

TECH LEVEL: 6 STORY POINTS: 2

MALDAK

Maldak and his fellow guards are the bottom run of the elite, men and women who do the scut work in return for being able to live in relative comfort. Maldak's a good soldier, who once spent eight days in the ventilation tunnels looking for someone, but he's starting to grow weary of Varos and its parade of horrors. Something needs to change, soon, and it's not just the channel...

MALDAK

AWARENESS	2	PRESENCE	4
COORDINATION	3	RESOLVE	3
INGENUITY	3	STRENGTH	4

SKILLS
Convince 3, Fighting 4, Marksman 4, Transport 3.

TRAITS
Brave
By the Book

WEAPONS: Guard sidearm 1/3/L, Anti-Hallucination Helmet (+3 to all Resolve checks in the Punishment Dome whilst wearing it)

TECH LEVEL: 6 STORY POINTS: 1

JONDAR

A leading rebel, Jondar became famous both for his good looks and the fact he was a guard before he revolted. To see a member of the ruling class turn against Varosian society entranced and enraged the populace in equal measure and Jondar's attacks, and eventual capture, were amongst the highest rated programs that month. Now, his torture, and execution, look set to break even those viewing records...

JONDAR

AWARENESS	3	PRESENCE	3
COORDINATION	4	RESOLVE	3
INGENUITY	3	STRENGTH	4

SKILLS
Fighting 4, Marksman 4, Survival 3, Transport 3.

TRAITS
Brave
Impulsive
Tough

TECH LEVEL: 6 STORY POINTS: 1

ARETA

Jondar's mate, Areta supported him but her own revolt was eclipsed by his celebrity. Now under detention, she waits for the inevitable moment of Jondar's death as well as her own. An intelligent, driven woman, she's every inch the rebel Jondar is and is far more articulate than he is. If Jondar is the new face of the rebellion, Areta is the new voice. The only question is whether or not she'll be allowed to speak.

ARETA

AWARENESS	3	PRESENCE	3
COORDINATION	3	RESOLVE	4
INGENUITY	3	STRENGTH	3

SKILLS
Convince 4, Fighting 3, Knowledge 3, Science 3, Subterfuge 3.

TRAITS
Brave
Voice of Authority

TECH LEVEL: 6 STORY POINTS: 1

ARAK AND ETTA

Arak and Etta are the only look we get at the lower levels of the Varosian population. Healthy, educated and moderately well off, the pair have completely opposing politics which they banter about constantly. They're also completely desensitised to violence, happily criticising torture for looking 'fake' even though it isn't. They're worn down, and resentful and charming for all that. They'd certainly be a pleasure to watch TV with, as long as you make sure you're not in the program they're watching...

ARAK

AWARENESS	3	PRESENCE	2
COORDINATION	3	RESOLVE	3
INGENUITY	2	STRENGTH	4

SKILLS
Craft 3, Fighting 2, Survival 1, Transport 3.

TRAITS
Argumentative
Face in the Crowd

TECH LEVEL: 6 STORY POINTS: 1

ETTA

AWARENESS	3	PRESENCE	3
COORDINATION	4	RESOLVE	4
INGENUITY	3	STRENGTH	2

SKILLS
Convince 2, Knowledge 3, Technology 2.

TRAITS
By the Book
Face in the Crowd

TECH LEVEL: 6 **STORY POINTS: 1**

VEHICLES

Varosian Guard Buggy
Small and fast, these small runabouts were born from the twin needs of mining and hunting down escaped prisoners.

They can carry a single driver plus up to three passengers and are unarmed. However, their speed and manoeuvrability makes it easy for guards to catch prisoners escaping on foot.

Armour	Hit Capacity	Speed
0	6	10

FURTHER ADVENTURES

- **Lights! Camera! Revolution!** The TARDIS arrives back on Varos to celebrate the 100th anniversary of its liberation and the characters are immediately arrested. Something has gone terribly wrong, the planet is covered in statues and temples to Sil, the AI running the Punishment Dome has his personality and the great god of Commerce, GMC, is worshipped by the entire planet. Now, trapped in an even more feral Punishment Dome, they must face trial by death trap.

- **The Diamond World:** The TARDIS arrives on Varos thousands of years before their first visit and find a different, far larger world. A solid nugget of Zeiton-7, the world is being strip mined by automated ships of Gallifreyan design. Advanced Gallifreyan design.

  Why are Time Lords from the future here? Why are they so well armed? What's the Time War? And why, in the heart of Varos, is a mechanical voice counting down. Something is sleeping in the Diamond World, and the Time Lords want to know what is. They won't like what they find.

- **The Varos Job:** The TARDIS is out of Zeiton-7 again and the Doctor, muttering that the old girl just likes it on Varos, coaxes her into land. In nothing.

  Varos has gone. The entire world has been spirited away and the only sign of it having been there is a small, automated beacon advertising "Sabalom Glitz's Solar System Removal Services. We've Got Your World On Our Shoulders!" Now, the Doctor and his companions must follow the exhaust trail of Glitz's ship in a limping, almost dead TARDIS, fight off the changes in environment and layout in the ship, find Varos and refuel.

THE MARK OF THE RANI

'What's he up to now? It'll be something devious and overcomplicated. He'd get dizzy if he tried to walk in a straight line.'

SYNOPSIS

England, 1820s

Something was very wrong in the English village of Killingworth. With the Luddite riots gripping the country, groups of enraged miners were attacking anyone with machinery. To make matters worse, the men were behaving brutal and savagely.

The Doctor and Peri saw this first hand when they arrived. Initially on course for Kew Gardens, they were drawn to Killingworth for reasons the Doctor didn't understand. Detecting an anomaly in time, he and Peri set out for the village, with his companion more than a little fed up that her fancy outfit would do nothing but get dirty.

Before they could get very far, they saw a group of men assaulting a horse and trap carrying machinery. The men fled and when the Doctor tried to help one with his wounds, he saw a distinctive red mark on the side of his neck. The man ran from him before the Doctor could do anything and he and Peri accepted a lift from the grateful trap driver into town. On the way, they passed an old lady running the local bath house and the time scanner spiked briefly.

Unknown to the Doctor, the old lady was the Rani, a Time Lady exiled from Gallifrey. And unknown to her, the Master was also in Killingworth and after sending a group of the Luddites to try and kill the Doctor, he visited the Rani. She admitted who she was, and explained that the inhabitants of the planet she had taken as her own, Miasimia Goria, had a problem. The Rani's experiments had destroyed their ability to sleep and she was using a parasite to alter the brain chemistry of the local men and use their cerebral fluid to help her people rest. The Master pointed out the Doctor was here and suggested they team up. The Rani reluctantly agreed.

The Doctor and Peri, meanwhile, had found out George Stephenson, an engineering genius the Doctor greatly admired, was in town. Even better, he was giving a talk to a group of equally historical vital figures. The Doctor and Peri bluffed their way to the meeting but were accosted by the Master's Luddites on the way. The attack left the Doctor hanging from a chain over a mineshaft and his time scanner destroyed. One of the Luddites had already plummeted to his death and the Doctor looked set to join him before Lord Ravensworth, the local mine owner, appeared and scared the men off. He berated the Doctor and Peri, revealing he knew they were impostors.

Discovering that several men in the village had disappeared and realising there was something unusual about the old woman they'd seen, the Doctor disguised himself as a miner and visited it. However, he was soon knocked out and woke up strapped to a gurney by the Rani. They bickered and the Rani admitted she'd been harvesting humanity for centuries. Peri was captured and the Master returned mockingly showing the Doctor his TARDIS being thrown down a mine shaft and ordering his Luddites to wheel the Doctor outside. The Doctor kicked the Master's weapon free and he and Peri escaped. However, his gurney was pushed the wrong way and the Doctor began hurtling back towards the open shaft, with Peri in desperate pursuit.

At the last possible moment, George Stephenson stopped the gurney and unstrapped the Doctor. Fleeing with Stephenson, Peri and the Doctor met his assistant, Luke, whose father was one of the men the Rani had taken. Stephenson explained that he was planning on assembling the various engineering geniuses so they could pool their talents but the Doctor was cautious about doing so in such a dangerous climate. Peri, a botanical specialist, suggested using a sleeping draft to knock the miners out and was told the herbs she would need were in Redfern Dell. Whilst they were talking the Master cornered Luke and hypnotised him into killing anyone who tried to stop the meeting. The Master's plan was simple; control the geniuses of the Industrial Revolution, shape their minds and use them to create an Earth that he would rule, at the centre of a vast empire.

As this was happening, the Doctor and Peri snuck back to the bath house and the Doctor discovered the Rani's TARDIS, hidden behind a screen print of a volcano that spewed actual mustard gas. Disarming the booby traps, he went aboard and was amazed to discover dinosaur embryos and, suddenly, the TARDIS dematerialising. Peri watched in horror as it vanished. He discovered dinosaur embryos in storage in her control room and was surprised both by this, and the TARDIS disappearing with him inside. The Master and the Rani came aboard, the Rani picking up a stack of land mines that she revealed she'd laid in wait for the Doctor in Redfern Dell. In the meantime, Peri, to try and get over her panic at seeing the Doctor vanish, had gone looking for the herbs she needed for the sleeping draft. She met Luke, who, unknown to her, realised she was a threat to the meeting. He took her to Redfern Dell, planning to kill her.

The Doctor arrived at the last possible minute, with Peri already terrified by the sight of Luke stepping on one of the mines and becoming a tree. The Doctor, holding the two other Gallifreyans hostage, forced the Rani to walk Peri out of the minefield and was taking them back to the TARDIS to face justice when the enraged Luddites appeared. The Rani and the Master mockingly pointed out the moral dilemma he faced, and Peri volunteered to hold them at gunpoint whilst he tried to save the miners. The Doctor did what he could but was captured, and strung up by the miners on a pole. When they walked through the minefield, the two men carrying him became trees and the Doctor only just avoided it himself.

Peri, in the meantime, had been holding the Master and the Rani hostage. The Rani faked a coughing attack and begged to be allowed to use her tablets. Peri relented and the Rani threw a 'tablet' at the ground, dispensing dust that knocked her out. The two Gallifreyans escaped and the Doctor found Peri, alive and unharmed, but guilty at letting them go. The Doctor reassured her he'd picked up a few tricks, something the Master and the Rani found out to their cost as the Rani's TARDIS accelerated far faster than normal. Stuck to a wall by the force of the acceleration, the two evil Gallifreyans watched in horror as one of the Rani's dinosaur embryos was knocked from its jar and began to grow...

Back in Killingworth, the Doctor and Peri said their goodbyes to Stephenson and Lord Ravensworth, who had arranged for the TARDIS to be retrieved from the mineshaft. The Doctor gives Ravensworth the vial of brain fluid the Rani had harvested (and he'd picked from her pocket) And they leave.

CONTINUITY

- This is the first time we've seen the Master since his apparent demise at the end of ***Planet of Fire***. Presumably he escaped, somehow.
- Time Lords are immune to rabies, or so Peri surmises.

RUNNING THE ADVENTURE

There's a lot of fun to be had in this adventure, with the historical setting, multiple Time Lords and some wonderfully nasty traps (the Tree Mines especially). There are three things to remember when running it:

Earth Doesn't Mean Safe

The Luddite Riots were a feverish, terrifying time for those in the middle of them. Look at the Doctor in this adventure, nearly pushed down a mine shaft twice, constantly interrupting or getting into fights and strung up on a pole at one point. Use the familiar setting to lull the characters into relaxing, then hit them with the first incident and see how they react.

Cat and Mouse

All three Time Lords we meet here are clearly playing a very different sort of game. The Master is so driven to kill the Doctor he purposely diverts the Doctor's TARDIS just so they will encounter one another, the Rani is happily using one race to give her what she needs to help another one and the Doctor views both of them as intellectual rivals far more than actual threats.

There's a real opportunity here, much like in ***Family of Blood*** (see **The Tenth Doctor Sourcebook**), to show just how alien he is. This adventure is a game of three-way chess, played between three alien geniuses. Make it feel like that.

With that in mind, don't be afraid to throw big ideas at your characters, the adventure certainly isn't. The Rani, the Master, the Luddite riots, human geniuses, the parasites, the brain fluid, the Rani's TARDIS, the tree mines and near constant peril all combine to make this a breathless story. Make sure your characters feel that. Once they hit the first reveal, keep them coming, as they're dragged further and further into the insane schemes of the Rani.

Historical Doesn't Mean Dull

Historical stories are just as action, and idea, packed as any other; they just have an added advantage: context. The Luddite riots are a fascinating, visceral period of history where people were, they felt, being forced to choose between their families and their jobs. Whilst the answer was never quite that simple, it's an emotive, exciting time for an adventure, as is the Industrial Revolution itself. This is the moment where Britain stood on the cusp of something massive and, as no less an authority than Captain Jack says, you've got to be ready. Keep it action packed and fast paced, but throw characters in there too and use technology level to show how this is just as alien a world as any other planet. After all, Killingworth is a place where you need to go to an entirely different building to bathe, there's every chance you'll be attacked on the way into the village and everyone works for the same person. Think of it like Varos, but cheerier and with more flat caps.

THE LUDDITES

The Luddites were part of a larger movement of popular protest throughout the UK in the 19th Century. A lot of these riots were about food, but the Luddites were protesting something more insidious;

a threat to their jobs. Initially textile workers protested the new machinery that was taking work away from them. They were often met with local support and were almost a private army, meeting on the moors at night to practice drills and manoeuvres. They were a persistent threat throughout Nottinghamshire, Yorkshire and Lancashire especially and even went as far as assassinating William Horsfall, a mill owner in West Yorkshire. In fact they were so feared that several mill owners had 'panic rooms' put in their buildings so they could hide during a Luddite attack. This level of fear couldn't be tolerated for long, and through the combination of a mass trial and the never-ending stream of innovation, the Luddite movement faded away.

In adventure terms, the Luddites are an interesting, ambiguous group. They were clearly a real threat to the Doctor in this adventure, but had the Master's plans to industrialise Earth worked, they would have come in very handy. The enemy of my enemy is my friend, after all.

GEORGE STEPHENSON

George Stephenson was the father of the modern railway. An engineer, he developed the rail gauge that is still used worldwide today. He was born in 1781 and is best known for building the first public inter-city railway line in the world to use steam locomotives in 1830. The Liverpool and Manchester Railway sealed an already renowned position as one of the figureheads of the self-starting, hard-working Victorian work ethic that included developing early locomotives and a working miner's safety lamp that was amongst the first of its kind.

When the Doctor meets him, it's instantly clear that Stephenson is not only a genius (so no psychic paper) but also a kindred spirit. He's fascinated by engineering, by the nuts and bolts of how things work and why they do, and finds real beauty and peace in that. He's also an idealist, a man who believes that any problem he can't solve simply needs more brain power. No wonder he and the Doctor get on so well.

GEORGE STEPHENSON

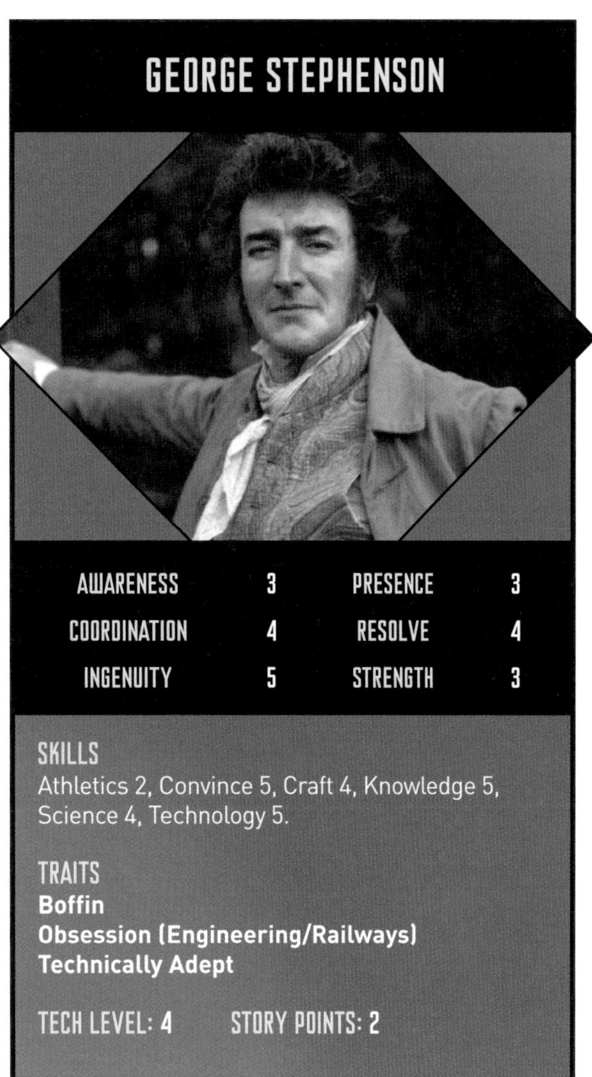

AWARENESS	3	PRESENCE	3
COORDINATION	4	RESOLVE	4
INGENUITY	5	STRENGTH	3

SKILLS
Athletics 2, Convince 5, Craft 4, Knowledge 5, Science 4, Technology 5.

TRAITS
Boffin
Obsession (Engineering/Railways)
Technically Adept

TECH LEVEL: 4 STORY POINTS: 2

LORD RAVENSWORTH

Lord Ravensworth was born in 1775 and succeeded his father in 1791. He owned family estates at Ravensworth Castle and Eslington Park, and had large interests in coal mining. He was also an MP and High Sheriff of Northumberland. He'd go on to be made Baron Ravensworth of Ravensworth Castle in 1821.

But what makes him really interesting, especially here, is how smart a patron he was. Ravensworth had his house demolished in 1808 and replaced with a new Gothic mansion and he employed George Stephenson at his Killingworth Colliery to research and develop steam power. This was then used to improve the efficiency of the wagons that transported coal to the Tyne, which made the colliery more efficient and the mine safer.

It also means he was a futurist, a man who saw the possibilities that could make life better, was smart enough to realise he wasn't smart enough to do it himself and decided to throw money at the people who could. That willingness to step aside is an admirable trait and, combined with his belief in Stephenson, made him a powerful ally for Stephenson and, potentially, your characters.

LORD RAVENSWORTH

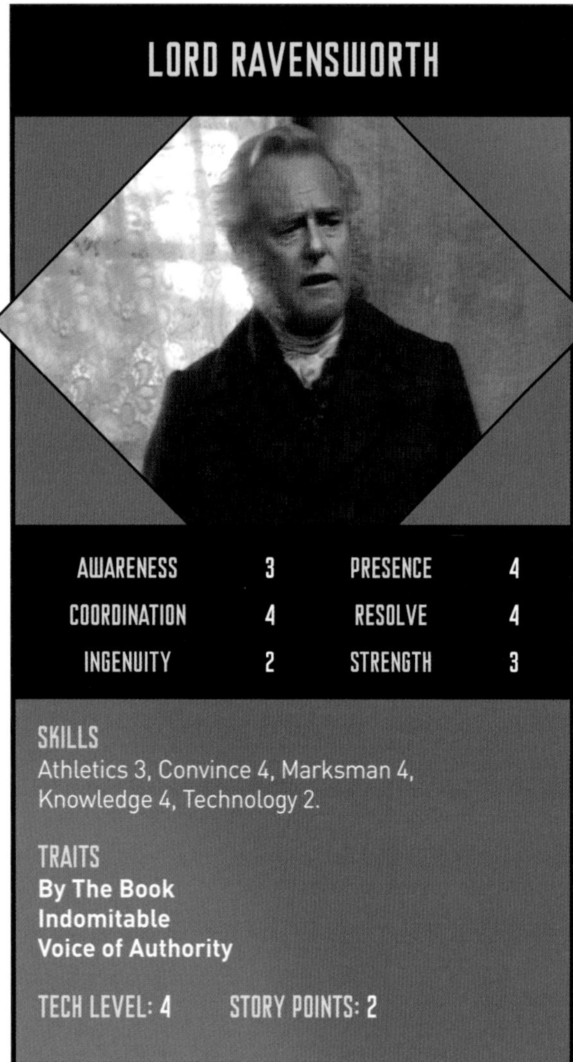

AWARENESS	3	PRESENCE	4
COORDINATION	4	RESOLVE	4
INGENUITY	2	STRENGTH	3

SKILLS
Athletics 3, Convince 4, Marksman 4, Knowledge 4, Technology 2.

TRAITS
By The Book
Indomitable
Voice of Authority

TECH LEVEL: 4 **STORY POINTS: 2**

LUKE

Stephenson's assistant, Luke is the son of one of the miners the Rani has taken. He's a smart young man, instinctively academic in a way that has isolated him from the other people in his village. As a result, he both views Stephenson as a mentor and a lifeline, and is desperate to get his father back.

LUKE

AWARENESS	2	PRESENCE	2
COORDINATION	3	RESOLVE	3
INGENUITY	4	STRENGTH	3

SKILLS
Athletics 3, Craft 3, Marksman 1, Knowledge 3, Science 2, Technology 3, Transport 1.

TRAITS
Brave

TECH LEVEL: 4 **STORY POINTS: 1**

MINERS

The men who've had their cerebral fluid drained by the Rani are just the same as they were before the process, aside from one thing. They're constantly aggressive and that aggression is coupled with a total lack of morality. These are good men, certainly but they're no longer in control and that makes them dangerous to everyone who crosses their path.

MINER

AWARENESS	4	PRESENCE	3
COORDINATION	5	RESOLVE	1
INGENUITY	3	STRENGTH	5

SKILLS
Athletics 4, Fighting 5, Marksman 1.

TRAITS
Impulsive
Quick Reflexes

TECH LEVEL: 4 **STORY POINTS: 1**

TECHNOLOGY

Time Scanner (Minor Gadget)

The Doctor's Time Scanner is a handheld offshoot of the TARDIS console itself. It detects the traces of temporal energy left on a time traveller from several miles away, emitting a rising tone as it gets nearer to the subject.

Traits: Scan

THE MASTER'S POCKET WATCH

Of course, the Master, and the Doctor, both use pocket watches later in their lives (see both ***The Family of Blood*** and ***Utopia*** in **The Tenth Doctor Sourcebook**). Whilst the Master is clearly himself in this adventure, there's nothing to stop the watch being part of his Chameleon Arch, just one he's repurposed a bit. Here are some ideas how:

Past Regeneration: The watch contains the memories of a past regeneration, giving the Master a sounding board as well as doubling his hypnotic abilities.

Future Regeneration: The Master was sent the watch by a future incarnation, who encoded his memories into it. It helps him out, as above, but has an ulterior motive, steering him just as the Master steers the Doctor in this story.

Other Time Lord: The Master has stolen the memories of another Time Lord and trapped them in the watch. Which means he gets extra help when he needs it and somewhere out there is a human who used to be a Time Lord, wondering why they have strange dreams...

Hypnotic Watch

Both the Doctor and the Master are gifted hypnotists, but the Master, like any good villain, likes his toys. This appears to be a normal, 20th century pocket watch from Earth. However, when the Master swings it in front of a subject's face, he gets an extra +2 to any attempt to get them to do something.

Tree Mines

The Rani's oddest, and cruellest, weapon, appear to be pressure-sensitive mines. In reality, they're disc-shaped containers with a pressure switch on top. When the switch is pressed, the container fires a concentrated burst of nanites straight upwards. These are programmed with one pattern; a large grey tree (which, rumour has it, was the Rani's favourite childhood hiding place) and when released, the nanites instantly rewrite the target's genetic coding into that tree. This, frankly horrifying, weapon has no known cure. Once the subject is turned, they can't be placed on another mine programmed with their own genetic coding because they're rooted to the spot. To make matters worse, the subject retains their memories and awareness, just distributed through the structure of the tree. Awareness + Survival Difficulty 9 is needed to spot the mines when they're loosely concealed and 11 when they're completely buried. When triggered they instantly reduce every attribute aside from Awareness and Presence to 0. Those get a +1 bonus.

THE CURE

Of course there's a cure. The Rani knows it. And if you do just a couple of little favours for her, she'll give it to you.

THE RANI

Gallifrey is home to a lot of geniuses but some of them are broken and, when you live as long as the Time Lords do, those broken individuals can cause some real trouble. The Rani was a brilliant chemist, with an instinctive understanding of her field and a tremendous aptitude for technology to go with it. However, she was cruel, her sense of humour and morality warped and broken by gazing into the Untempered Schism. The fault wasn't detected at first and the Rani worked as a trusted Time Lady for some time. Then, an unfortunate 'accident' involving forcing mice to grow to huge size led to a scandal. That in turn led to exile. The Rani was still brilliant, but now she was alone. That couldn't stand.

The Rani found Miasimia Goria and with it, a new sense of belonging, a place she could call home and a planet-sized laboratory. Since then she's ruled the planet, happily experimenting on the subjects and seeing how she can make them better. However, a side effect of her work has recently become apparent; the Miasmia Gorians can no longer sleep, and it's killing them. Desperate to save her subjects, the Rani discovered a cure on Earth. The cerebral fluid of human males, if their inhibitions were dropped and aggression lifted, produced exactly the chemicals she needed. The Rani began harvesting what her people needed and, eventually found herself in Killingworth. Setting up the bath house was a perfect cover for the work she needed to do but what the Rani didn't realise was she was far from the only Gallifreyan in the village...

Personality
The Rani is elegant and clinical, the epitome of the brilliant doctor who is unconcerned with her patients. To her, anyone who isn't a Time Lord isn't really any more than an animal to her. Certainly she has favourite pets, but they don't really have feelings. While she is polite and mannered, she is also utterly ruthless and used to getting what she wants. She always works to a precise plan and engages enemies with her intellect, which is also her greatest weapon. She views the Master and the Doctor as both beneath her and deeply foolish, obsessed with their own rivalry to the exclusion of getting any of the real work done.

Background
The Rani is not only a graduate of the same year but the same class at the Prydonian academy as the Doctor and the Master. Like them she found the rules of Gallifrey not to her taste, and as a result was exiled. Not even the Time Lords should be allowed to meddle with her experiments. As she keeps to herself and has few plans to take over the universe the Time Lords mostly leave her alone. A cynic might suggest they hope to benefit from the incredible discoveries she has made, even if they are at the cost of so many lives.

THE RANI'S TARDIS

The Rani's TARDIS appears to be a more recent model than the Doctor's. It's certainly got a functioning Chameleon Circuit and can be controlled remotely, although the Doctor seems to think that's something she developed herself. The interior is stone work with an orrery-like time rotor instead of the Doctor's cylinder.

Stattenheim Remote Control
The Rani's TARDIS has a Stattenheim Remote Control enabling her to summon it to her. The Sixth Doctor is openly impressed, and envious of both this and the one his Second incarnation has when they meet. The Stattenheim can be keyed to a specific TARDIS and allows the holder to summon that TARDIS to wherever they happen to be at that point in space and time. It's an immensely useful device, especially for a pilot with the eccentricities of the Second Doctor.

Clearly the Doctor loses the Stattenheim sometime between his second and sixth lives. We'd suggest he look down the back of the sofa, but as the sofa could be on the other side of the infinite, constantly shifting interior of the TARDIS, it may take a while

Trait: Transmit
Cost: 1 Story Point

THE PARASITES

The parasites the Rani uses are unusual creatures. These small worms attach themselves to the base of the target's brainstem, most commonly from a position on either side of the neck, leaving a distinctive red circular mark. It then disperses over half its body weight into the neural pathways of the brain, both sampling the chemical make-up of the subject and blocking the pathways for sleep and relaxation inducing chemicals. These are diverted back to the body of the parasite itself, which grows and distends to over five times its normal size. The parasite can also be tailored to make the subject docile, imprinting on the first person they see when the parasite takes effect and following their orders.

The parasite's presence creates a red mark on the neck of the subject as the soft tissue bruises from constant pressure. At this point the parasite can either be removed surgically, or, if left unchecked, swells to the point where its presence proves fatal to the host. Once this happens, the parasite can, again, be removed and milked, the fluid its collected removed for later use. The parasite takes so little of the fluid, and filters it so effectively, its ready for medical use immediately. More importantly, it acts as a powerful soporific (-4 to all Resolve rolls to stay conscious if the subject has been fed the fluid) and, when introduced to the brains of a similar species, will encourage relaxation, restfulness and sleep.

Effects

- The subject gains the Impulsive trait.
- The subject loses 1 level of Resolve for every day the parasite is in place
- The subject gains 1 level of Strength for every day the parasite is in place
- The subject stops sleeping and becomes enraged at the slightest provocation

THE RANI

AWARENESS	4	PRESENCE	5
COORDINATION	4	RESOLVE	6
INGENUITY	9	STRENGTH	2

SKILLS

Athletics 3, Convince 3, Craft 1, Fighting 1, Knowledge 5, Marksman 2, Medicine 4, Science 4 (Biology, Chemistry), Subterfuge 4, Survival 2, Technology 3, Transport 3.

TRAITS

Attractive (Minor Good): +2 bonus to any rolls that involve the Rani's looks.
Biochemical Genius (Major Good): May create biological and chemical 'gadgets'. Using science instead of Technology for jiggery pokery.
Boffin (Major Good): Allows the Rani to create Gadgets.
Doctorate (Minor Good): +3 when using Biology or Chemistry.
Indomitable (Major Good): +4 bonus to any rolls to resist psychic control.
Reverse the Polarity of the Neutron Flow (Major Good): May reverse a test result once per adventure.
Quick Reflexes (Minor Good): The Rani always goes first in her Action Round unless taken by surprise.
Technically Adept (Minor Good): +2 to any Technology roll to fix a broken or faulty device.
Time Lord (Special Good)
Time Traveller (Major Good): Familiar with Tech Level 5 and below.
Tough (Minor Good): Reduce total damage by 2.
Voice of Authority (Minor Good Trait): +2 bonus to Presence and Convince rolls.
Vortex (Special Good): The Rani may pilot time craft through the Vortex, and gains +2 when doing so.
Insatiable Curiosity (Minor Bad): The Rani will investigate anything that sparks their curiosity unless they pass a Resolve or Ingenuity roll at -2.
Obsession (Major Bad): Experimentation and biological advancement.
Selfish (Minor Bad): The Rani puts her own needs first.
Wanted Renegade (Special Bad): The Rani is actively hunted by her own people who may catch up with her at awkward moments to bring her to justice.

EQUIPMENT: Mind Control Worms (Special Gadget): Hypnosis (Special), Weapon (4 /L /L)

REGENERATIONS USED: 1

TECH LEVEL: 10 **STORY POINTS:** 7

- Five days in to implantation, with the parasite swelling, the subject begins to feel light headed (-1 to Resolve rolls) and experience blinding headaches. This only enrages them further. Removing one of the parasites is a Coordination + Medical roll (Difficulty 16). The subject must be unconscious before the procedure takes place. If the roll is failed by 4 or less, the parasite floods the host's system with adrenalin and they wake up. If it fails by 5 or more, the subject goes into cardiac arrest and a Coordination + Medical roll (Difficulty 20) is required to revive them.

THE RANI IN HISTORY

The Rani has an interesting relationship with Earth, almost the mirror image of the Doctor's. Where he leaps in feet first to help at every opportunity, she insinuates herself into established historical conflicts and makes them just a little bit worse for reasons that, from a certain angle, look altruistic. Combined with the sort of absent-minded genius it takes to leave live dinosaur embryos lying around it shows she and the Doctor have a lot more in common than she'd care to admit.

After all, it's the Master who wants to take over the planet, whereas the Rani just wants to fix her people. She's cruel and callous, certainly, but she's as close to the Doctor in approach as the Master and that makes for some interesting ambiguities that you can have a lot of fun exploring.

You could play her as troubled by what she's had to do and furious at being put in exile. Alternatively you could play her as revelling in the chance to be free of the stifling hierarchy of Gallifrey (sound like anyone we know?) or as a scientist in the purest sense, a woman utterly unfettered by questions of morality and concerned only with "Can I?" not "Should I?" However you choose, the Rani's combination of intellectual curiosity and amorality makes her a fascinating antagonist and, on occasion, an ally too.

THE MASTER

The Doctor's oldest enemy and closest rival has, like the Rani, seen better days. He's tried everything to deal with the Doctor and none of his elaborate, elegant, savage plans have come to fruition. Defeated, again, the Master found himself faced with a choice: move on or try, once again, to defeat his nemesis. A sane man would have moved on. The Master went to Earth. The Doctor's beloved second home, a place he was sure to come.

Once there, the Master isolated the one thing that the Doctor most admired; the industriousness of humanity, and worked out how to turn it against him. He would control the Industrial Revolution, steer Earth towards his own special brand of greatness and steal humanity out from under the Doctor's nose. The plan was perfect, elegant and simple. There was only one problem; the Doctor had no idea he was there. So, the Master directed his old foe's attention to his plans. It was only then that he realised there was a Time Lady on the board now too...

FURTHER ADVENTURES

- **Fellow Travellers:** There are ghosts in the TARDIS, echoes of companions, and Doctors, from the past, present and future. They're being caused by something that should be impossible: a branch in the Vortex, a place where all of time divides like a river along two wildly different paths. The Doctor takes the TARDIS there and finds a second TARDIS, its size circuits completely broken, at the centre of the branch. It's the Rani's TARDIS and it's hours from exploding, an action that will have disastrous consequences for all of time. The Doctor and companions must enter the feral TARDIS, discover who else the Rani was travelling with and repair the TARDIS before it's too late.

- **Life In A Northern Town:** Saltaire, just outside Bradford, is a utopian town at the height of the Industrial Revolution. There's no alcohol allowed inside the town, everyone is housed, schooled and fed. So why are the streets patrolled? Why have four patrol men been killed? What's being built inside Salt's Mill? And why are there Time Agents guarding it? With the help of a very unusual Consulting Detective and her staff, the Doctor and his companions must find out the secret of Salt's Mill, before the utopian town becomes a slaughterhouse.

- **Lives of the Rani:** Stopping by 2012 London to enjoy the Olympics (again), the Doctor is astonished to find a statue of the Rani in the grounds of Thames House. She's dressed as a nurse and the inscription reads: NURSE AGNES RANIER, ANGEL OF THE EASTERN FRONT

  He discovers that she was a nurse, and nursing pioneer, during the First World War and instrumental in saving hundreds of men's lives. Her sisters were equally extraordinary, Giselle Ranier becoming the first French aviatrix and Dominique Ranier lying about her gender and serving on the front lines. There are statues to the other two in France, and the Sisters of Ranier are an established, well-respected charity organisation. Except, of course, it's the Rani. The Doctor begins investigating but everything seems above board. The Sisters of Ranier carry out great work, the historical records all agree that they were three extraordinary women and nothing seems out of place.

  Has the Rani finally made peace with herself and her work? Did she die happily and at the end of a long life in the early 20th century? Or is the woman sitting in UNIT headquarters' holding cells insisting that she's Agnes Ranier and her life has been stolen telling the truth?

THE MASTER

AWARENESS	3	PRESENCE	4
COORDINATION	4	RESOLVE	6
INGENUITY	9	STRENGTH	3

SKILLS

Convince 5, Craft 2, Fighting 4, Knowledge 6, Marksman 3, Medicine 3, Science 4, Subterfuge 5, Survival 4, Technology 4, Transport 4

TRAITS

Adversary (The Doctor, The Daleks) Block
Transfer Specialist
Boffin
Charming
Eccentric
Hypnosis
Indomitable
Obsession (Major, Beat the Doctor, Control the Universe)
Percussive Maintenance
Photographic Memory
Reverse the Polarity of the Neutron Flow
Selfish
Technically Adept
Time Lord*
Time Lord Engineer
Time Lord (Experienced x12)
Time Traveller (All)
Voice of Authority
Vortex Born
Wanted Renegade
Weakness (Minor-Gloating)

EQUIPMENT: Tissue Compression Eliminator (2D6/L/L): The Master's weapon of choice is a hideous device that compresses the space between molecules. This not only kills the victim but shrinks their body down to a precise, seemingly unharmed, doll-like version of itself. A direct hit from it instantly kills living creatures and destroys complex mechanical or electrical circuitry but even a graze will still cause serious damage.

REGENERATIONS USED: 12+

TECH LEVEL: 10 **STORY POINTS:** 6

*The Master can no longer regenerate, nor does he have any of the anatomical advantages of a Time Lord.

THE TWO DOCTORS

'Dastari, I have no doubt you could augment an earwig to the point where it understood nuclear physics, but it would still be a very stupid thing to do!'

SYNOPSIS

Camera Station, and Spain, 1985

The Second Doctor and Jamie McCrimmon were en route to Camera Station. The last time the Doctor had visited, it was a tiny research lab but it had grown into a huge complex since then. He complained about the Time Lords forcing him to come there, pocketed the remote control for the TARDIS and told Jamie to stand back and admire his diplomatic skills. On the way to the Head of Projects' office, they encountered Shockeye, an Androgum who worked in the kitchens. Shockeye asked whether Jamie was for sale as he wished to cook him and the Doctor angrily faced him down.

The Doctor had been sent there on behalf of the Time Lords to persuade the station chief, Dastari to suspend time travel experiments being carried out by Kartz and Reimer, two of the scientists aboard. The Time Lords were deeply concerned that the research would damage the Vortex but Dastari angrily dismissed the concerns. He pointed out the Time Lords had refused to help, the Doctor demanded that the experiments be shut down and the two men began to argue.

At the same time, Chessene, Dastari's assistant and an Androgum whose brain he'd enhanced, disabled the station's security to allow a Sontaran battle fleet to board it. As the drugs Shockeye had put in the last meal he'd prepared took effect, Dastari passed out and the Sontarans stormed the station. The Doctor told Jamie to flee even as he was arrested.

Elsewhere, the Sixth Doctor and Peri were fishing, the Doctor far more enthusiastically than his companion. Making their way back to the TARDIS, Peri was horrified to see the Doctor suddenly pass out. Meanwhile, on Camera Station, Jamie watched in horror as his Doctor, trapped in a glass tube, appeared to die.

When the Sixth Doctor came round he decided to visit Dastari, the most experienced geneticist he knew, to find out what was wrong with him. He also expressed concern that time may be unravelling following his death in a previous incarnation. When they arrived, the station stank of rotted food, and the computer began using its defences to try and kill them. Barely making it to Dastari's office, they found it abandoned. To make matters worse, Dastari's last log entry expressly blamed the Time Lords for the massacre on the station.

Refusing to believe his people were capable of this sort of horror, and revelling in the fact that the computer couldn't detect them because Dastari's luxurious carpet was masking their heat signals, the Doctor opened the service tunnels and led Peri in to reach the computer and shut it off.

Arriving at a hacienda in Andalucia on Earth in the 1980s, the Sontarans and Androgums took possession of the house and began setting up a lab. Unknown to them Oscar Botcherby and Ada, a couple out walking in the hills, saw them arrive. Seeing a Sontaran and Dastari carry the unconscious Second Doctor into the hacienda, Oscar assumed it was a plane crash and began looking for help.

Back on Camera Station, the Sixth Doctor and Peri were clambering through the service tunnels. The Doctor found the circuit box he needed and began to work. Peri was attacked by a humanoid in rags and, startled, the Sixth Doctor triggered a booby trap and fell, suspended from wires. Peri knocked her attacker out, rescued the Doctor, who revealed he'd shut down his respiratory passages to survive the gas and unmasked her attacker: Jamie.

The Sixth Doctor hypnotised him into reliving what happened, and recognised the aliens Jamie described as Sontarans. Heading back to Dastari's office to examine the station records further, the Doctor was horrified to see Peri in agony in the tube. Frantically trying to turn it off, he saw Dastari, the Second Doctor and himself in there as well. Realising the animation system had been left on and captured their likenesses, the Doctor also deduced it was a trap meant to make people think he was dead. His previous incarnation had been the target all along.

He explained that the symbiotic link a Time Lord has with their TARDIS is the key reason why time travel is possible. That genetic imprint, known as the Rassilon Imprimatur, gives the traveller and time machine the molecular stability they need and was clearly what the Sontarans were looking for. Even worse, he deduced they kidnapped Dastari as he was the only biogeneticist able to isolate the symbiotic nuclei that were central to the process. He put himself in a telepathic trance to try and find out where his second

incarnation was being held and, hearing the bells of the Great Cathedral of Seville, realised he's being held in Spain.

At the hacienda, Chessene explained that Earth had been chosen because it was a convenient staging post for a strike the Sontarans wished to make against the Madillon Cluster, currently held by their ancient enemy, the Rutan Host. Shockeye was also delighted to be there, having always wanted to eat human. Dastari dismissed him as nothing more than an animal and reminded Chessene she was so much more advanced than a simple Androgum anymore.

The Sixth Doctor's TARDIS arrived in the grounds of the hacienda and was seen by Oscar and Anita. Oscar assumed the Doctor, Peri and Jamie were InterPol officers and told them what happened. Playing along, the Doctor asked him to lead them to the hacienda. When they got there, the Doctor told everyone else to hide and snuck up to a side window.

Inside, Dastari explained to the Second Doctor that he was planning on isolating his symbiotic nuclei and giving them to Chessene so she could use the Kartz-Reimer time module, perfected and transported with them to the hacienda. The Second Doctor argued that her Androgum nature and that level of power would make her a near unstoppable threat but Dastari would have none of it. Outside, the Sixth Doctor slipped and the Second Doctor was left alone whilst his captors went outside to investigate. Field Marshal Stike entered the room and the Second Doctor tried to goad him into an honour duel so he could escape, with no luck.

Outside, the Sixth Doctor made it back to his companions unharmed and told them the situation. Anita revealed there was a passage to the cellar from the nearby ice house and the Doctor told Jamie to come with him to rescue the Second Doctor whilst Peri created a distraction. The other two were to stay out of harm's way, something Oscar, terrified of blood, welcomed.

Peri's arrival delayed Dastari's attempt to isolate the symbiotic nuclei and Chessene met her at the door. Peri claimed to be an American student looking for party accommodation, Chessene claimed she lived alone and explained Shockeye was her servant. Neither woman trusted the other and Chessene sensed thoughts of the Doctor in the younger woman's mind. When the Second Doctor was put in a wheelchair and pushed past Peri, the younger woman didn't recognise him whilst Chessene explained he was an ill relative. Peri left, just as Shockeye moved to attack her and Chessene told him if she did have friends they'd be suspicious. He ignored her and chased after Peri who he knocked out and brought back to the hacienda.

Meanwhile, the Sixth Doctor and Jamie had made it to the cellar. The Sixth Doctor explained about the Rassilon Imprimatur just as Stike appeared. He held Jamie hostage and threatened to kill him unless the Doctor primed the time machine. The Doctor did so, just as Jamie stabbed the Sontaran in the leg. The two made their escape upstairs and found the Second Doctor at last, only to be interrupted by Shockeye returning with Peri. The Sixth Doctor and Jamie hid, whilst the Second Doctor pretended to be unconscious.

Dastari and Chessene entered, with Chessene expressing concern. She'd realised that the Doctor in Peri's thoughts wasn't this one, meaning two Time Lords were involved. She suggested a fallback plan; Dastari would implant the Second Doctor with some of Shockeye's genetic material, turning him into an Androgum. That way he would be much easier to control. They discussed betraying the Sontarans, as, earlier, Stike had made it clear to his lieutenant, Varl, that their plan was to steal the now-active time machine and use the self-destruct on their own ships to kill everyone else.

Shockeye, meanwhile, was preparing to butcher Peri for cooking. Chessene stunned him and helped Dastari transfer his genetic material into the Doctor. Upstairs, the Sixth Doctor and Jamie waited until she'd gone then revived Peri. The Sixth Doctor revealed he knew Stike was there and had deliberately fed him misinformation. He'd also removed the briode nebuliser from the time machine meaning it wouldn't work.

Downstairs, Shockeye woke up, enraged. The Second Doctor followed and had already developed the same eyebrows as Shockeye, as well as an instatiable appetite. The two took themselves into Seville. Outside, the Sixth Doctor and companions watched as Dastari lured the Sontarans into the cellar of the hacienda. Chessene killed Varl and severely injured Stike by dropping two canisters of coronic acid into the passageway they were in and leaves. Stike managed to escape, and reached the time module. Without the nebuliser it injured him even more severely and he staggered out of the hacienda to his ship. Forgetting it had been set to self-destruct, it exploded, taking him with it.

The Sixth Doctor and his companions set off to rescue the Second Doctor but were running behind. The conversion process would be permanent if it wasn't stopped quickly and the Sixth Doctor was already craving food as well. Following the trail of violence the two other men left, they found themselves in Seville, where Chessene and Dastari had also come in search of their missing companions. The transformation process needed a second operation to become permanent and without it the Androgum genetic material would be rejected. Both groups began checking restaurants whilst, nearby, the Second Doctor and Shockeye found Oscar's restaurant. They ran up a massive tab and, when Oscar asked them to pay it, Shockeye stabbed him to death. The Sixth Doctor and companions arrived just too late, and Shockeye fled whilst the Second Doctor slowly reverted to normal. They left the restaurant and were immediately found and taken hostage by Chessene and Dastari.

The two took their hostages back to the hacienda, where the Doctor assured them the time machine had been primed. They searched him, found the nebuliser and sent Peri on a short trip with the machine to prove he was telling the truth. When she returned unharmed, Chessene gave Shockeye permission to cook Jamie and took him through to the kitchen. Alone, the Second Doctor complimented his future self on his intelligence and the Sixth Doctor admitted he'd sabotaged the nebuliser, spreading a thin interface layer over it so it would work for one trip. The two Doctors found the keys to their chains and the Sixth Doctor had freed himself when, upstairs, Jamie screamed. The Second Doctor told his future self to go and rescue him, but to leave the keys.

Upstairs, the Sixth Doctor freed Jamie but was attacked by Shockeye, who stabbed him. Bleeding, the Sixth Doctor fled, with Shockeye in pursuit. Unable to stop herself, Chessene licked at the blood trail the Sixth Doctor had left and Dastari saw it. Horrified, he realised that she would always be an Androgum and therefore a threat and went inside to free the Second Doctor and his companions.

In the grounds, the Sixth Doctor had weakened badly. With Shockeye closing in, he found the moth net and killing jar that Oscar had left there earlier in the day and hid in the nearby tree. When Shockeye came past, the Doctor put the net over his head, stuffed a cloth full of the poison from the jar over his mouth and killed him.

Back at the hacienda, Chessene interrupted Dastari freeing the prisoners and killed him. She was about to do the same to the Second Doctor and Peri before Jamie threw a knife at her wrist, causing her to drop the gun. Chessene fled into the module, but without the interface layer it exploded. She died as a pure Androgum, all Dastari's work undone.

The Second Doctor and Jamie say their goodbyes, the Second Doctor using a Stattenheim remote control to summon his TARDIS much to the Sixth Doctor's jealousy. The Sixth reassured Peri that their TARDIS was nearby and that from now on, they would be on a strict vegetarian diet as they set off for home.

CONTINUITY

- The Doctor has a variety of famous historical geniuses, including Leonardo da Vinci, Christopher Columbus, Archimedes, and Isambard Kingdom Brunel, in his address book.

- Ripples in time are measured on the Bocca Scale. The Kartz-Reimer experiments registered a 0.4 on this. Presumably the Doctor has a whole level to himself on the opposite end of the dial past where it goes red.

- The Doctor is no longer "flavour of the month" on Gallifrey – although it's not entirely clear which of his many fallings out with the Time Lords this refers to.

- As did the Fourth Doctor, the Sixth Doctor enjoys fishing (see ***The Androids of Tara*** in **The Fourth Doctor Sourcebook**).

RUNNING THE ADVENTURE

This is a particularly difficult adventure to run given that you have the time machine, the two Doctors, the two sets of companions, not to mention Dastari, Chessene and Shockeye and the Sontarans and their conflicting agendas to keep track of. Here are some things to remember and ways to keep on top of it.

Pace

Keep the action bouncing along, just like in the adventure. Or, cut the Second Doctor and Jamie arriving at Camera Station completely and begin with the Sixth Doctor having the fainting episode. Keep everything moving and drive the pace until you get to the first point the characters are all in the same place, then slow down.

The Time Machine

Everyone wants the time machine. The Sontarans want it because of their war, Chessene and Dastari want it because of the freedom it will give them, the

Doctors want it so they can stop everyone else having it and the Time Lords want it because then no one else will have it. Make the time machine the centre of as many scenes as possible, whether in discussion or actively.

No One Likes The Time Lords
Not even other Time Lords like the Time Lords, judging by the Second Doctor's embittered reactions to them. The Time Lords are so despised by the Third Zone governments that Chessene can plausibly frame them for a massacre. They're an unseen force, always on a pedestal, always out of reach and never responding to entreaties for help. This adventure's a great starting point for a campaign focusing on that, or, a gateway into a visit to Gallifrey to discuss why time machines keep being developed and why the Time Lords are acting like they are.

No One Trusts Anyone Else
Every single plan within a plan is based on mutual distrust. Weirdly, only the Sontarans genuinely trust each other in this adventure and look how far it gets them! Always be looking for an angle for each character to get one over on the others and, of course, to get one step closer to the time machine...

Space Station Location Location
The two different locations in this adventure give you a real chance to play with the tone and feel of scenes. Emphasise the contrast between the stench and the carnage on Camera Station with the beautiful Spanish countryside and how odd the Sontarans and Androgums seem in the middle of it all. Think about the scenes like an Androgum would; what would the characters smell? What would they hear? How would the air taste?

THIRD ZONE GOVERNMENTS

The Third Zone is an unusual place and one that humanity hasn't quite reached when the Second Doctor arrives there. However, the governments of the Third Zone clearly know about the Time Lords, given how frustrated Dastari is at their refusal to help with the time machine. What's unusual is that whilst they're advanced enough to pool their scientific resources in Camera Station and build a time machine, they see nothing wrong with employing the Androgums as what appear to be indentured slaves.

WHO ARE KARTZ AND REIMER?

We never see the two scientists, but we certainly see the consequences of their work. The fact they've perfected a time machine, essentially from scratch, is astounding and has terrifying implications for history. After all, by their own admission the Time Lords made horrifying mistakes when they started out, which is why they're so cautious about other races developing time travel.

In terms of this adventure, Kartz and Reimer are ideas rather than characters, with their machine very much in the spotlight instead. However, if you want to go back to them at any point, here are some ideas about who they are:

The Androgum Legacy: Kartz and Reimer are the descendants of two of the Androgums thrown back in time in the original experiments. They've developed the time machine for two reasons: firstly to ensure their own existence and secondly to use to evacuate the remaining Androgums to a better life (at least, once they develop a larger model...)

The Time Lord Option: Kartz and Reimer are the Rani and the Master, having lost their TARDISes, trying to work out a way to get back to their respective homes. Of course, developing a time machine from scratch with backwater science might just be enough to impress the council into granting them pardons...

The Other Time Lord Option: Kartz and Reimer are the Doctor and the Master, at the Prydonian Academy, acting out. It's all an elaborate prank that backfires horribly, gets the Master exiled and leads to everything starting all over again...

Here are a couple of different ways you can play the Third Zone Governments:

Benign Dictatorship: The Third Zone Governments have banded together to raise the standard of living for every species in the zone through the focused scientific innovation seen on Camera Station. Each has pooled their resources and staff in an effort to ensure they all benefit.

The Time Rush: There is an area of weakness, similar to the Untempered Schism, in the Third Zone that has allowed Vortex energy to leak and meant the races of the Third Zone have evolved at a far faster rate. As a result, they are on the brink of developing time travel by the end of the 20th century on Earth. The Androgums are the first species encountered beyond the temporal effects and as a result are still primitive and easily conquered.

The Third Zone governments are well aware that they are further ahead than they should be and are desperate to capitalise on this. This is why they founded Camera Station and why they are racing to build a time machine, so they can capitalise on their lucky break and take a seat next to the Time Lords and the Daleks as a major galactic power.

THE ANDROGUMS

The Androgums are a controversial species, with distinctive bushy red eyebrows and grey wart-like facial markings. Governments of the Third Zone use them for service work and they particularly excel in catering. The reason for this is the Androgums are driven by a constant, insatiable hunger. They value not just fine food but new fine food above all things bar their clan, or Grig, to which they remain utterly loyal.

When they're not eating vast amounts, they're thinking about eating vast amounts and Androgum law is built around this. Anything is permissible: the consumption of vermin, other intelligent species, even Androgums themselves in the never ending search for a new culinary high.

What makes the Androgums a genuine threat is how physically strong they are. An Androgum can easily overpower a human or a Time Lord and, it's implied in this story, give a Sontaran a serious fight if it comes down to it. This combination of total lack of impulse control and tremendous strength makes them a real threat, and Androgums that work with other races have their movements and appetites closely controlled. Either way, the Androgums and how they're treated, for all their violence, is an area of real moral ambiguity and one you can explore for several adventures if you want to.

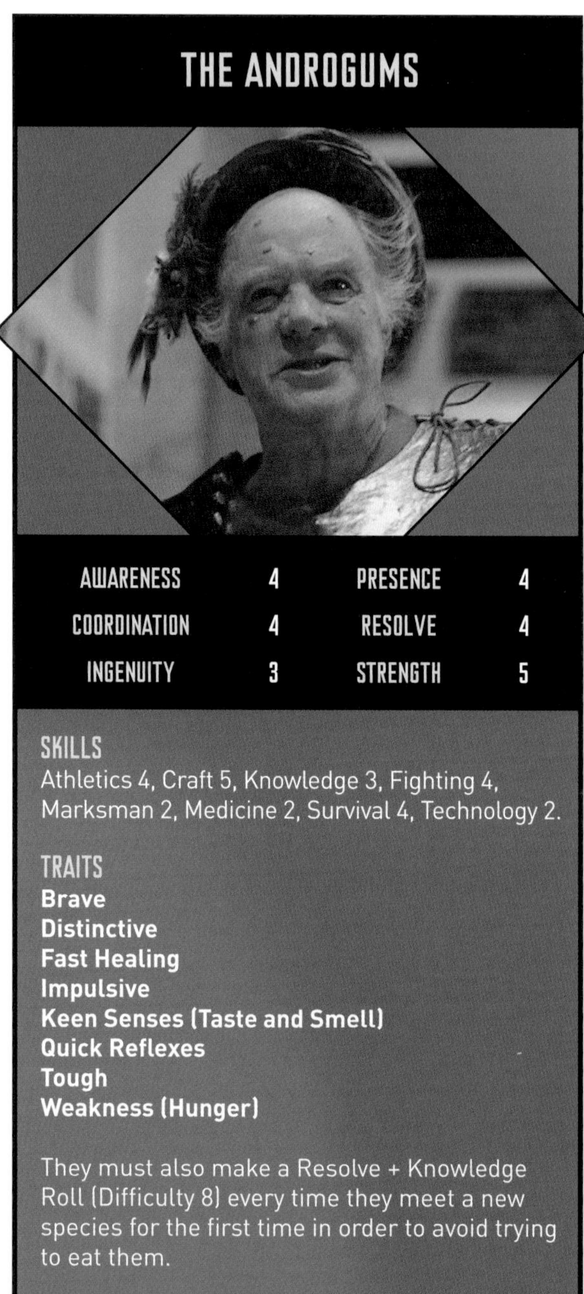

THE ANDROGUMS

AWARENESS	4	PRESENCE	4
COORDINATION	4	RESOLVE	4
INGENUITY	3	STRENGTH	5

SKILLS

Athletics 4, Craft 5, Knowledge 3, Fighting 4, Marksman 2, Medicine 2, Survival 4, Technology 2.

TRAITS

Brave
Distinctive
Fast Healing
Impulsive
Keen Senses (Taste and Smell)
Quick Reflexes
Tough
Weakness (Hunger)

They must also make a Resolve + Knowledge Roll (Difficulty 8) every time they meet a new species for the first time in order to avoid trying to eat them.

Information and rules for both the Second Doctor and Jamie McCrimmon can be found in **The Second Doctor Sourcebook**.

DASTARI

Dastari was a pioneering bio-geneticist working on Camera Station, attempting to recreate Kartz-Reimer's experiments into time travel. Amongst his creations was the hyper-evolved Androgum, Chessene, who he had made into a genius in her own right.

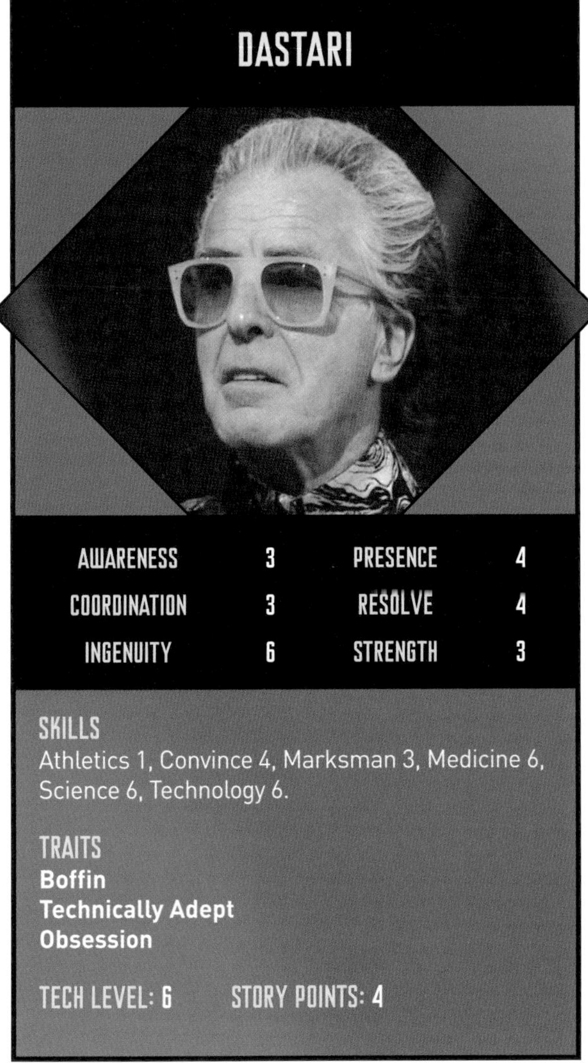

DASTARI

AWARENESS	3	PRESENCE	4
COORDINATION	3	RESOLVE	4
INGENUITY	6	STRENGTH	3

SKILLS
Athletics 1, Convince 4, Marksman 3, Medicine 6, Science 6, Technology 6.

TRAITS
Boffin
Technically Adept
Obsession

TECH LEVEL: 6 STORY POINTS: 4

CHESSENE

Chessene was an Androgum servant working for Dastari, who he augmented to possess a vast intelligence. At heart she remained a savage Androgum, however, a fact that dawned on Dastari after he caught her instinctively lapping the blood off the injured Doctor.

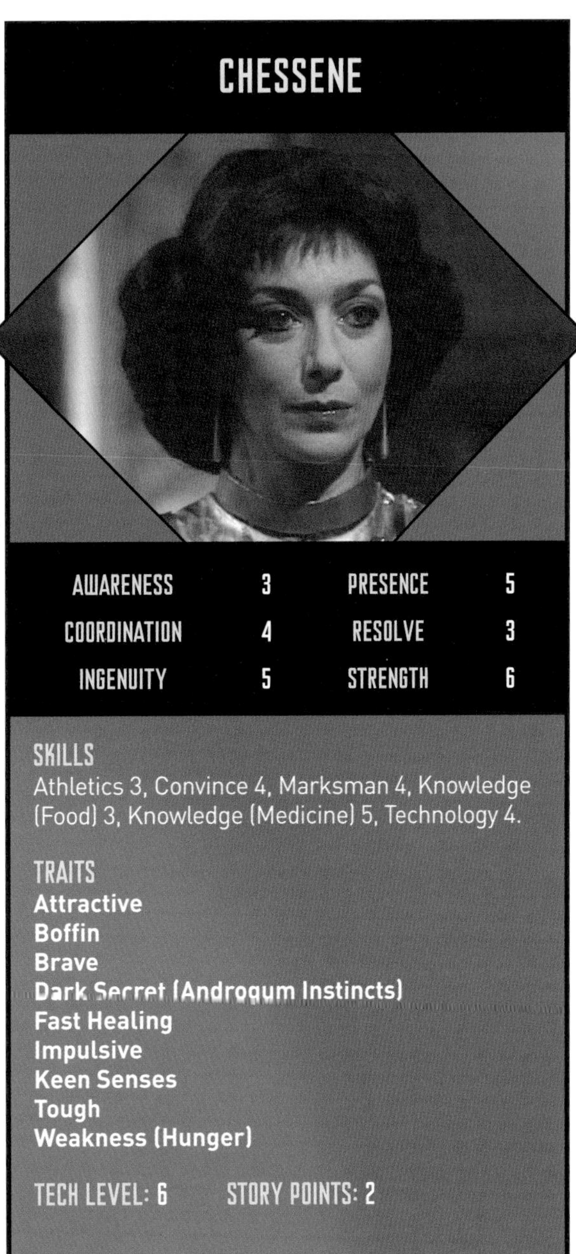

CHESSENE

AWARENESS	3	PRESENCE	5
COORDINATION	4	RESOLVE	3
INGENUITY	5	STRENGTH	6

SKILLS
Athletics 3, Convince 4, Marksman 4, Knowledge (Food) 3, Knowledge (Medicine) 5, Technology 4.

TRAITS
Attractive
Boffin
Brave
Dark Secret (Androgum Instincts)
Fast Healing
Impulsive
Keen Senses
Tough
Weakness (Hunger)

TECH LEVEL: 6 STORY POINTS: 2

SHOCKEYE

Shockeye was an Androgum chef onboard Camera Station. He had a constant craving for human flesh, and tried to eat both Peri and Jamie on several occasions. He was killed by the Doctor.

SHOCKEYE

AWARENESS	3	PRESENCE	4
COORDINATION	4	RESOLVE	2
INGENUITY	2	STRENGTH	8

SKILLS
Athletics 4, Fighting 4, Knowledge (Food) 6.

TRAITS
Brave
Distinctive
Fast Healing
Indomitable
Impulsive
Keen Senses
Quick Reflexes
Tough
Weakness (Hunger)

TECH LEVEL: 6 STORY POINTS: 1

MARSHAL STIKE

AWARENESS	3	PRESENCE	5
COORDINATION	4	RESOLVE	6
INGENUITY	5	STRENGTH	6

Stike is tired of losing and so are his men. Victory is near, he senses it.

SKILLS
Athletics 2, Convince 4, Fighting 5, Knowledge (War) 3, Marksman 5, Medicine 1, Science 4, Subterfuge 4, Survival 4, Technology 4, Transport 3.

TRAITS
Adversary (Rutans)
Alien
Alien Appearance (Minor)
Armour (5)
Brave
By the Book
Special-Probic Vent
Tough
Voice of Authority
Weakness (Major – Coronic acid)

TECH LEVEL: 6 STORY POINTS: 10

VARL

AWARENESS	3	PRESENCE	3
COORDINATION	4	RESOLVE	6
INGENUITY	3	STRENGTH	6

Varl knows war, victory and pain. He also knows defeat, something he'd prefer to stay joyously ignorant of. However, Varl also knows he isn't clever enough to change the fortunes of his campaign. That's what Marshal Stike is for and Varl knows he'll deliver them to victory.

SKILLS
Athletics 2, Convince 2, Fighting 5, Knowledge (War) 3, Marksman 5, Medicine 1, Science 3, Subterfuge 3, Survival 4, Technology 3, Transport 3.

TRAITS
Adversary (Rutans)
Alien
Alien Appearance (Minor)
Armour (5)
Brave
By the Book
Special-Probic Vent
Tough
Weakness (Major – Coronic acid)

TECH LEVEL: 6 STORY POINTS: 3

TECHNOLOGY

TA Process
At one point Dastari refers to Chessene as 'Androgum TA' and that she's now at 'Mega-Genius Level'. Dastari was a genius and his peculiar specialty was the Transcerebral Addition (or TA) process. This involved treating the brain of his subjects with a combination of his own, cloned cerebral tissue and enhancing chemicals to massively increase not just their intelligence but their capacity to learn. He carried this process out on Chessene numerous times and the end result was one of the most gifted, if doomed, strategic thinkers of her age.

Anyone undergoing the TA process must remain in the lab where it's taking place for a full day. In that time, they are anaesthetised and the cloned cerebral tissue solution introduced to their skull. It's encouraged to bond with the brain by a series of light bursts that trigger specific neurons, culminating in the material being fully absorbed by the brain. The subject must then rest but will notice the effect almost immediately. Namely, a +1 increase in Ingenuity or Awareness for every process undergone.

The downside to the process is that it requires a second, stabilising operation within a short period of time. Once this is complete, the increase in intelligence is permanent. Without it, the increase fades after an hour. The upside is the process, thanks to Dastari's equipment, is very simple; an Ingenuity + Medicine (Difficulty 15) roll for each operation.

GA Process
Dastari's Gene Acquisition (or GA) Process is essentially the same in reverse. The subject is anaesthetised (or at least restrained) and a gene scanner is used to isolate the particular sequence the Doctor is looking for. This is then isolated and transferred, in the same chemical solution as before, into the new host body, or put in storage until needed. If it's implanted, once again, a stabilising operation is needed. On waking the character the material has been harvested from will be at -1 all attributes for several rounds, but otherwise unharmed. As they recover, one attribute, the one closest to the function of the material used, will remain at -1. The roll to operate the equipment is as above.

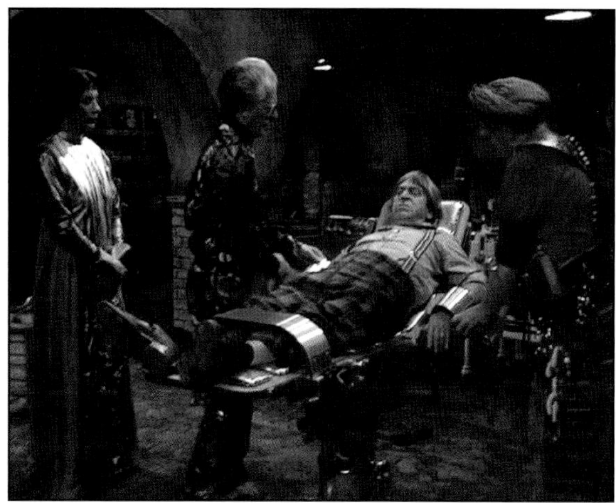

Interface Layer (Minor Gadget)
Interface Layer or 'Interface Lazy' as its sometimes referred to is one of the most useful inventions in the Third Zone. A slightly coloured, clear gel, it's the best friend of harried engineers and Time Lords everywhere. The gel adapts to whatever situation its placed in on electrical circuit, whether acting as a fuse, a conductor, or insulation. There is some speculation that the gel may technically be alive as no one knows how it adapts so well, but so far, the companies that sell the gel aren't answering any questions.

The downside is Interface Layer burns off after one usage but, if you're in a fix, or need a quick fix, then it's essential. The Interface Layer adds a +2 bonus to the next roll, be it Science, Technology, Medicine or Transport, using the piece of equipment it has been spread on.

Traits: One Shot
Cost: 1 Story Point

Holo Generator (Minor Gadget)
A passive system, designed to map the movements and features of anyone in a room, the holo generator was designed to give the impression that the Second Doctor had been killed. However, devices like this

are frequently used for much happier purposes, including providing a holographic view of the area outside a ship or to break the ice at parties.

Traits: Scan, Restriction (Immobile), Huge
Cost: 1 Story Point

NEW GADGET TRAIT: HUGE (MINOR BAD)

The gadget is larger than the characters themselves, or is woven into the structure of the building they found it in. It can't be moved, or at the very least, will have to be completely disassembled in order to do so.

VEHICLES

Sontaran Battle Cruiser
The force Stike uses to take Camera Station is very small, as the ship we see at the hacienda only carries a few people, including Chessene, Dastari, Shockeye and the Doctor. Despite this, the cruisers are still fearsome warships.

Armour	Hit Capacity	Speed
9	20	10

Kartz-Reimer Module
The Kartz-Reimer Module may not look like much but it's actually a historic breakthrough. This is the first working time machine developed by a race in centuries so no wonder the Time Lords are concerned. It may not be much to look at, little more than a triangular cupboard with windows and a seat, but this small ship has the potential to change the galaxy forever.

Armour	Hit Capacity	Speed
2	4	10

FURTHER ADVENTURES

- **Late for Dinner:** Shane Crossley is the new darling of the foodie set, a burly, heavyset man in his late '40s with red bushy eyebrows and a deep, sonorous voice. He's an astounding cook, working with subtlety and flavour no one else can come close to. He also doesn't exist before 1976. Summoned to Earth by UNIT, who have been asked to investigate a series of disappearances around major London restaurants, the Doctor and his companions soon find Shane a prime suspect. The Androgum Dastari thought lost in the time stream landed on their feet, and one of them has a TV and book deal now. But is Shane really the killer?

  Why is his house so well fortified? And what are the shadowy, flickering figures that always seem to show up around him if he stays still for too long? The Doctor and his companions must not only find out the truth, but work out how to help a man out of time, prove his innocence and get his life back.

- **Message in a Bottle:** The TARDIS lurches sideways as, suddenly, a familiar looking closet appears in the control room. When the Doctor gets the ship back under control, the characters realise this isn't the Kartz-Reimer machine but rather, the Kartz-Reimer Mark 2. Someone has been continuing the research Kartz and Reimer began, and they're in trouble. Because in the cockpit is blood, a spent Time Agent firearm and a note scrawled in the condensation on the window: LONDON, 2013, COME GET ME, JH

  When the characters arrive, they find an injured Captain Jack hiding out by the river. The only problem is, he hasn't met them before, they haven't met him before and he's still working for the Time Agency. Why is Jack in London? Why are odd, short, masked police officers guarding the Royal Observatory? And who built the KR Mark 2?

- **The Gauntlet:** A message is delivered to the TARDIS by a postman as it leaves the hacienda. It reads; HONOUR REQUIRES YOUR PRESENCE. MADILLON CLUSTER. STIKE.

  When the TARDIS arrives, the Doctor and companions find Stike, or rather one of his clone brothers. The last surviving member of that batch, he and his brothers have fought for years to clear the name of Stike, the Sontaran Marshal responsible for the Medillon Cluster disaster. Now, only one thing is left; to face the Doctor in honourable combat. The only problem is, the Medillon Cluster is far from empty and, when Cyberman warships appear in orbit over the world Stike is on, its clear he has bigger problems than the Doctor. Can the characters persuade the Sontaran to work with them to stop the Cyberman threat? Or will honour defeat all?

TIMELASH

'The stories I've heard about you. The great Doctor, all knowing and all powerful. You're about as powerful as a burnt out android.'

SYNOPSIS

Karfel, the Future, and Scotland, 1885

The Doctor and Peri were arguing about where their next destination should be. Peri was complaining that the Doctor kept suggesting the Eye of Orion when the TARDIS was suddenly caught by a Kontron corridor. The Doctor explained this was a tunnel through time that someone had constructed and that if the TARDIS wasn't steered correctly, the consequences would be disastrous.

At the same time, on the planet Karfel, Aram, Gazak and Tyheer, three members of an oppressive society were trying to escape to meet up with the rebels. Despite splitting up, all three were captured and brought before the Maylin. Aram was taken to the private vault of the Borad, the overall leader of Karfel, whilst Gazak and Tyheer were cast into the Timelash, a corridor in space and time. Both disappear when thrown in, whilst elsewhere Aram met the Borad, is horrified by his true face and aged to death.

Vena, Maylin Renis' daughter and Mykros, a councillor and her future husband, discussed the situation and both realised that something needed to be done. Mykros followed Maylin Renis to the Power Room, the location where the power needs for the settlement were controlled and confronted him. Despite the sentence for being in the room being death, Mykros argued eloquently in favour of bringing down the Borad. Renis, as he was responsible for power distribution, argued with him. However, when Renis opened his orders and saw that the Borad was asking all power at the hospital to be transferred to his chambers, killing the Borad's wife, who was on life support there, the older man changed his mind. He told Mykros he wouldn't oppose him and to be careful for the sake of Vena. Mykros agreed and they left, only to be confronted by one of the Borad's androids. Mykros was summoned to an emergency council meeting whilst Renis was summoned to the Borad. He thought the conversation was secure, as the delta rays put out by the power system in the settlement interfered with communications but was horrified to find out the Borad had bugged his amulet. The Borad revealed that he had heard everything, showed Renis his true form and then killed him using a Time Web, a weapon that accelerated the ageing of its target.

Mykros arrived at the council chamber to discover he was under arrest for treason and would be thrown into the Timelash. Vena begged for his life as, to her horror, the council were informed that Maylin Renis had had a seizure and died and Tekker was the new Maylin. Tekker's sadistic nature was a perfect fit and

Vena was faced with the horrific choice of letting her fiancé be cast out or becoming a traitor to the society that her father had served. Mykros begged for help and she acted, snatching the amulet from Tekker and leaping into the Timelash.

In the TARDIS, the Doctor and Peri strapped themselves to the console as the ship was thrown around by the turbulence. The Doctor frantically worked to stabilise the ship and did so, just as the ghostly form of Vena floated through the console. Her passage caused the ship even more damage as, on Karfel, Tekker watched the TARDIS move up the Timelash and began formulating a plan.

When the Doctor arrived he was pleasantly surprised. He'd visited Karfel before and Tekker greeted both Peri and he warmly. However, whilst Peri was fascinated by the plants on display, Tekker was summoned away to talk to the Bandril ambassador. The Bandrils, a nearby intelligent race, were protesting the fact the grain shipments the Borad had promised them had not arrived. Tekker cut them off, confident the Borad would deal with them in time.

Elsewhere, Peri was remarking on how boring life was on the mirrorless, bland Karfel when she and the Doctor were handed a mysterious message: "Sezon at the Falichian rocks". Peri pocketed the message as Tekker returned to lead her off on a tour with Councillor Brunner. Tekker discussed the situation with the Timelash with the Doctor and claimed that Vena fell through it by accident. He asked for the Doctor's help in retrieving the amulet but he refused whilst, elsewhere, Brunner ordered a Guardolier to kill Peri. She evaded him by hurling an acid-spitting plant in his face and fled through a door way to the caves outside the Citadel. Rapidly getting lost, Peri was soon cornered by a Morlox, a huge animal. She was rescued by a group of rebels and, as they escaped, were surprised by the appearance of a burning android in the middle of the room. The rebels were suspicious at first until Peri said she was with the Doctor. They showed her a picture that she identified as the Third Doctor's companion Jo Grant and they agreed to help her.

Back in the Citadel, the Borad was watching video recordings of Peri and decided to have her found and brought to him. Tekker told the Doctor they were holding Peri hostage and he reluctantly set off to look for Vena and the necklace. He traced her to 1885, where she had landed in a small Scottish village. Herbert, a young teacher who witnessed her arrive mistook both her, and the Doctor, for spirits and tried to exorcise them to no avail. Vena reluctantly agreed to return with the Doctor and, despite Herbert's pleas, he refused to let the younger man come too. On the way back to the TARDIS, the Doctor picked up a mirror, suspecting it might be useful.

Back on Karfel, the rebels explained the situation to Peri. The Borad had nearly driven Karfel to war with the Bandrils and if the other race deployed the bendralypse warheads they'd developed they would certainly be. The warheads were designed to kill anything with a central nervous system whilst leaving inanimate objects undamaged. When one of the other rebels called someone Sezon she realised this was the group that had reached out to them. She also realised the note had gone and before she could warn anyone, Guardoliers arrested them.

Back on Karfel, the Doctor returned and discovered that Herbert had stowed away in the TARDIS. Before he could do anything about it, Tekker demanded the amulet and the Doctor refused, asking to hand it to the Borad alone. Tekker threatened to kill Peri and, with the TARDIS crew reunited and the rebels captured, the Doctor handed the amulet over. Tekker immediately sentenced everyone to the Timelash, with the Doctor going first. At the last second, he used the mirror he'd taken to distract the android and it became confused at seeing a reflection for the first time. The rebels seized the opportunity and overpowered the Guardoliers, sealing the room. They were under siege and Peri was still being held by the Borad.

To give them a fighting chance, the Doctor had himself lowered on a rope through the Timelash. The walls of it were lined with Kontron Crystals and he, Herbert and Mykros were all almost lost trying to retrieve some. They succeeded and the Doctor began frantically working on building them some weapons to fight off the Borad's guards. He succeeded, building a Time Break that would project an image of him ten seconds into the future, and a crystal that would absorb and redirect any energy fired at it back on the attacker. Things were looking up until Mykros spotted the Bandril attack heading for Karfel.

The guards attacked, using the Borad's weapon to age the doors, but were driven off. The android with them was destroyed and projected back in time an hour to when Peri was rescued from the Morlox. The Doctor sets off to confront the Borad and rescue Peri, who had been taken to the Morlox caves again, and Herbert insisted on coming with him. The Doctor tried to talk him out of it, but, finally, demanded he watch from a high gallery rather than take part in the confrontation.

The Doctor and the Borad met and the Borad's horrific true nature became clear; he was half man, half Morlox. In reality a scientist named Megelen, the Borad had been turned in to the council for unethical experiments on the Morlox. The Third Doctor reported him to the Council and Megelen, whilst criticised, refused to stop his experiments. This led to a horrific accident when he sprayed himself with the chemical Mustakozene-80. A Morlox attacked him and the chemical fused them together.

Whilst his appearance became hideous, he gained both intelligence, strength and a longer lifespan, leading to his plan to provoke a war with the Bandrils. He planned to manipulate them into destroying the population of Karfel so he could repopulate them with his own people. He planned to make Peri, trapped in the Morlox caves with some Mustakozene-80 strapped to her, the first.

The Doctor activated his Time Break. The two men played a tense game of temporal cat and mouse that culminated in the Doctor warning the Borad, the Borad firing at the Doctor and him redirecting it using his secondary crystal. The Borad died and the Doctor dispatched Herbert to the caves to rescue Peri whilst he searched for the release mechanism. He found it but it released both Peri and the Morlox and she was only saved by Herbert's swift arrival.

The three returned to the Council Chamber where Mykros told them the bad news; the Bandrils weren't answering communications and had already fired their bendalypse warhead. The Doctor tried to reason with them but without proof of the Borad's death they refused to negotiate and cut transmission.

The Doctor rushed back to the TARDIS where Peri confronted him about planning to sacrifice himself. He insisted that he could only deactivate it alone and she finally relented and left. It was only when the TARDIS had set off that the Doctor realised Herbert was still aboard. The two apparently died, sacrificing themselves to take the hit from the warhead.

On Karfel, Peri and the others were initially overjoyed to see the warhead hadn't detonated and assumed the Doctor had defused it. When the Bandril fleet contacted with condolences, Peri was crushed and then, horrified, to find herself back in the hands of the Borad. He explained the Borad they'd seen was just a clone and that unless the incoming Bandril diplomatic party were captured and held hostage, Peri would die. Just as all seemed lost, the Doctor and Herbert returned, the Doctor mocking the Borad and smashing a nearby wall panel, showing him his own hideous reflection. Horrified, the Borad let Peri go and the Doctor shoved him into the Timelash and then overloaded it, shutting it down. He explained that the Borad would arrive in Inverness in 1179 and perhaps be mistaken for the Loch Ness monster. Herbert asked to stay but the Doctor refused and reluctantly the young man returned to the TARDIS. The Doctor promised to tell Peri how he escaped and she asked who Herbert was. The Doctor showed her the calling card he'd dropped: HERBERT GEORGE WELLS

CONTINUITY

- The Third Doctor and Jo Grant visited Karfel in the past, although we never saw their adventures there.

- The Doctor and Peri use – for the first and last time – TARDIS seatbelts as it passes through the Timelash. The Eleventh Doctor would later add make-shift seatbelts to his home-made junk TARDIS though (see ***The Doctor's Wife*** in **The Eleventh Doctor Sourcebook**).

- The Doctor makes mention of the fact that he is Lord President of Gallifrey (see ***Invasion of Time*** in **The Fourth Doctor Sourcebook** and ***The Five Doctors*** in **The Fifth Doctor Sourcebook**).

- The Doctor suggests that the Borad could be the origin of the legend of the Loch Ness monster, but so too could the Skarasen (see ***Terror of the Zygons*** in **The Fourth Doctor Sourcebook**).

RUNNING THE ADVENTURE

This is a surprisingly adaptable adventure that, appropriately, can be approached from both ends of the story.

It's absolutely possible to run this as an adventure set entirely on Karfel, aside from the disappearance of Vena and the necklace. Play up the drab nature of the place, the lack of mirrors, the fact that even the guards have their faces masked. Think of it as Ancient Rome with occasional blue-skinned centurions and play out the intrigue plot for all it's worth, culminating in the hideous reveal of the Borad.

Likewise, you could start the adventure in Scotland. Centre the adventure more solidly around Wells, with Vena as a mystery to be investigated (like the time traveller in ***Hide*** – see **The Eleventh Doctor Sourcebook**) and have blue-skinned androids and Morlox running loose in the Scottish foothills. Done this way it becomes a very traditional affair, complete with disbelieving villagers and a big reveal of just what the Loch Ness monster is to round things off.

THE BORAD'S (MANY) EVIL PLANS

You could shift the focus of the adventure so it's on any one of the Borad's evil plans; after all, he does have an awful lot of them. Let's recap:

1.The Bandril War

Add in regular propaganda broadcasts about the drab nature of the settlement and how it's because of the awful things the Bandrils did to the outside world. Describe Guardoliers picking people off the corridors for 'looking alien' or 'sympathising'.

The Bandrils are repeatedly described as vile creatures intent on stealing Karfel away, and the inhabitants are spoiling for a fight, which, of course, is exactly what the Borad wants.

2. Genetic Mixing
The Borad's idea of combining the Morlox with the Karfelons could be portrayed far more openly. What if the Borad android we see is presented as the end result, with the Borad as the halfway point. The Karfelons would be against the process at first but one or two 'accidental' M80 leaks would soon ensure public opinion turned to the Borad.

Then of course, there's the possibility he'd just go all out, spray the entire complex with M80 and open the doors to the Morlox caves, making this a far more urgent, action-packed adventure than anyone thought it would be.

3.The Timelash
The Timelash has so many possibilities in a game that you can't list them all, but here are just a few:

Bandril's Past: The Timelash is sending dissidents (and, if the Borad is feeling particularly horrible, toxic chemicals) to Bandril's past to poison the planet. If they die before the present, then he doesn't have to worry about provoking a war. If they make it to the present, they'll be so sickly they'll be easily conquered. Unless of course, some of the dissidents explain what's going on.

Karfel's Past: The Timelash goes to Karfel's past, where the dissidents are fed to the ancestors of the Morlox. Or, sent through to find particularly fine specimens of Morlox to retrieve for the Borad's program.

Invasion Earth: Maylin Tekker saw which way the wind was blowing some time ago. The Borad's insane scheme would get them all killed and wipe the planet out. The Karfel needed a new home, and Tekker realised that Earth was the perfect place to make a new start, provided they had the right weapons...

There's a massive idea every five minutes and it's all too easy for them to get lost. Keep the action going, as always, but don't be afraid to explain things. The characters will need help. Make sure you provide it.

HG WELLS

Herbert George 'HG' Wells was born in September 1866 and is remembered as one of the most influential science fiction writers of the modern age. Often referred to as the Father of Science Fiction he wrote *The War of the Worlds, The Time Machine, The Invisible Man* and *The Island of Doctor Moreau.* He was also an immensely prolific writer in other fields including politics and social commentary, literary fiction and war gaming rules. He was clearly a genius, so it's a relief that the Sixth Doctor didn't try to use his psychic paper on him.

The Wells the Doctor meets in this adventure is a very young, desperately enthusiastic and relentless man who desperately wants adventure and doesn't understand the word no. He's also a keen spiritualist, a man completely open to the idea of ghosts but astounded at the thought of aliens. All of which is, of course, about to change...

HG WELLS

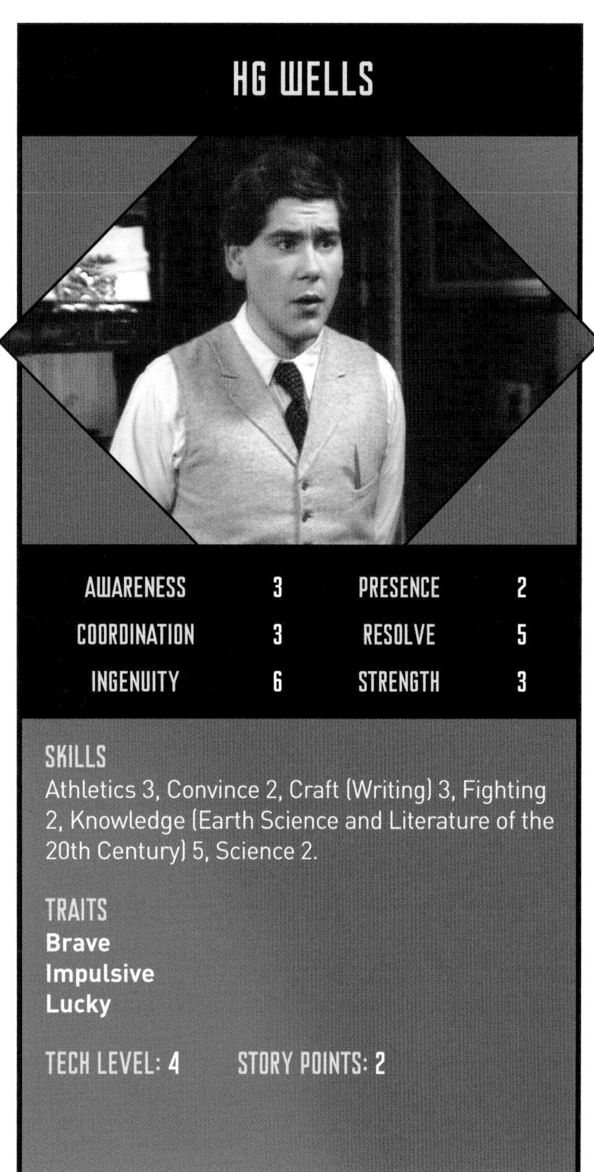

AWARENESS	3	PRESENCE	2
COORDINATION	3	RESOLVE	5
INGENUITY	6	STRENGTH	3

SKILLS
Athletics 3, Convince 2, Craft (Writing) 3, Fighting 2, Knowledge (Earth Science and Literature of the 20th Century) 5, Science 2.

TRAITS
Brave
Impulsive
Lucky

TECH LEVEL: 4 **STORY POINTS: 2**

THE BORAD

Once a Karfelon scientist called Megelen, the Borad was fascinated by the Morlox, the huge race of reptiles he shared his planet with. His experimentation with their genetic material culminated in a hideous accident that left him fused with one and an outcast from both species. Now, he plans to eradicate the Karfelons and replace them with a race just like him; not quite either, and yet not quite both...

THE BORAD

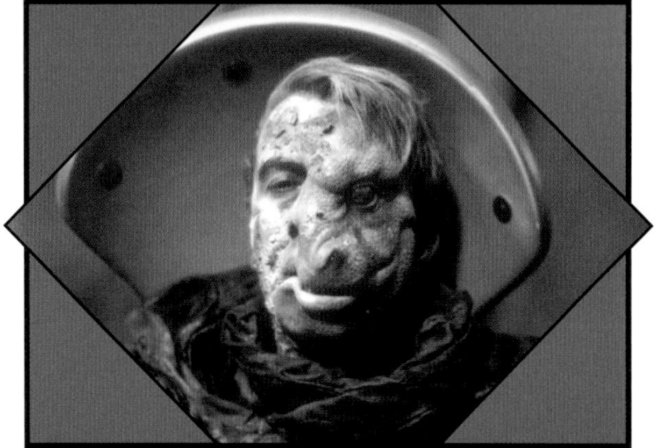

AWARENESS	5	PRESENCE	5
COORDINATION	2	RESOLVE	6
INGENUITY	6	STRENGTH	5

SKILLS

Athletics 3, Convince 3, Fighting 4, Knowledge 6, Medicine 7, Science 7, Survival 3, Technology 4.

TRAITS

Alien
Alien Appearance
Boffin
Clone
Dark Secret
Distinctive
Fast Healing
Technically Adept

TECH LEVEL: 6 STORY POINTS: 6

Clones

The Borad also perfected clone bodies and, in reality, the Borad that the Doctor talked to the most was a clone of the original. The records of how he did this have been lost, so we have no idea how many clones he had, how fast the gestation process was or how successfully he could transfer his consciousness between them.

NEW TRAIT: CLONE (SPECIAL GOOD)

Clone is a Special Good Trait costing 3 character points and 1 Story Points. The character has a clone; a perfect physical copy of themselves stored securely. If they ever die, the clone will be automatically activated and take their place. In order to make sure the clone knows everything they know, they must regularly visit the storage facility to update the clone's memory engrams (say, between each adventure). If they don't, then when the clone is activated, it will only have memories up to the last update.

Effect: The character literally has another life, which has the attributes, skills, traits and memories of whenever it was last updated.

VENA

AWARENESS	3	PRESENCE	5
COORDINATION	4	RESOLVE	3
INGENUITY	5	STRENGTH	6

The daughter of Maylin Renis, Vena was born to a position of power on Karfel. Where others would have been blinded to the problems of her world by this, Vena had her eyes opened and campaigned with increasing energy, and fear, to try and stave off the worst excesses of the Borad. She met Mykros through these works and, when her father was made Maylin, thought things might change. They have, but not for the better.

SKILLS

Athletics 3, Convince 4, Fighting 3, Knowledge (Karfel) 6.

TRAITS

Attractive
Empathic
Lucky
Run for your Life!

TECH LEVEL: 6 STORY POINTS: 3

MAYLIN RENIS

Renis wanted more. He wanted a life of quiet service to the state and the knowledge that he'd protected his world. But, when his wife fell ill, and the Borad came to power, Renis found nothing of the sort.

The Borad's increasingly greedy demands and belligerent stance terrified him and whilst he still carried out his orders, his heart had long since stopped being in it. Now, with Vena and Mykros, he sees a chance to start to undo some of the damage.

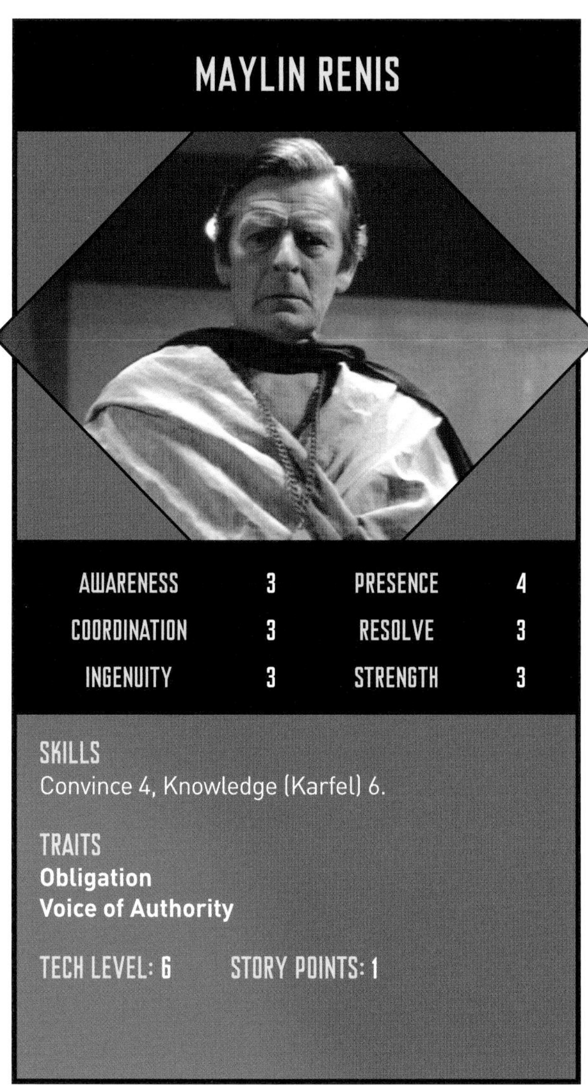

MAYLIN RENIS

AWARENESS	3	PRESENCE	4
COORDINATION	3	RESOLVE	3
INGENUITY	3	STRENGTH	3

SKILLS
Convince 4, Knowledge (Karfel) 6.

TRAITS
Obligation
Voice of Authority

TECH LEVEL: 6 STORY POINTS: 1

MYKROS

A member of the Council of Five, Mykros should be satisfied with his life. He's a powerful man, about to marry a powerful woman and has the ear of the Maylin. But Mykos has seen the way Karfel is going, the shortages, the deaths. He wants something to change and he's desperate to lead that change.

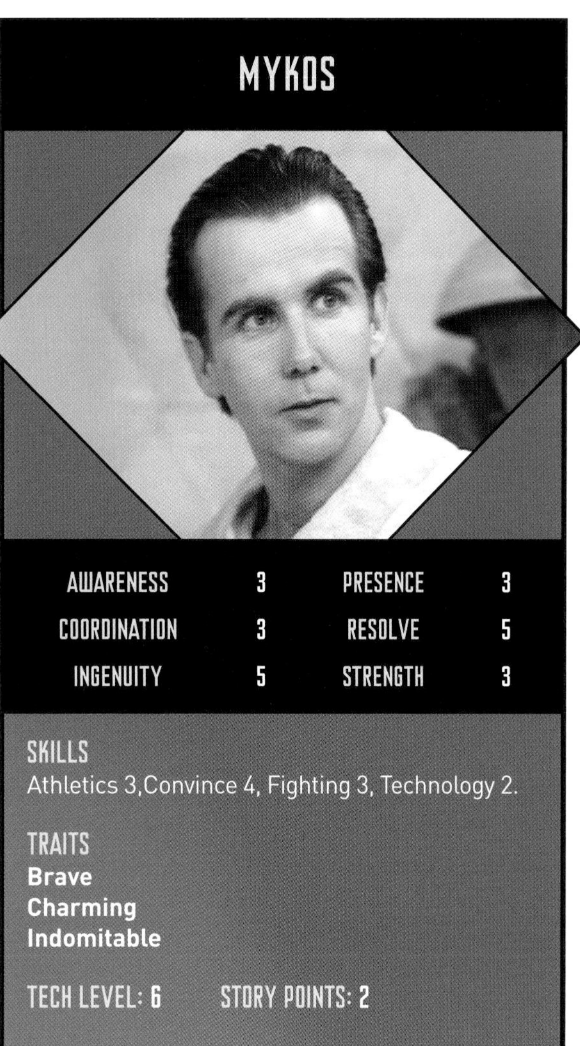

MYKOS

AWARENESS	3	PRESENCE	3
COORDINATION	3	RESOLVE	5
INGENUITY	5	STRENGTH	3

SKILLS
Athletics 3,Convince 4, Fighting 3, Technology 2.

TRAITS
Brave
Charming
Indomitable

TECH LEVEL: 6 STORY POINTS: 2

TEKKER

Tekker has no problem with the Borad. He has no problem with his increasing demands on Karfel or the coming war. The only problem Tekker has is he isn't Maylin yet and he'll do everything he can to make sure that changes, and soon.

TEKKER

AWARENESS	3	PRESENCE	3
COORDINATION	3	RESOLVE	4
INGENUITY	5	STRENGTH	3

SKILLS
Convince 5, Fighting 2, Knowledge (Karfel) 5.

TRAITS
Charming
Lucky
Selfish

TECH LEVEL: 6 STORY POINTS: 3

THE BANDRILS

AWARENESS	4	PRESENCE	2
COORDINATION	5	RESOLVE	3
INGENUITY	3	STRENGTH	3

The closest neighbours of the Karfelons, the Bandrils are a reptilian race. They rely, at least partially, on grain from Karfel and are accomplished warriors and engineers. Their bodies are ridged and pitted and they have wide, cobra-like hoods across the back of their skull.

SKILLS
Athletics 2, Convince 3, Fighting 3, Knowledge (Bendalypse) 6, Science 3, Technology 3, Transport 3.

TRAITS
Alien
Alien Appearance
By the Book

TECH LEVEL: 6 STORY POINTS: 1

ANDROID

AWARENESS	3	PRESENCE	4
COORDINATION	2	RESOLVE	3
INGENUITY	1	STRENGTH	7

Taller than a human or Karfelon, these blue-skinned androids act as the Borad's hands, enacting his will with precise, machined calm and ruthlessness.

SKILLS
Athletics 1, Fighting 3, Marksman 2.

TRAITS
Robot
Slow Reflexes

TECH LEVEL: 6 STORY POINTS: 1

SEZON

AWARENESS	3	PRESENCE	3
COORDINATION	3	RESOLVE	4
INGENUITY	3	STRENGTH	5

Sezon was a Karfelon rebel, assisting the Doctor in defeating the Borad.

SKILLS
Athletics 3, Fighting 4, Marksman 4, Knowledge (Karfel Caves) 4.

TRAITS
Face in the Crowd
Outcast

TECH LEVEL: 6 STORY POINTS: 1

GAZAK

AWARENESS	4	PRESENCE	3
COORDINATION	4	RESOLVE	4
INGENUITY	3	STRENGTH	3

Gazak assisted the Doctor in defeating the Borad, rebelling against his dominion of Karfel.

SKILLS
Athletics 4, Fighting 4, Knowledge (Karfel Caves) 5, Technology 3, Subterfuge 4.

TRAITS
Attractive
Outcast

TECH LEVEL: 6 **STORY POINTS:** 1

MORLOX

AWARENESS	5	PRESENCE	8
COORDINATION	5	RESOLVE	3
INGENUITY	1	STRENGTH	4

The other race to inhabit Karfel, the Morlox are huge, savage, reptilian quadrupeds. Dark green in colour, they have long necks, dinosaur-like snouts and razor sharp teeth.

TRAITS
Alien
Alien Appearance (Major)
Weakness (M80)

NATURAL WEAPON: Bite (Skill 2) 2/6/10.

Of course if you really wanted to make things interesting, you could decide that the real reason the Borad was obsessed with the Morlox was because they're at least as intelligent as the Karfel. A sentient, carnivorous, dangerous race, waiting just next door for your characters to try and make peace with them.

GUARDOLIER

AWARENESS	3	PRESENCE	4
COORDINATION	3	RESOLVE	2
INGENUITY	3	STRENGTH	3

The Guardoliers served as the guards on Karfel, enacting the orders of the Borad or the Maylin.

SKILLS
Athletics 3, Fighting 4, Marksman 3.

TRAITS
By the Book

WEAPON: Guardolier Rifle 2/**4**/8

TECH LEVEL: 6 **STORY POINTS:** 1

TECHNOLOGY

Time Acceleration Beam (Major Gadget)
The Borad's chair is equipped with a Time Acceleration Beam, in turn powered by a Kontron Crystal. He uses this to age to death those who displease him and whilst the weapon can only be fired twice at a time, it's still terrifyingly effective.

The sheer power involved is huge, meaning the beam must be mounted to an external power generator, such as the one that powered the Borad's chair.

The effects of the beam can be reversed using Ingenuity + Technology Difficulty 14. However, fine tuning them to exactly the character's original age requires a roll of Difficulty 18 and the beam can't return someone from the dead.

Damage: 3/L/L
Traits: Huge, Restriction (One Shot).
Cost: 2 Story Points

The Timelash
The Timelash appears to be a doorway set into a four-sided closet in the Council of Five's chamber. However, when it's activated (placing a massive drain on Karfel's resources) it opens a tunnel through time to Scotland on Earth in 1179. Anyone thrown into the Timelash will land there, nauseous and faint but otherwise unharmed.

Anyone thrown into the Timelash must make a Resolve + Survival roll (Difficulty 10) to stay calm in the immensely disturbing Vortex. The sheer weight of information, as time hurtles past on all sides, can drive people mad if they spend too long inside the Vortex. Anyone who fails the roll loses a point from their Presence for the rest of the game.

Kontron Crystals
Kontron Crystals are crystallised time. The unusual minerals form naturally on the walls of tunnels and rifts in time and are highly prized as symbols of status as well as weapons in their own right. Kontron Crystals absorb time, refracting it like light, meaning that with the right expertise and tools you can make them do almost anything. Due to their incredible capacity for destruction, mining of Kontron Crystals has been banned by Gallifrey. Which doesn't mean the Third Zone worlds aren't trying, of course...

Kontron Crystals give characters a +1 bonus on any roll involving temporal mechanics or time travel. They give Time Lords a +4 bonus.

KONTRON CRYSTAL GADGETS

Kontron Crystals are remarkably adaptable and can be used for anything involving the manipulation of time. However, they're also very complex. Any gadget construction involving kontron crystals needs be an Ingenuity + Technology Roll (Difficulty 16).

Timebreak (Major Gadget)
The most common use for Kontron Crystals is to create a Timebreak. By running a charge through the crystal a specific way, it projects an image of

BUT WHAT IS THE TIMELASH ACTUALLY FOR?

The Borad clearly has a plan, involving repopulating Karfel with Karfel/Morlox hybrids and picking a war with the Bandrils. None of which involves the Timelash you'll notice. Which is a shame as the Timelash is actually a rather lovely idea, and one that really could do with some exploiting. Earlier we looked at some of the things the Borad could have done with it now. Let's take a look at some of the things the characters could use it for.

Exploration: If the characters decide to make Karfelons their home for a while, it's entirely possible to steer the far end of the Timelash. It's not easy by any means (Ingenuity + Technology with a Difficulty 18) but if they manage it, they'll be able to step through a stable hole in time to anywhen that isn't timelocked in history.

Reconnaisance: Heard a rumour about Cybermen massing in the Andromeda Galaxy? Saw an unusual ship the last time you were on Varos? Want to find out the truth about something that's always bothered you? Move the Timelash, step through and find out. But be careful what you wish for...

Putting Right What Once Went Wrong: Perhaps your characters lost a friend thanks to cruel fate, or a battle went against them. Perhaps there's something in the timestream that they just know is wrong and want to fix. With the correct coordinates, the Timelash can take them there and, perhaps, help them do some good.

Safe Haven: Karfel is a small world with a smaller population. It's relatively peaceful, enjoys the protection of the Bandrils and has been taken under the Doctor's wing twice now. It's not perfect but nowhere in the universe is. Karfel could be a sanctuary, a port of call for people displaced by the horrors of war or time, with the characters helping them into the Timelash to their new home.

the wearer 10 seconds into the future, allowing the wearer to act with impunity for that time. However, this relatively minor temporal alteration drains the charge rapidly and most Timebreaks can only be used twice. This means all rolls attacking the character with the active Timebreak are at +8 difficulty for that turn

Traits: One Shot
Cost: 2 Story Points

Deflection Ray (Major Gadget)
Kontron Crystals can also be used to refract other kinds of energy within themselves. Any attack, involving physical projectiles or beam energy, is absorbed by the crystal. 10 seconds later, its released in the exact opposite direction, striking the attacker.

This means that whatever successful roll the attacker made to fire at the target, then automatically becomes the defending character's roll to hit them.

Traits: One Shot
Cost: 2 Story Points

Time Visor (Minor Gadget)
Placing a Kontron Crystal, or fragment of one, correctly in any form of camera or telescope will enable it to see through any temporal distortions in the room. The field of detection is limited only to what's directly in front of the lens, but will show any temporal anomalies in that field of vision.

Traits: Scan
Cost: 1 Story Point

ACIDIC PLANTS

Imported from the Bandril homeworld, these beautiful flowering plants conceal a deadly secret; if the leaves are touched by a living creature, their natural electric field closes a circuit which triggers the release of organic acid directly into the target's face. Untreated, they die in seconds and their slow decay feeds the plant.

The effect of this is simple; if a character touches the plant for more than a turn, the acid is released, causing the following damage:
3/**L**/L

BENDALYPSE

Bendalypse is a radioactive ore that, when refined, is almost impossibly stable. The Bandrils have perfected its use not only as a power source but a

weapon. In both cases, the reaction is so difficult to achieve that large, 100-ton pieces of bendalypse must be fired at one another in order to achieve a reaction. In reactors this is done in the central chamber. In warheads this is done at the point of impact, the two halves being driven together by the final stage of the missile.

The result is instantaneous; a massive release of almost entirely clean radiation. The missile spreads the radiation over a 100km radius instantaneously. Anyone caught within that radius is vaporised, instantly. No structures are harmed. This clean weapon is as horrifying as it is absolute and the Bandrils have used the threat of it as a means of keeping the peace with the several nearby races for centuries.

Effects: If you're caught in a bendalypse explosion, you're going to die. Unless, of course, you have other plans. A character using a Deflection Ray, for example, would receive the following damage, depending on their success: 3/1/0.

If they succeed completely, then the radiation in the cone immediately around them is absorbed by the crystal and, 10 seconds later, fired back the way it came. If they don't succeed enough, their wounds can be treated. And if they fail? Then they won't feel a thing.

MUSTAKOZENE-80

The most controversial substance developed in Karfel history, M-80 is a contact mutagen. Simply placing it on exposed skin will trigger low level, instantaneous mutation.

M-80 works by stimulating the stem cells of the subject in much the same way as the Varosian Cell Mutator. Megelen intended to use this as a means of experimenting with growth and modification of the Karfelon gene but, instead, found that the substance excited the Morlox. The one he was working with broke free, attacked him and dumped an entire container of M-80 over him. The two beings were fused together and the Borad was born.

Effects: Treat M-80 exposure in same way as exposure to the Cell Mutator (see pg. 41), but with a couple of differences. Here what matters isn't the amount of times it's happened but the amount of M-80 the characters has been exposed to. Check the exposure table first and either take the result from there or go to the Mutation Table.

FURTHER ADVENTURES

- **Scaling Mount Kontron:** En route to Karfel for the formal closing of the Timelash, the Doctor decides to take the 'short cut' one last time and ride up the tunnel. Halfway up, there's a shuddering crash as the TARDIS smashes into an outcropping of Kontron Crystals that wasn't there before. The ship is stuck and badly damaged, and the Doctor and companions have no choice but to climb the rest of the way. Assailed by glimpses of their past, present and future, they realise something is badly wrong.

  A group of Sontarans are mining the crystals, the Timelash is already starting to heal and, in the middle of it all, they find Captain Edmund Hillary, a man out of space and time.

- **Any Port In A Storm:** A Bandril missile has gone rogue. Armed with a bendalypse warhead it's headed right for Karfel. There's no way to stop or move it in time, so the Doctor has one choice; evacuate the planet down the Timelash. But how do you hide thousands of Karfel and Morlox in 1179 Scotland? And, out in the loch, the Borad is waiting.

- **Time's Wing'd Chariot:** An android from Karfel appears in the TARDIS control room and immediately tries to kill the Doctor. When it's subdued, the characters discover information in its visual memory apparently showing the Doctor assassinating the Council of Five and claiming the seat of Maylin for his own. The characters realise the Doctor on screen is a clone, taken and grown in secret by the Borad. They have one hour to stop him killing the Council of Five, but, if they succeed, how could the android have appeared in the TARDIS?

MUSTAKOZENE-80 EXPOSURE TABLE

M-80 EXPOSURE	STRENGTH + SURVIVAL DIFFICULTY	DAMAGE IF UNSUCCESSFUL
Very small (Fingertip)	10	Skin reacts (-1 to resolve) but no after effects
Small (Finger)	15	Systemic shock. Character passes out and is -1 all attributes. No further effects if M-80 cleaned off immediately
Medium (Hand)	17	Roll once on the mutation table
Large (Limb)	25	Roll twice on the mutation table
Very Large (1/2 or more of the body)	30	Roll three times on the mutation table

MUTATION TABLE

2D6 ROLL	RESULT	EFFECT
2	Giant size	+2 Presence, +1 Strength, -1 Coordination and the Alien Appearance trait.
3	Tail and claws	+1 Presence, +1 Coordination, Alien Appearance trait.
4	Full extra limb	+2 Coordination, Alien Appearance trait.
5	Translucent skin	+3 Presence, Alien Appearance and Outcast traits.
6	Character develops spines all over their body	+1 Presence, -1 Coordination, Outcast (Quills do 1/3/L damage).
7	Character develops brilliant and diverse skin pigmentation	+2 Presence, Alien Appearance trait.
8	Reptilian appearance	+1 Presence, Alien Appearance trait, Outcast
9	Gills	Character can breathe underwater. At your discretion may only be able to breathe underwater.
10	Fur all over body	Alien Appearance trait.
11	Skin hardens and expands	+2 Strength, -2 Coordination, Distinctive trait.
12	Fused with nearest living organism	Add all attributes and skills together and divide by 2. Presence + Resolve (Difficulty 19) to not go insane during the process.

With an Ingenuity + Technology roll (Difficulty 16), any character stuck with some serious mutations can be cured. Of course, you'll have to go to Varos to the Cell Mutator to do it...

REVELATION OF THE DALEKS

'Ah, I see you have been busy.'
'Whereas you have been stupid, Doctor!'
'Prerogative of a Time Lord.'

SYNOPSIS

Necros, the Future

The TARDIS arrived on Necros, the location of the Tranquil Repose funeral home and suspended animation centre. The Doctor wanted to pay his respects to Doctor Arthur Stengos, a deceased friend, and insisted that Peri and he both wear blue clothes, the official colour of mourning on the world. They had barely left the TARDIS when the Doctor was attacked by a hideously disfigured man. He attempted to hypnotise him but it only made the attacker more aggressive. Peri was ultimately forced to kill him before he throttled the Doctor and, as the man was dying, he both absolved Peri and explained he had been made this way by the 'Great Healer'.

At Tranquil Repose, where a DJ played old Earth tunes and read messages to the residents, Mr Jobel, the Chief Undertaker, was frantically coordinating staff for one of the most important jobs of his life. The President was en route with the body of the First Lady, and the entire staff were scrambling to be ready in time. Mr Jobel's arrogant, abrasive style rubbed every one of his staff up the wrong way, aside from his adoring assistant Tasambeker. Mr Jobel treated her even more cruelly than the rest. Undeterred, she was honoured to be summoned to the presence of the Great Healer – revealed to be Davros, reduced to a head in a life support system. He asked her to spy for him and she agreed.

As this was going on, Natasha Stengos, Arthur's daughter, and her friend Grigory, had broken into the facility. They were also looking for Arthur and were disturbed to find his suspended animation capsule empty. They looked further and discovered a room filled with living brains held in nutrient tanks and a glass Dalek with a red mass of flesh at its centre. To their horror, it opened its eyes and said Natasha's name. It was Arthur Stengos. Arthur explained that each brain in Tranquil Repose was being experimented on to be changed into a new wave of Daleks and that he had been conditioned to serve the 'Great Healer'. His voice rising and becoming more Dalek-like with every moment, he begged his daughter to kill him and she did so just as his transformation was complete. Numbed, the two made their escape and were captured by Takis and Lilt, two of Mr Jobel's staff. Natasha and Grigory were tortured even as they tried to explain what was really going on.

Elsewhere on the planet, Madame Kara and her assistant Vogel were reluctantly dealing with the Great Healer, sick of the hold he had over not just Tranquil Repose but the protein extract factories she operated here. In reality, the 'Great Healer' had developed the protein extract from the bodies of the Tranquil Repose clients, keeping their brains to use in his experiments. Kara hired a mercenary to kill Davros. Orcini, a former member of the Grand Order of Oberon, and his squire, Bostock, were hired to find Davros and kill him, detonating a bomb with a five figure passcode that Madame Kara equipped them with. She asked them to enter the code as soon as they located Davros and, unknown to them, planned to detonate the bomb remotely to kill them as well. The two men agreed to take the job, Orcini revelling in the idea of, for once, killing someone for a good reason.

The Doctor and Peri had made their way to Tranquil Repose and were just about to enter when the Doctor saw a huge statue with his face on it. Used, by now, to arriving places where the Doctor had already been, Peri joked about it being a good likeness. The Doctor was disturbed though, realising that the placing of the statue in the Garden of Fond Memories meant he'd died and it was a memorial. Suddenly, the statue collapsed on him and Mr Jobel appeared, assuring Peri that he was quite dead and attempting to flirt with her. The Doctor, unharmed because the statue wasn't actually made of stone, dusted himself off, confronted Mr Jobel and they left.

Inside Tranquil Repose, the pair were met by Tasambeker. The Doctor asked to be taken to whoever had erected the statue of him and suggested Peri go and see the DJ, as she was amused by how familiar he sounded. Reluctantly, as she had Mr Jobel as a traveling companion, Peri set off. When she arrived, the DJ helped her get rid of Mr Jobel and they chatted. The DJ was amazed to find that Peri was from Earth and explained he'd copied his style from the old records his grandfather had brought him.

Elsewhere, Orcini and Bostock spotted and destroyed a Dalek. Davros was alerted and he realised Kara had sent assassins to kill him. He dispatched Daleks to her office, killed her secretary and ordered her brought to him. Realising what was coming, Tasambeker attempted to warn Mr Jobel out of misplaced love. He refused to believe her and, enraged, she snapped and stabbed him to death. Stricken with guilt, she was chased down and exterminated by a Dalek.

The Doctor had already been captured by the Daleks and was put in the same cell as Natasha and Grigory. Orcini rescued them, easily overpowering the Doctor, who mistook him for another foe. Releasing the prisoners, Orcini and Bostock pushed through to Davros' chamber. A battle ensued and for a moment Bostock thought they were victorious. However, the

head in the centre of the room was a decoy and the pair were quickly overpowered, Orcini's artificial leg getting blown off in the process. Kara was brought in and her true motives emerged. She bragged that at least they would both die and Orcini deployed a small knife from his sleeve and killed her.

Natasha and Grigory had returned to the incubation chamber, planning on putting the brains out of their misery. However, Natasha's gun had run out of charge and whilst Grigory was looking for a self-destruct system on the control console, a second glass Dalek began to materialise. The two ran for the door but the glass Dalek had disappeared. They looked up and were killed by a second Dalek.

The Doctor was able to warn Peri, telling her to stop the President landing by using the TARDIS radio. She was getting ready to go when the DJ pointed out it would be suicide and that she could make contact using the equipment at the station. Davros overheard the transmission and dispatched Daleks to the radio station. The DJ used a sonic cannon to kill two Daleks but was exterminated by a third. The Doctor tried to save her but was caught, as was Peri, and taken back to Davros. There, the Dalek creator told his captives the truth: there was an army of Daleks prepared for war and stored in the catacombs beneath the lab. Bostock, badly injured, shot Davros' hand off and, enraged, the Dalek creator killed him.

Elsewhere, Takis had seen enough and done the only thing he could; called the Supreme Dalek on Skaro. A troopship from the other Dalek faction arrived and made their way to Davros. There, he tried to have them capture the Doctor but they refused, not recognising him post-regeneration. A battle ensued and the Imperial Daleks won, taking Davros back to Skaro to stand trial for crimes against the Daleks.

Orcini told the Doctor that he wanted to detonate the bomb before Davros' ship left. He agreed to wait whilst the Doctor, Peri and Takis evacuated Tranquil Repose. The Dalek ship left before Orcini, embracing the body of his fallen Squire, could detonate the bomb. Unaware, he detonated it anyway. Outside, the Doctor comforted a grief-stricken Peri, pointing out Orcini had died with immense honour, destroying the next wave of Daleks. He then told Takis, worried now he was unemployed, that they could always harvest the flowers on Necros and promised Peri he'd take her on a real holiday next time.

CONTINUITY

- This adventure continues on from the end of ***Resurrection of the Daleks*** (see **The Fifth Doctor Sourcebook**), Davros having escaped in an escape pod.
- Daleks can be created from human stock, as we later see in ***Bad Wolf*** (see **The Ninth Doctor Sourcebook**) and, by a different means, in ***Asylum of the Daleks*** (see **The Eleventh Doctor Sourcebook**). Presumably the Progenitor Device would reject these Daleks too (see ***Victory of the Daleks*** in **The Eleventh Doctor Sourcebook**).

- Davros has his hand shot off in this episode, which explains why he has a robotic claw in ***The Stolen Earth*** (see **The Tenth Doctor Sourcebook**).

RUNNING THE ADVENTURE

This is a surprisingly streamlined adventure, especially after the previous escapades. As a result, it's possible to use this one as both a change of pace and a slow ramping up of the stakes. The key is atmosphere: Tranquil Repose is a funeral home and Necros is a quiet, peaceful world.

Even better, this is a story set in a workplace. Mr Jobel is a familiar figure – the bullying boss – and how the characters react to and around him will set the atmosphere and raise the stakes when you roll the Daleks out.

Think of this as an episode of a sitcom or soap opera, set at Tranquil Repose. There's the same jealousies and alliances, the same jockeying for power you get in any workplace but its mixed with a constantly increasing horror. The Daleks aren't on their way, the Daleks are already here and when they make themselves known, all hell will break loose.

Once that happens, go all out in terms of pace and action. Orcini's a great opportunity to drive both, as is the ticking clock of the President's arrival. At the centre of it all though should always be Davros, the King Spider, the Dalek's creator, orchestrating every event around him. This is one of Davros' moments to truly shine, his vindictive plan to trick the Doctor into arriving playing out perfectly. The Daleks' master may have reduced resources these days, but he's as terrifying as ever he was. Use him as the centre of everything.

DAVROS

The creator of the Daleks had seen better days when the Doctor met him on Necros. Still reeling from the Movellan virus he'd been infected with and with his forces all but gone, Davros had retreated to Necros to recover and plan. His work with Madame Kara gave him unlimited resources and relative anonymity. However, when he realised the Doctor knew Arthur Stengos, he saw a chance not only to regain power, but to be revenged on his ancient enemy.

On Necros, he seems apparently powerless, reduced to a mere head in a jar. However, Davros is still heavily armed and there's much more of him than meets the eye...

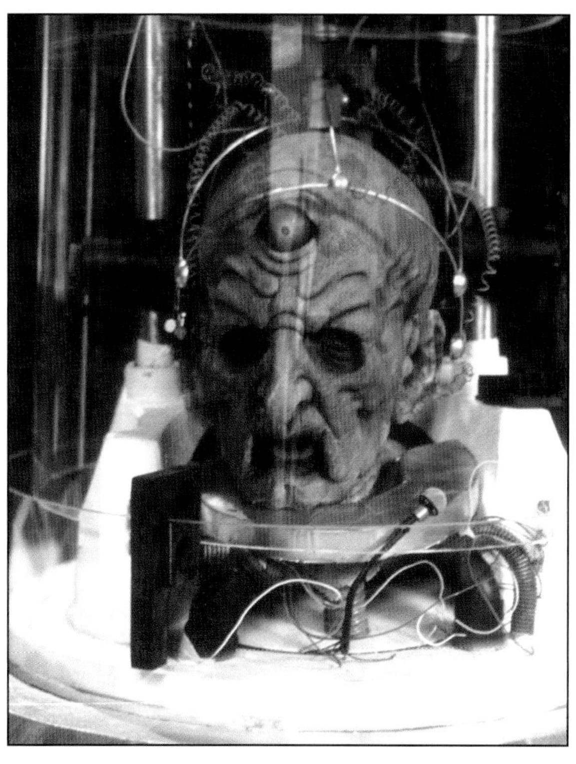

DAVROS / 'THE GREAT HEALER'

AWARENESS	2	PRESENCE	2
COORDINATION	2	RESOLVE	6
INGENUITY	7	STRENGTH	2

SKILLS
Convince 1, Craft 6, Knowledge 6, Medicine 6, Science 6, Subterfuge 4, Survival 2, Technology 6, Transport 2.

TRAITS
Boffin
Cyborg
Dependency (his life-support system)
Fear Factor 1
Flight (Minor)
Indomitable
Immortal
Obsession
Technically Adept

WEAPON: Lightning Projection System 3/**6**/L

TECH LEVEL: 6 **STORY POINTS:** 12

DALEK

The Daleks presented here are advanced models but still lack the ability to fly — only to hover.. They rely on Dalek Troopers to go where they can't.

DALEK

AWARENESS	3	PRESENCE	5
COORDINATION	2	RESOLVE	4
INGENUITY	4	STRENGTH	7*

SKILLS
Convince 4, Fighting 4, Marksman 3, Medicine 3, Science 8, Subterfuge 3, Survival 4, Technology 8.

TRAITS
Armour (Major)
Cyborg
Environmental (All)
Fear Factor (3)
Flight (Minor)
Natural Weapon – (Exterminator)
Technically Adept

WEAPON: Exterminator - The legendary Dalek weapon usually kills with a single shot – 4/**L**/L.

TECH LEVEL: 8 STORY POINTS: 5-8

GLASS DALEK

The Glass Dalek was designed to act as a nursery of sorts for the successful mutants Davros was creating. The brains were placed inside the chest cavity of the Dalek and tissue grown around them at an accelerated rate to mould them to the shape required. This combined with a massive surge in their Dalek conditioning, preparing them for combat and their true body. Glass Daleks aren't made of glass but they are fragile, the reinforced structures of their body unarmoured and making the mutant inside a very easy target. However, their weapon systems are fully active, meaning the mutant can defend itself if fully grown and under attack.

GLASS DALEK

AWARENESS	2	PRESENCE	4
COORDINATION	1	RESOLVE	4
INGENUITY	3	STRENGTH	5

TRAITS
Armour (1)
Cyborg
Environmental (Major)
Fear Factor (4)
Natural Weapon (Major x2)
Scan
Special (Self Destruct)
Technically Adept

WEAPON: Exterminator 4/**L**/L

STORY POINTS: 3

TRANQUIL REPOSE RESIDENTS

The residents of Tranquil Repose know nothing about the horrors being visited on the staff. All they can hear are the soothing sounds of the DJ, and all they can see are their best and happiest memories. But the lights are going out in Tranquil Repose, people are disappearing and the best and happiest are starting to lose their lustre.

Awareness 2, Coordination 1, Ingenuity 3, Presence 2, Resolve 1, Strength 1

MR JOBEL

A legend in his own mortuary, Mr Jobel is the greatest undertaker alive. He feels the need to remind his staff of this constantly, his cruel, savage put downs reducing many to tears. But Jobel doesn't care. Great work requires sacrifice and as long as that sacrifice isn't his, who is he to argue?

TASAMBEKER

Mr Jobel's biggest target and yet his biggest fan, Tasambeker does nothing without his say so and is never far from his side. Her reward for this is relentless, vile bullying but she doesn't mind. Great work requires sacrifice, and after all, so does great love...

MR JOBEL

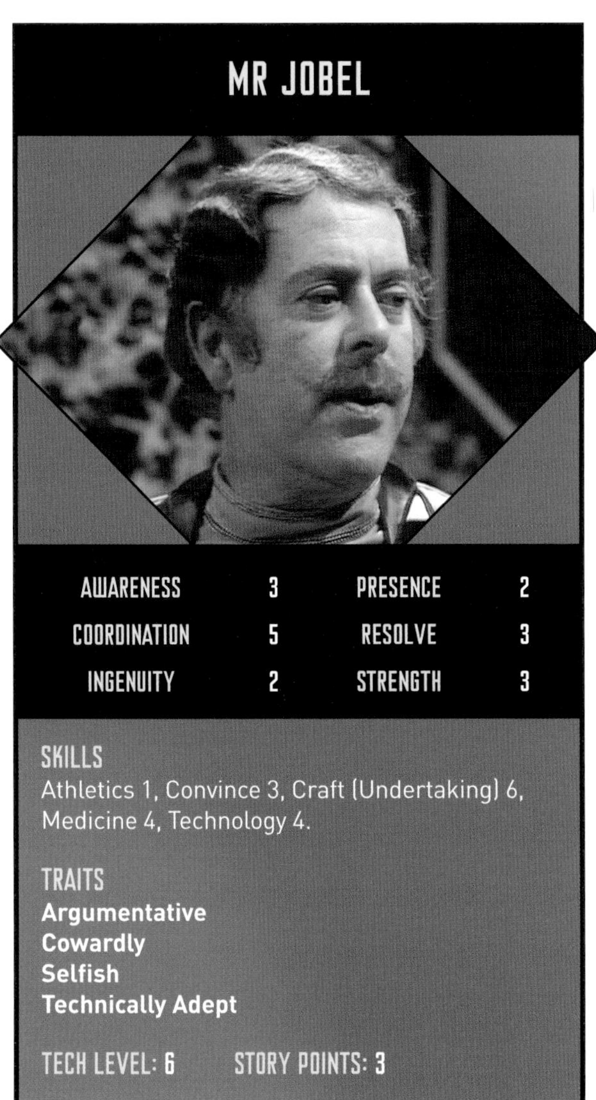

AWARENESS	3	PRESENCE	2
COORDINATION	5	RESOLVE	3
INGENUITY	2	STRENGTH	3

SKILLS
Athletics 1, Convince 3, Craft (Undertaking) 6, Medicine 4, Technology 4.

TRAITS
Argumentative
Cowardly
Selfish
Technically Adept

TECH LEVEL: 6 STORY POINTS: 3

TASAMBEKER

AWARENESS	3	PRESENCE	2
COORDINATION	4	RESOLVE	4
INGENUITY	3	STRENGTH	3

SKILLS
Athletics 1, Convince 3, Knowledge (Necros) 5, Medicine 3, Science 3, Technology 3.

TRAITS
Argumentative
Obsession

TECH LEVEL: 6 STORY POINTS: 3

THE DJ

All the DJ ever wanted was to play the records his grandfather had brought from Earth and to be cool. Elvis, Jim Morrison, Glen Miller, the greats of pop music towered over him, urging him on but never quite letting him catch up. When he was offered the gig on Necros, he thought all his ships had come in at once. But now, sitting alone in a radio studio that's also his apartment, the DJ is starting to wish he'd dreamt a little bigger.

THE DJ

AWARENESS	2	PRESENCE	3
COORDINATION	2	RESOLVE	3
INGENUITY	6	STRENGTH	3

SKILLS
Athletics 2, Convince 3, Knowledge (Earth Culture and Music) 6, Technology 5.

TRAITS
Brave
Charming
Forgetful
Unlucky

TECH LEVEL: 6 STORY POINTS: 2

MADAME KARA

Madame Kara runs Necros. Madame Kara is rich and powerful. Madame Kara is trapped, between her idiot staff on one hand and the Great Healer on the other. It can't last. And she will do anything she has to to make sure it doesn't.

MADAME KARA

AWARENESS	5	PRESENCE	4
COORDINATION	3	RESOLVE	5
INGENUITY	4	STRENGTH	3

SKILLS
Convince 6, Knowledge (Necros) 6, Science 5, Subterfuge 5.

TRAITS
Attractive
Friends
Selfish

TECH LEVEL: 6 STORY POINTS: 3

VOGEL

Madame Kara's aide, Vogel is sick of it all. He's sick of Necros and its miserable weather, sick of the endless demands placed on him by Madame Kara and most of all, sick of the Great Healer. The sooner he's dealt with, the better. Then Vogel's life may finally get a little more peaceful.

VOGEL

AWARENESS	3	PRESENCE	2
COORDINATION	2	RESOLVE	4
INGENUITY	4	STRENGTH	3

SKILLS
Athletics 3,Craft (Administration) 6, Fighting 2, Knowledge (Necros) 6, Medicine 3, Science 3, Technology 3.

TRAITS
By the Book
Face in the Crowd
Indomitable
Slow Reflexes

TECH LEVEL: 6 STORY POINTS: 2

NATASHA STENGOS

Natasha Stengos wants her father back. The rumours she's heard about Necros are terrifying and if true... she can't think about it. Not yet. She'll find and rescue her dad. That's all that matters.

NATASHA STENGOS

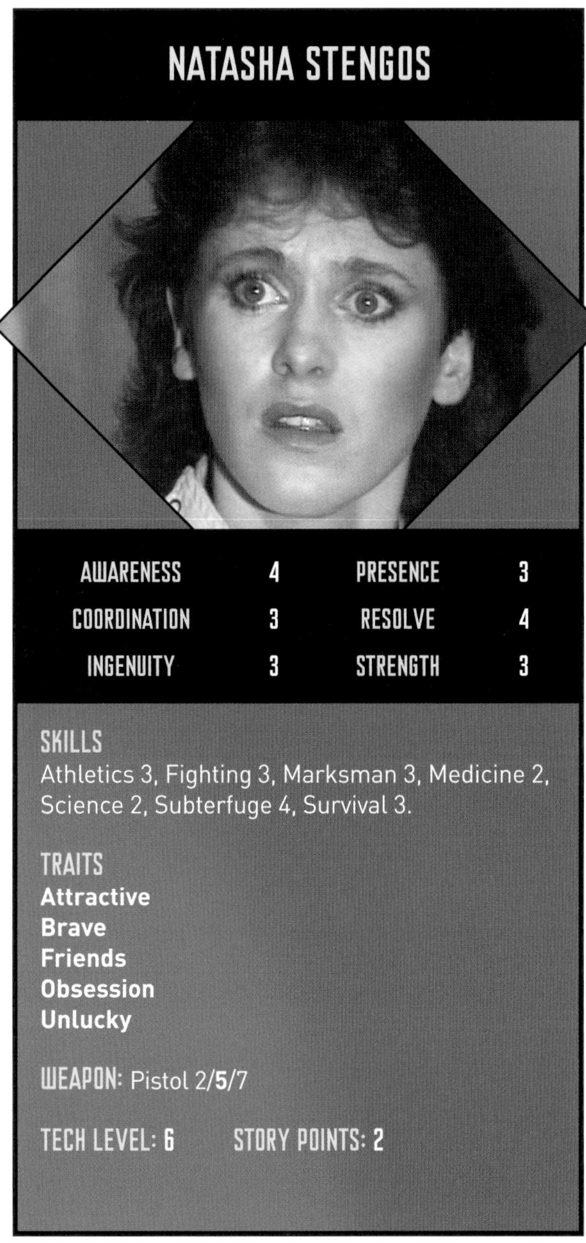

AWARENESS	4	PRESENCE	3
COORDINATION	3	RESOLVE	4
INGENUITY	3	STRENGTH	3

SKILLS
Athletics 3, Fighting 3, Marksman 3, Medicine 2, Science 2, Subterfuge 4, Survival 3.

TRAITS
Attractive
Brave
Friends
Obsession
Unlucky

WEAPON: Pistol 2/**5**/7

TECH LEVEL: 6 **STORY POINTS: 2**

TAKIS

The funeral business just isn't the same any more for Takis. Oh sure, he likes the work, likes the pageantry and enjoys the occasional violence but... something's off. Since the Great Healer came there's been constant tension, and it's only been getting worse. He's thinking about packing it in, maybe selling flowers...

TAKIS

AWARENESS	3	PRESENCE	4
COORDINATION	4	RESOLVE	3
INGENUITY	4	STRENGTH	4

SKILLS
Athletics 3, Fighting 4, Knowledge (Necros) 5, Marksman 4.

TRAITS
Adversary (Tasambeker)
Face in the Crowd
Indomitable

TECH LEVEL: 6 **STORY POINTS: 2**

GRIGORY

Grigory wants out, but, he also wants to look after Natasha. Her father helped him when he needed it and now, reluctantly and with growing horror, Grigory's returning the favour. He just hopes the old man is alive to thank him.

GRIGORY

AWARENESS	3	PRESENCE	3
COORDINATION	4	RESOLVE	4
INGENUITY	3	STRENGTH	4

SKILLS
Athletics 3, Fighting 3, Marksman 3, Medicine 5, Science 3, Subterfuge 2, Survival 2.

TRAITS
Boffin
Brave
Technically Adept
Unlucky

WEAPON: Rifle 3/**6**/9

TECH LEVEL: 6 **STORY POINTS: 2**

LILT

Lilt and Takis have been friends since Morturary School and they've always divided the labour equally; Takis did the office politics and flowers and Lilt did the occasional violence and flowers. It's a good system, but it's just not... fun any more. Takis is thinking about changing career and Lilt's thinking about coming too, especially if there's the odd bit of violence and flower arranging involved.

LILT

AWARENESS	3	PRESENCE	2
COORDINATION	4	RESOLVE	4
INGENUITY	2	STRENGTH	3

SKILLS
Athletics 3, Convince 3, Fighting 4, Knowledge 6, Medicine 7, Science 7, Survival 3, Technology 4.

TRAITS
Face in the Crowd
Friends
Unadventurous

TECH LEVEL: 6 **STORY POINTS: 2**

ORCINI

Orcini lost his honour years ago. His leg followed not soon after. Now, he's tired and sore, his bones ache and the days of the Order are long behind him. There's no honour left in the universe, no such thing as a good clean fight. There's just paying the bills, keeping moving and keeping ahead of the most implacable hunter he's ever run from: time. And Bostock. Faithful as ever.

But now, Orcini has one last chance to die with honour, one last life to end. Orcini gets to be a hero again and his pain is all gone. He's a Knight again, even if it is just once more.

ORCINI

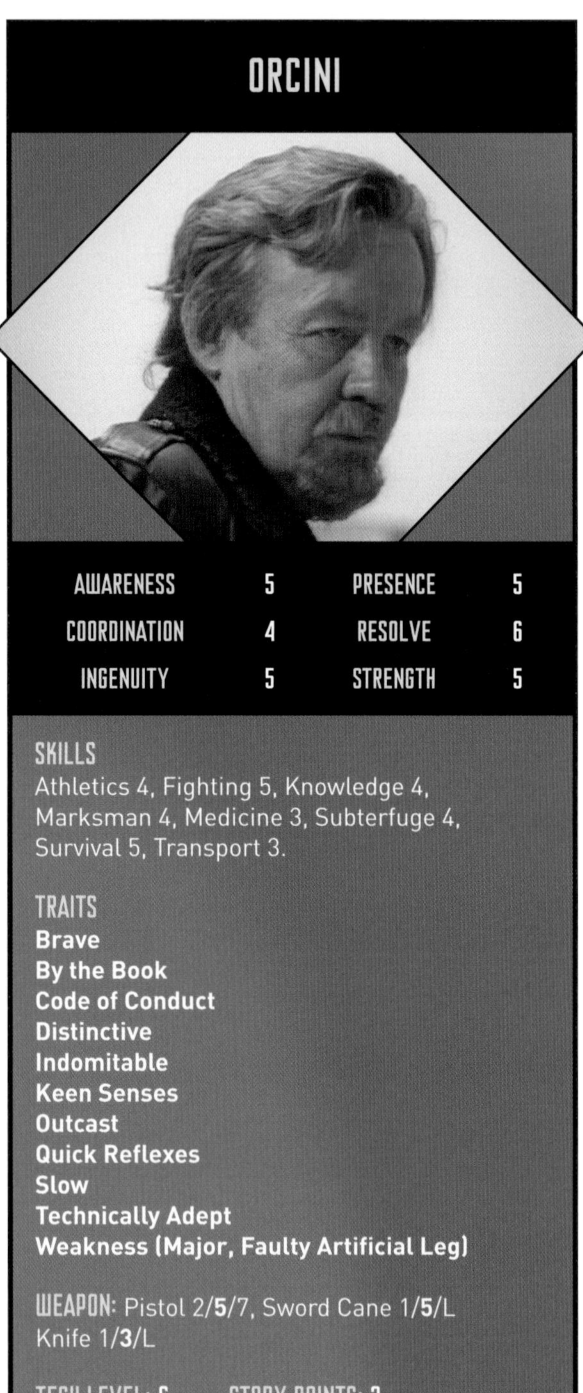

AWARENESS	5	PRESENCE	5
COORDINATION	4	RESOLVE	6
INGENUITY	5	STRENGTH	5

SKILLS
Athletics 4, Fighting 5, Knowledge 4, Marksman 4, Medicine 3, Subterfuge 4, Survival 5, Transport 3.

TRAITS
Brave
By the Book
Code of Conduct
Distinctive
Indomitable
Keen Senses
Outcast
Quick Reflexes
Slow
Technically Adept
Weakness (Major, Faulty Artificial Leg)

WEAPON: Pistol 2/**5**/7, Sword Cane 1/**5**/L Knife 1/**3**/L

TECH LEVEL: 6 **STORY POINTS: 3**

WHO ARE THE GRAND ORDER OF OBERON?

Stories of the order have echoed down through the years, many contradictory. Here are a few of them:

Dalek Veterans: The Order were formed from the survivors of the units that had held back the Daleks on Neptune's moon Oberon in the 22nd century.

Oberon's Children: The Order were all descended from Oberon Van Statten, great grandfather of Henry Van Statten and the first man on Earth to encounter a hostile alien and survive. They each carry his memories and skills.

Leading by Example: The Order were founded in the late 23rd century by Oberon Van Statten, a descendent of Henry's, who had become obsessed with the concepts of knightly honour and martial combat. He built the Order as a private army but, instead of hiring them out as mercenaries, donated their services to the weak and needy.

BOSTOCK

Bostock stays with Orcini because he's his Squire. He's stayed with him through the glory days, the dark days and everything in between. They've patched each other up in foxholes and dined out in the best hotels in the universe. He loves Orcini completely and knows that love is returned. The two men are at the end of their run but if this is their last windmill to tilt at, then Bostock will be right there with Orcini, one last time. There's nowhere else in the universe he'd rather be.

BOSTOCK

AWARENESS	5	PRESENCE	2
COORDINATION	5	RESOLVE	4
INGENUITY	4	STRENGTH	3

SKILLS
Athletics 4, Fighting 4, Knowledge 4, Marksman 5, Medicine 5, Subterfuge 4, Survival 6, Transport 4.

TRAITS
Brave
Code of Conduct
Distinctive
Indomitable
Sense of Direction
Tough

WEAPON: Rifle 3/**6**/9

TECH LEVEL: 6 STORY POINTS: 3

MUTANT

Created as part of Davros' experiments, the mutant attacked the Doctor – driven to hostility and rage by the Great Healer. Peri killed him.

MUTANT

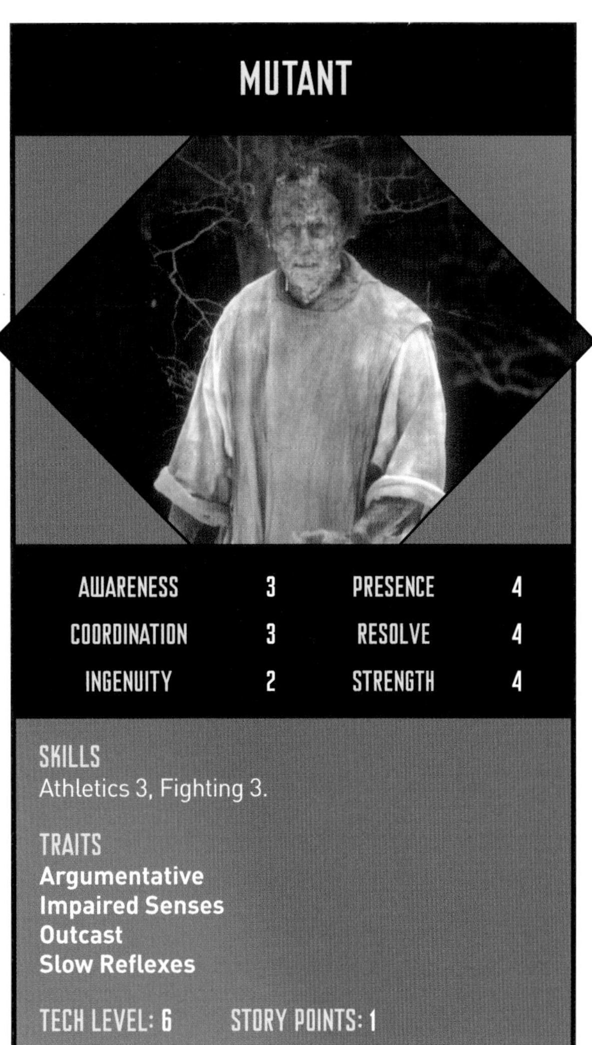

AWARENESS	3	PRESENCE	4
COORDINATION	3	RESOLVE	4
INGENUITY	2	STRENGTH	4

SKILLS
Athletics 3, Fighting 3.

TRAITS
Argumentative
Impaired Senses
Outcast
Slow Reflexes

TECH LEVEL: 6 STORY POINTS: 1

NEW TRAIT: MAIL IN KNIGHT (SPECIAL GOOD)

Orcini claimed to be the last of his order and he may well have been right. But there are some who still follow the code of Oberon, reconstructed through years of research. They don't have the Knights' monastery or the ability to apprentice knights to an experienced master, but they do have the Galactic Communications Network. Anyone who finds their contact details, and anyone who's interested can become a Knight of the Grand Order, training their mind and body to a level they never thought possible.

This Special Good trait is available in two 'levels'. The first costs 3 Character Points and is for characters who've reached the Squire level. They get the following:

+1 Awareness, +1 Athletics, +2 Fighting,
+1 Marksman, Code of Conduct (Major Bad).

The second version of this trait costs 6 Character Points and is for the – exceptionally few – who make it this far:

+1 Awareness, +1 Coordination,
+2 Athletics, +2 Fighting, +2 Marksman,
By The Book, Code of Conduct (Major),
Keen Senses.

TECHNOLOGY

Suspension Technology

The suspension process is by all accounts pleasant. The subject picks the memories and experiences they want to experience, is anaesthetised and placed under. What they don't know, of course, is that their bodies are then broken down and used to make protein extract whilst their brains remain in a state of suspended bliss.

Any character killed on Necros can be put through this process, either by the staff or the other characters with an Ingenuity + Medicine roll (Difficulty 16) needed to complete the procedure. If that's done, the character wakes up surrounded by their happiest memories and the others wait for the awkward moment to tell them they're now a brain in a jar.

The suspended character shouldn't despair though. After all, the Borad has developed cloning and the Varosian cell mutator (see pg. 41) could be used to revive their body (Ingenuity + Medicine at Difficulty 18 for that one). Death isn't the end on Necros. Just make sure you like rock and roll and you'll be fine.

Of course you could also combine the suspension tech here with the Matrix or Crozier's Conscious transferral machine and have an adventure set inside a Suspended character's mind.

'Rock and Roll' Cannon

The DJ's sonic cannon was a typically flamboyant weapon for him. It was actually a sonic lance, originally used to carve the tunnels that the Tranquil Repose was built in and left in the DJ's studio by a departing miner. He tinkered with it and worked out how to supercharge it simply by feeding the entirety of modern rock music through its central transmitter. The end result was destructive, over the top and very, very him.

Sonic Lance	2/**4**/8
Rock and Roll Cannon	3/**6**/12

FURTHER ADVENTURES

- **The Dalek Blues:** Visting Necros several years later, the Doctor is pleased to find Takis and Lilt have successfully marketed and sold the flower protein. He's even more pleased to see they've begun a reclamation effort on Tranquil Repose, assisted by Earth Military's Anti-Dalek forces, of course. As the old tunnels are opened up, the hope is to renovate the complex and help erase the memory of the horrors that were perpetrated there. But then the workers start hearing a mournful voice, with an American twang, singing the blues.

  Somewhere in the suspension system at Tranquil Repose is the digital ghost of the DJ. He's not alone either. Harsher, more strident voices join the chorus as the rescuers dig deeper. There are Daleks alive in the tunnels, driven mad by the solitude and the only thing keeping them from going into a frenzy is the DJ. If they can't rescue him before his ghost fades, the Daleks will go on the rampage. But who or what do they replace him with? And what is the Asylum of the Daleks?

- **Hive Mind:** Six months after the events of this adventure, the Doctor collapses mid-sentence, his mind filling with images of a decaying, run down mansion at sunset and hundreds of people in the grounds screaming his name. The vision happens again and again until finally he realises that it's showing him Tranquil Repose.

  The clients who weren't turned into Daleks are still alive beneath the rubble and with the power failing, their brains have connected to each other in order to survive. Time is running out and the characters must organise a rescue mission before the brains freeze and die. All is going well until the Doctor has the vision again and this time, there are Daleks in every window of the mansion. The characters must race against time, and the Daleks, to save the clients.

- **The Necros Job:** Sabalom Glitz has a business proposition for the Doctor. He knows that things went south on Necros, but he also happens to know that there is a particular person in suspension who really shouldn't be there. Because he owes Glitz money, first of all, and secondly because he's there against his will. Declan Ziato, Glitz's old drinking buddy and a former star athlete was put in Tranquil Repose so his perfect body could be put on the clone market. The only problem is, Declan was in hock to Glitz for a lot of...mismanaged bets.

  Now, Glitz wants his money and his friend and he knows the Doctor can't resist helping those in need. There is one problem though: Glitz has rivals and they all want Declan's mind too. Now, the characters must race the Daleks, the debt collectors and Glitz to save Declan Ziato and get out without being noticed.

CHAPTER FOUR
THE TRIAL OF A TIME LORD

'Madam, this revelation should halt this trial immediately. Surely even Gallifreyan Law must acknowledge that the same person cannot be both prosecutor and defendant!'

INTRODUCTION

This chapter details one of the most tumultuous periods of the Doctor's life, when he was put on trial by the Gallifreyan High Council. Facing a mysterious prosecutor called the Valeyard and suffering from Temporal Amnesia, the Doctor still, somehow managed to discover the truth and prove his innocence. This is one of the most demanding, and rewarding, sets of adventures you can run and this chapter will walk you through the multiple ways that you can approach them as well as places to go after this campaign. But first, hold tight, because the TARDIS is about to take an unscheduled detour... The reasons behind the trial, and the mysterious Valeyard, will be dealt with first.

This section includes a possible explanation for the Valeyard's appearance and connection to the Ravolox incident, different origins for him and ways you can use him and the Justice Station in your games. Later, you'll find full write-ups for the four adventures that make up The Trial of a Time Lord.

THE VALEYARD AND THE JUSTICE STATION

THE RENEGADES

Following the disastrous reigns of Chancellors Goth and Borusa, the Time Lords were in crisis. Their leaders were riddled with corruption and insanity and if a third scandal was to break, their entire culture would be at risk. To make matters worse, House Prydon, the house that many of their greatest politicians were chosen from, was also home to the largest number of renegade Time Lords.

Have one guess which house the Doctor is part of. Well done.

With the Doctor, the Master, the Rani, the Corsair and countless others careening around the universe, the Time Lords' non-interference doctrine was a joke. To make matters even worse, each one of the renegades was a point of unpredictability, their actions constantly throwing off the predictive capabilities of the APC Net otherwise known as the Matrix. Their leaders were corrupt, their citizens were using the universe as their personal laboratory and the whole while the governments of the Third Zone were pushing to create a time machine of their own.

They weren't alone either. The Time Lords were threatened in a way they hadn't been since the Sontaran invasion and this problem was even more insidious. Previously, the Time Lords had been content to give their renegades their head, confident that they would police each other as well as provide useful intelligence when needed. It was time for that to stop.

THE VALEYARD

The project was championed by the Valeyard. A precise, older Time Lord who dressed in black robes, the Valeyard had arrived on Gallifrey several months previously and had presented credentials that allowed him access to both the High Council and the President. His argument was both simple and compelling. It was the nature of time that societies, especially great ones, fell. The Time Lords were in the early stages of what would become the total collapse of their civilisation and, unless the Council policed the renegades and brought them into line, the collapse couldn't be stopped. With all the renegades back in the fold, it was entirely possible that Gallifrey would survive and the Time Lords would continue to be one of the major powers in the galaxy.

The council did what they always did; debated the matter. They consulted the Matrix and were horrified to find evidence bearing out the Valeyard's fears. In a few centuries, Gallifrey would be a barren wasteland following a second Sontaran attack, be at the core of the New Cyberiad or, worse still, have fallen to the Daleks forever. War was coming, change was coming and the Time Lords had to be made to stand together.

THE THEFT

Then the unthinkable happened; a group of Andromedans hacked into the Gallifreyan Matrix, stole the central secrets of Gallifreyan culture and fled. Their work was good but Time Lords are relentless and they eventually tracked the thieves down to Earth. They had hidden in the London Underground, creating a shelter and entering suspended animation whilst they waited for the robotic retrieval vessel from Andromeda to reach Earth.

If they escaped, the Time Lords wouldn't be safe. Worse, they wouldn't be unique any more.

The Council debated for days. Altering Earth's time line was considered, crossing Gallifrey's time line to prevent the theft before it happened was for a time the most popular option but, in the end, the Valeyard won out once again. His idea was simple, effective and utterly chilling.

The Andromedans needed to be stopped but there was no way to find a single vessel as it made its

DOES THE VALEYARD SHOW THEM THE TIME WAR?

That's up to you. Given when the Valeyard's from it seems perfectly reasonable to assume he knows about the Time War. If he's sincere in trying to warn them then the halfway mark of the Doctor's life would be the perfect place to start to prepare, especially as the war doesn't really go hot until his eighth life. Alternatively, the Valeyard could be manipulating the Matrix for his own ends.

way across the galactic border. Therefore the only thing left was to ensure the ship no longer had a destination to reach. Earth needed to be moved by the Time Lords. The Magnetron hadn't been used for centuries but the Valeyard's logic seemed inescapable. After all, what were a few trillion lives across centuries on Earth compared to the lives that would be lost if Gallifrey were to be attacked again?

The Magnetron was activated and, on Earth, it seemed like a colossal solar flare was about to hit. The governments did what they could and, far beneath London, the Andromedan robots manipulated events to ensure they had a viable workforce. Their colleagues would come, their charges would be retrieved. All they had to do was wait.

Earth and its entire solar system were hauled light years through the galaxy and the damage was, as expected, horrifying. But, as the planet slowly cooled, two things now became clear; the Andromedan ship would miss its target and the Valeyard now knew exactly what the Council had done. His price for keeping quiet about that knowledge was simple: to be allowed to lead the charge against the renegade Time Lords and forcibly bring them home.

THE JUSTICE STATION

The solution the Valeyard championed was both drastic and simple; construct a special Justice Station to travel space and time, find the renegades and bring them in. The station would be equipped with courtrooms, direct Matrix links and scoops designed to compel Time Lords to return to their TARDIS and drag them to the station. Quarters would, of course, be provided for the accused (which were, of course, guarded) and re-education centres would be used to show the guilty the error of their ways and bring them back into the fold.

THE TRUE PRICE

The Valeyard could have demanded a seat on the Council or any other price for his silence. Instead, all he did was ask that when the Justice Station sought out the Doctor, he would be allowed the Doctor's remaining regenerations when he was found guilty. The Council, sick of the Doctor's meddling and his petty refusal to act in a Presidential way, happily accepted. The Justice Station was built in Gallifreyan orbit and its crew were selected from the best and brightest of all the houses. Gallifrey was going to bring it's errant children home or end them once and for all.

> Rumours about the Justice Station abound, suggesting that it was the Valeyard's TARDIS or belonged to a secret Time Lord Intelligence Agency.

USING THE JUSTICE STATION

The Justice Station is unlike anything the Time Lords have used before or since, and as a result it and its mission offer some interesting challenges. The easiest way to run it is to have the Doctor be its first target, which would make a lot of sense given the Valeyard's agenda. However, it does seem like overkill, even by the Valeyard's usual standards, to send an entire station (that clearly contains multiple courtrooms) against a single Time Lord.

The other option is that the Justice Station is a TARDIS (perhaps the Valeyard's? Or what the Doctor's TARDIS will become?) and that it goes on one voyage, acquires all the renegades at once and tries them simultaneously. Or the Station could be halfway through its voyage when you encounter it, with several Time Lord renegades already detained waiting to be forcibly returned home. Of course, keeping that many brilliant people in one place is positively inviting a jail break...

Or, if you wanted to have the final diplomatic negotiations before the Time War as a backdrop, the Justice Station could be hoovering up the renegades, the Doctor in particular, as a show of good faith to the Daleks. The hope of being able to mollify them is, of course, a vain one but it's still an interesting idea, and opens up the two elements the Justice Station needs to embody: fear and conflict. This is a station set up specifically to find, try and, where necessary, execute its own people and that, for all the Gallifreyan pomp and circumstance, is a genuinely frightening thing. It's also completely against everything the

Time Lords have done since the Dark Times and, given that there are multiple scoops aboard, and by implication multiple courtrooms, it's likely some of the extensive crew will be more concerned about this than others. You could use the Justice Station as a real point of conflict for a Gallifreyan campaign, with elements of the crew choosing to aid the renegades rather than imprison them.

THE JUSTICE STATION

AWARENESS	1	PRESENCE	6
COORDINATION	4	RESOLVE	4
INGENUITY	4	STRENGTH	6

SKILLS
Fighting 5, Knowledge 6, Science (Temporal Science) 6, Technology 6, Transport 4.

TRAITS
Indomitable
Tough
Voice of Authority
Fast Healer
Feel The Turn Of The Universe
Psychic
Resourceful Pockets
Sense of Direction
Telepathy
Vortex
Justice Machine
By The Book
Code of Conduct
Obsession

GADGET TRAITS
Justice Machine, Hostile Action Displacement System, Matrix Interface, Real World Interface, TARDIS Sensors, Sensor Preset Controls (Time Lord renegades), TARDIS Scoop.

ARMOUR: 40

SPEED: 12 (MATERIALISED)

STORY POINTS: 20

COST: 20

NEW TRAITS

Justice Machine (Minor)
The Justice Station has spent a good deal of its life in the service of the High Council. As a result it's very focused on enforcing the laws of Time and assisting in the capture of Time Lord renegades, especially the Doctor and the Master.

A TARDIS with this trait actively resists any use of its system to contravene the Laws of Time. Any use of the TARDIS Story Points to allow a Time Lord to cross their own timestream after a fixed point in time or create a paradox of any sort using its systems, costs twice the normal amount.

The TARDIS will also keep a record of Time Lord renegades and, if it encounters one will refuse to move in any direction other than in pursuit of that renegade. It gains 3 Story Points whilst hunting its target and will not allow itself to be used by a Time Lord with the Wanted Renegade trait.

Real World Interface (Major)
The Real World Interface or RWI connects the outer shell of the TARDIS and its internal architecture. In a normal TARDIS this would appear as a black void when the TARDIS doors opened, that would dissipate when stepped across it, maintaining the illusion of the TARDIS and its outer shell being the same size. Alternatively, the doors themselves are sometimes designed to function as the RWI, although anyone opening them will see a seemingly impossibly space inside when they do.

The Justice Station works a little differently, with the TARDIS interior intersecting with the ship's exterior at multiple locations. Each courtroom is part of the TARDIS interior, as are each set of quarters and the engine room. Everywhere else, including every area where prisoners are detained, is part of the exterior and each RWI is completely sealable. Getting through a set of these doors requires advanced technology of at least TL 7, and, given that each renegade is searched the moment they arrive, that's very unlikely to happen.

But not impossible. After all, Time Lords are ingenious and all it takes is one sympathetic guard...

Hostile Action Displacement System (Minor)
The HADS system takes advantage of both the TARDIS' clairvoyance and its ability to travel in time by dematerialising shortly before an attack takes place. It's a highly effective system and that's been

a problem for Time Lords in the past (or future) who've left the system on, left their TARDIS and then watched it dematerialise without them as soon as they get in trouble. The system on the Justice Station lacks this problem due to the fact the crew rarely, if ever, leave.

Matrix Interface (Special)
All TARDIS units have Matrix Interface links installed. These can be used by the Time Lord to access the vast amount of information stored in the Matrix, aside from anything restricted by the High Council. The link is, unfortunately for some, two way, allowing the Council to spy on the whereabouts and movements of renegade Time Lords. This is one of the reasons why renegades tend to favour outdated models as they are harder to track and tend not to be missed as quickly.

Use of the Matrix interface reduces the difficulty of any research task by 3 when using the TARDIS computer. However, it also leaves the TARDIS open to direct Time Lord interference. The link can be disabled but it's an Ingenuity + Technology roll (Difficulty 30) to do it. Worse, failure will damage the circuit, crippling the navigation controls which will in turn add +30 to the difficulty of piloting the TARDIS until the Interface is repaired (Difficulty 27 task).

The Justice Station has multiple links to the Matrix, one in each courtroom and a second in every set of quarters used by counsel.

TARDIS Sensors (Minor)
TARDIS sensors are able to pick up and identify any kind of energy or matter in the universe and a few which aren't from round here as well. General use of them requires an Awareness + Science roll at (Difficulty 12). A success will gather general information about the surroundings including radiation levels, atmospheric thickness and make up and so on.

A Good success will show trace elements in scans and also pick up objects, such as a TARDIS, moving in and out of 3-dimensional space. Normally, this would only be detectable on a Fantastic Success but the Justice Station's sensors are specially designed to pick up temporal anomalies and radiation. Finally, Failure will either give an incomplete or inconclusive reading or, in the case of a Disastrous Failure may overload the system, blowing out D6 Sensor Controls.

Sensor Preset Controls (Minor)
These are settings that the sensors can be locked to, meaning they will always search for them first. Once a character using them makes a Sensor roll, they

don't have to roll to detect that energy or matter for the rest of the adventure. The Justice Stations preset controls are set to the specific exhaust wake of a TARDIS, to enable them to track down and retrieve renegade Time Lords.

Time Scoop (Major)
The Time Scoop is keyed to the Sensor Preset Controls and is designed to be the penultimate stage in bringing a renegade to justice. The sensors allow the Justice Station to zero in on an errant Time Lord and, using the Matrix Link in their TARDIS, take control of their body. This is done using a Presence + Convince roll (Difficulty 25). If Successful, the Time Lord is compelled to return to their TARDIS and activate the HADS system. Once this is done, the Time Scoop redirects the HADS so the TARDIS appears directly above the Justice Station where a tractor beam takes hold of it and brings it inside. The process is instantaneous if successful and the trauma of it can trigger Temporal Amnesia in the Time Lord or any other people in the TARDIS at that time.

If the roll is Unsuccessful, the TARDIS dematerialises without the Time Lord, stranding them in their present location. If this ever occurs Justice Station personnel are trained to send an Extraction TARDIS to allow the renegade Time Lord to escape what is usually a dangerous situation. Whilst renegades know that they're heading for the Justice Station, or at the very least some form of Time Lord authority, that's often a lot more preferable than being trapped without a TARDIS on a hostile world.

Tractor Beam (Major)
The final stage of retrieving a TARDIS is guiding it into land at one of the Courtrooms. Once the TARDIS has materialised in the same space and time as the station, the tractor beam is activated. The operator has to make an Ingenuity + Technology roll at a

THE INQUISITOR

'Planets come and go. Stars perish. Matters disperse, coalesces, forms into other patterns, other worlds. Nothing is eternal.'

The Inquisitor is focused entirely on her job. Her people are entering what could be their darkest hour and the time for the sort of frivolity the Doctor embodies has long since passed. She has no time for him, and is content to let the Valeyard's prosecution lead the case, so long as he too doesn't become too theatrical. The Inquisitor is a gifted Time Lord who gravitated towards the Judiciary at a young age. She's well aware of how important the Justice Station's mission is, and is very concerned with doing her job well.

AWARENESS	3	PRESENCE	5
COORDINATION	3	RESOLVE	5
INGENUITY	7	STRENGTH	3

SKILLS
Athletics 2, Convince 6, Craft 3, Fighting 1, Knowledge 6, Marksman 2, Medicine 2, Science 4, Subterfuge 4, Survival 2, Technology 4, Transport 4 .

TRAITS
Indomitable
Keen Sense
Technically Adept
Time Lord
Time Traveller
Tough
Voice of Authority
By the Book
Code of Conduct
Feel the Turn of the Universe
Time Lord (Experienced)
Vortex

REGENERATIONS USED: 1

TECH LEVEL: 10 STORY POINTS: 8

difficulty determined by the size of the object being pulled in to ensure it's grabbed successfully. Once it's in place, the Time Scoop activates one last time, dropping the TARDIS into place, dematerialising then materialising the TARDIS 30 seconds later outside a courtroom. This gives the guards ample time to move into place if needed and also disorients the Renegade TARDIS.

JUSTICE STATION GUARD

The Station Guard are amongst the youngest, and highest scoring, members of the Academy. These are Time Lords who've shown a tremendous aptitude for justice and enforcement and a slightly more flexible morality than their peers. They aren't as connected to Gallifreyan society as the senior staff and as a result are far more able to deal with the rigours of space travel.

The Guards are the tip of the spear aboard the Justice Station. They are all too aware they're dealing with not only the best in Time Lord society but the most dangerous and unpredictable. As a result, they are constantly on guard for anything the renegades may try.

THE KEEPER OF THE MATRIX

The Keeper is one of the most respected Time Lords, and is more than a little put out by having to come to the station, let alone the Doctor's ridiculous accusations. He has kept the Key of Rassilon for millennia, he has walked with the greatest minds in Time Lord history and he knows the Doctor is wrong. He has to be. The Keeper loves process. He loves the ritual and calm of maintaining the Matrix and watching the immensely complex micro-universe be shaped by the greatest minds in history. He is proud of his people, prouder still of his work and believes the best of all the Time Lords who work with him. After all, they are of the highest rank.

AWARENESS	3	PRESENCE	3
COORDINATION	4	RESOLVE	3
INGENUITY	7	STRENGTH	3

SKILLS
Craft 2, Knowledge (The Matrix +2) 6, Science 6, Technology 6, Transport 3.

TRAITS
Boffin
Cloistered*
Psychic Training
Technically Adept
By the Book
Code of Conduct
Slow Reflexes
Time Lord
Time Lord Engineer
Vortex

EQUIPMENT: **The Key of Rassilon** - The Time Lords never met a bit of ceremony they didn't like and that's rarely truer than with the Key of Rassilon. Not to be confused with the Great Key, the Key of Rassilon is held by the Keeper of the Matrix and is used to open a physical doorway directly into the Matrix, without needing to use the usual Mind Linkage equipment. If the user makes a Resolve + Technology roll (Difficulty 21) they can open a door into the Matrix in any solid surface anywhere in space time.

*see **The Fourth Doctor Sourcebook**.

REGENERATIONS USED: 1

TECH LEVEL: 10 **STORY POINTS:** 3

JUSTICE STATION GUARD

AWARENESS	4	PRESENCE	3
COORDINATION	4	RESOLVE	4
INGENUITY	3	STRENGTH	4

SKILLS
Athletics 4, Convince 3, Craft 2, Fighting 4, Knowledge 4, Marksman 4, Medicine 2, Science 5, Subterfuge 1, Survival 2, Technology 3, Transport 3.

TRAITS
Brave
Friends
Keen Senses
Technically Adept
Tough
By the Book
Time Lord

PERSONAL GOAL: To assist in bringing the renegade Time Lords to justice.

WEAPON: Staser Pistol

TECH LEVEL: 10 STORY POINTS: 8

PLAYING THE VALEYARD

The Valeyard is the most difficult element of the trial, already a challenge itself, to handle. From a game by game point of view he's relatively easy: you simply have him pressure the Doctor as much as he can, be obsequious to the Inquisitor and push his own agenda. He's a perfect villain at this level, so much so he's even dressed in black.

He's an odd figure, thought, wrapped up in one of the most important events in Time Lord history, the Ravolox incident, and yet it seems almost incidental to him, a means to an end. His focus is always the Doctor, and what the Doctor has that he doesn't. That puts him front and centre in the action here and also gives him a central role in the plot that pays off neatly by the end of the trial.

First off, we can take the Valeyard at face value and assume everything the Master says is true and he's the culmination of the Doctor's dark impulses, sitting somewhere between his twelfth and last life. That in turn suggests that he's not a full incarnation but rather a halfway house, similar to the Watcher or, to a lesser extent, metacrisis Tenth Doctor. It also provides you with a bunch of interesting origins for exactly how this dark echo of the Doctor got a body of his own. Even better, these are all useful options for creating a Valeyard-like figure for other Time Lord characters in your own game.

THE MANY ORIGINS OF THE VALEYARD

The Doctor: What if the Doctor, heading towards the end of his twelfth life, realised that the Valeyard was becoming ever more powerful and arranged to have his consciousness transferred to a new body. He could have done out of survival or, perhaps, out of a need to protect the time line.

After all, sooner or later, the Doctor will be on the other side of the equation here, looking back at his sixth life and the events that marked it. He has a responsibility to send the Valeyard back and create the course of events that followed.

Except, of course, he could choose not to. The implications of the Valeyard not existing are almost as staggering as his existence itself. The Sixth Doctor would never be put on trial, it's entirely possible Ravolox would never be moved and, arguably, the events of the Doctor's lives prior to this would also be radically changed. The denial of his dark instincts at this late stage might ripple back down his life and change countless decisions he's made for the better or, more interestingly, for the worse. What if the Valeyard's instincts cause the Fourth Doctor to stop the Daleks ever being born? Or lead the Third Doctor to command UNIT on a planet-wide mission to capture all alien life? The Valeyard may be the very definition of a necessary evil, and there's lots of potential in your characters travelling forward down the Doctor's timeline to make sure the Valeyard is born.

The other possibility is that the Valeyard is the reason why the Doctor is such a boundless champion of the weak and defenceless. The part of his personality that craves danger and risk is actually the Valeyard, constantly pushing him forwards, making him take risks and using the consequences of the Doctor's actions to weaken his resolve and make him easier to control.

The Time Lords: It's equally possible that the Time Lords capture the Doctor at that point in his life and forcibly remove the Valeyard from him. The effect that would have would surely echo down each of the Doctors previous incarnations, all of whom would be aware that the Sixth Doctor was the one who caught the brunt of the Valeyard's attacks and immediately go to him for help and assistance.

As to what would drive the Time Lords to do this, all sorts of options present themselves. Perhaps a desperate faction had the Valeyard created to fight in the Time War only to have him abandon his people in order to claim the Doctor's lives. Or, perhaps by the time the Twelfth Doctor is alive, the Time Lords have made some form of return to the universe and opt to remove the Valeyard from the Doctor as an act of kindness or a scientific experiment. After all, he is a

THE VALEYARD

'I really must curb these urges. I've no wish to be contaminated by your whims and idiosyncrasies.'

The Valeyard is cold, intellectual and controlled. He's formal and polite, even obsequious with figures of authority but aggressive and belligerent with the Doctor. He resents his other self not only for his youth and arrogance, but the lives he's squandered.

AWARENESS	4	PRESENCE	5
COORDINATION	3	RESOLVE	4
INGENUITY	8	STRENGTH	3

SKILLS
Athletics 3, Convince 6, Craft 5, Fighting 3, Knowledge 6, Marksman 3, Medicine 5, Science 6, Subterfuge 6, Survival 3, Technology 6, Transport 6.

TRAITS
Adversary (The Doctor)
Argumentative
Artron Battery*
Boffin
Charming
Dark Echo
Dark Secret
Fast Healing
Feel The Turn of the Universe
Hypnosis
Indomitable
Insatiable Curiosity
Keen Senses
Lucky
Obsession
Psychic Training
Quick Reflexes
Sense of Direction
Technically Adept
Time Lord**
Time Traveller
Tough
Voice of Authority
Vortex

*see **The Time Traveller's Companion.**

**The Valeyard cannot regenerate.

TECH LEVEL: 10 STORY POINTS: 8

THE ARCHIVISTS

A group of Time Lord explorers sent to the far future, the Archivists missed the Time War entirely despite finding records of it in the time periods they reached. Desperate to return home and help, they discovered the awful truth; history recorded that they were trapped in the future and they had to adhere to that. The archivists spent centuries investigating what, to them, was the distant future and finally discovered a record of their arrival in what we would view the present. They arrived and presented themselves to a very surprised Doctor. He was even more surprised when they offered to extract the Valeyard from him for further study and to ensure the time line remained intact. Now, they travel the Vortex cataloguing the differences in narrative between the events they read about and the ones they experienced, watching the remains of their civilisation slowly fade from the universe.

living, breathing specimen of the sort of evil that got them into the Time War and would be a fascinating study. Until he escapes, of course.

The Daleks: The Valeyard appears out of nowhere in Time Lord society, hacks the Matrix and almost succeeds in having their best and brightest killed. If he isn't a Dalek plant he does a very good impression of one. Also, there's some interesting parity to the Valeyard's actions, and the Fourth Doctor's actions on Skaro.

The Valeyard wants to steal the Doctor's remaining lives and ensure the countless millions his future selves would save would instead have died whilst the Time Lords wanted to commit retroactive genocide and make sure the Daleks never existed. Both moves have immense strategic value.

Davros' Fifth Column: The Daleks have had ample opportunity to sample the Doctor's genetic material over the centuries. They grow the Valeyard from this and use him to infiltrate Gallifreyan society, steal the plans for the Magnetron and put in motion the first major Dalek offensive of the Time War.

The Andromedans: The Andromedans are a completely logical choice for the origin of the Valeyard because both are introduced at the same time, both have access that they shouldn't to the Matrix and both are peculiarly concerned with Earth; the Valeyard through his link to the Doctor and the Andromedans for its properties as a bolt hole. The Andromedans are discussed in more detail later but the idea of them kidnapping the Doctor, extracting the Valeyard from him and using him as an inside man makes a lot of sense. It also opens up the possibility of a trip to Andromeda as a follow up. Or, if you choose the Andromeda Singularity option discussed later, maybe Andromeda mistakes the Doctor as a senior figure in the galaxy and creates their own version to facilitate communication, only for it go horribly wrong.

The Great Intelligence: We know that the Great Intelligence is there at every single one of the Doctor's most pivotal moments, trying to make him fail (see ***The Name of the Doctor*** in **The Eleventh Doctor Sourcebook**). We also know that Clara is at every single one of these moments too trying to stop him. Even better, we know she largely succeeds. But what if there was one attack on the Doctor so insidious that she didn't notice it? What if the Great Intelligence knew that each time he tried to defeat the Doctor it'd lose?

What if the Great Intelligence chose his battles in such a way that each time he attempted to change the Doctor's life, it nudged him a little further down the road that would lead to the Valeyard? Not even the Impossible Girl could save the Doctor from that. Or, what if the Valeyard is what is left if the Great Intelligence does succeed in corrupting every one of the Doctor's victories?

Twelfth Hour Syndrome: The Valeyard isn't an artificial creation or the result of tampering by the Doctor or the Time Lords, he's a disease given form and voice. Twelfth Hour syndrome is an incredibly rare Time Lord condition that alters the structure of the brain over the course of their lives, culminating in a partial regeneration during the twelfth life. The release of energy supercharges the disease, allowing it to lay down new neural pathways and take control of the regeneration. No Time Lord has suffered from this disease for over a millennia but ,then again, no Time Lord has travelled quite as much as the Doctor has. The cure is possible, but to reach it the characters must travel deep into Gallifrey's past to find it. Or, the cure may only be possible through awakening all the Doctor's incarnations, leading to the Doctor hooking himself up to the Matrix and the characters going in to find his other selves. Which may, of course, be what the Valeyard wants.

This is a radically different approach but it's one which still lets the events you see here play out entirely as they do, still establishes the Valeyard and still gives you plenty to work with. Plus, for a disease this complicated, why ask for a second opinion when you can get another ten?

NEW TRAIT: DARK ECHO

The character is a dark, future incarnation of a Time Lord, dedicated to acquiring more life for themselves at their 'creator's' expense. It costs 3 Character Points, can be bought multiple times and the character gains the following:

- 1 level of Experienced Time Lord.
- Adversary (Name of Time Lord they echo)
- Obsession
- Owes Favour (Major, Creator)

Regardless of what origin you choose, the Valeyard should be an implacable enemy, someone who knows the Doctor's every move because he's already made them himself. Of course, given his fate at the end of this story, that leads to the inevitable question; why is he beaten? Perhaps this is all part of a much larger plan and, again, there are multiple ways to explore that, including the campaign seed below.

CAMPAIGN SEED

THE ENEMIES OF TIME

The Cloister Bell sounds, out of the blue, even though nothing bad is happening to the Doctor's TARDIS. The Doctor tracks the problem down to a room that's always been locked and is so old even he's forgotten what's in it. To the characters' surprise, there's nothing in there but a series of coordinates on an ornate, brass plaque.

The characters set the coordinates and when the TARDIS materializes, they find themselves on what seems to be a village green in the UK in the mid-1980s. A group of people are playing cricket whilst others sit in deckchairs, read and watch the game. Every one of the players is in full Gallifreyan regalia.

The Umpire turns and greets the characters and introduces himself as Rassilon. Rassilon explains that they have passed a test he set millennia ago and hard coded into every TARDIS. Once a Time Lord had travelled enough, their TARDIS would come to this place, a small, secret Matrix Adjunct located in an asteroid high above the galactic plain. The asteroid was placed there during the Dark Times as a final redoubt should the Time Lords succeed in destroying themselves. Now, it's a refuge for the great minds of Time Lord history and the Doctor has, by travelling as far and as often as he has, been selected to act as their agent. Because, there's a problem, well, 12 problems, scattered around the known history of the universe.

Rassilon didn't want his people to become the plague they were threatening to and so, with the help of Time Lord scientists like Omega, he built the Apocalypse Clock. The Clock is hidden on the asteroid and requires 12 cylinders to spin up. When it does, it will activate and turn the time period it's in into a fixed point in time, meaning no changes can ever be made and the Time Lords' excesses will be curbed.The only problem is, they've lost track of six of the cylinders.

Now, the Doctor and his companions are faced with a choice. Trust that Rassilon is Rassilon and seek out the cylinders for him or ignore the pleas of the Time Lord and leave the greatest weapon in the universe out in the open.

NOTABLE CHARACTERS

- Rassilon, a Matrix personality imprint of an early incarnation of the legendary Time Lord. Desperate to retrieve the 12 cylinders of the Apocalypse Clock.
- Omega, his closest friend and occasional rival. Another personality imprint but, unlike Rassilon, one painfully aware of what his later selves became.

- The Watchmaker, a mysterious personality imprint who designed the Apocalypse Clock and seems to know the Doctor.
- The Folded, a demented Time Lord who has eight other incarnations trapped in his pocket watch. A former agent of the Adjunct who discovered the truth about the Apocalypse Clock and was driven mad.
- Geneva Van Statten, Henry Van Statten's grand daughter and obsessed with clearing her family's name. She sunk the last of the family fortune into time travel research and was able to have herself thrown 80 years into the future. She now rules a reinvigorated Van Statten Industries and is building the first time machine in Earth history, hundreds of years too early, in Switzerland.

ADVENTURES

The First Time
Discovering the Adjunct, meeting Rassilon and then setting off to retrieve the first cylinder, frozen in ice at Earth's North Pole in the latter days of the 21st century. There, the characters must negotiate with an Ice Warrior engineering team for the cylinder and stop them from killing a Van Statten Industries squad sent to retrieve the cylinder.

The Second Best
The second cylinder is located on Camera Station, in the offices of Kartz and Reimer, the two scientists who would go on to invent the KR Module. Even worse, they have no idea what they have and even worse than that, not only the Second but also the Sixth Doctor visited the station at this exact moment in history.

The characters must steal the cylinder from Kartz and Reimer without being discovered by either of the Doctor's other selves and also work out whether anyone can be saved from the imminent Sontaran massacre.

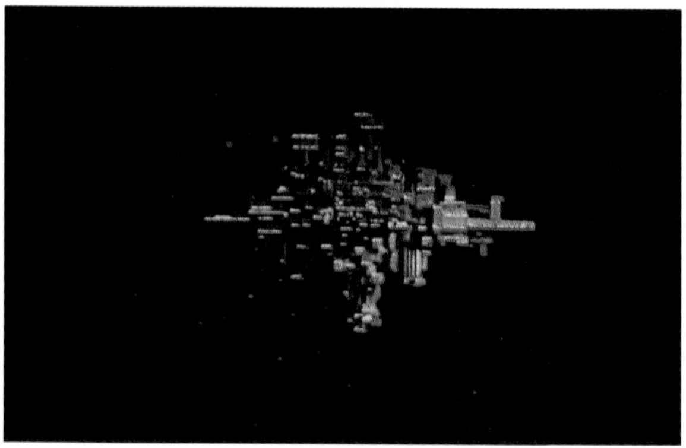

The Third Way

The third cylinder is the centrepiece of a temple in the 52nd century that's home to an order of outcast Cybermen. They pray and do good works in penance for the awful crimes committed by their species and have attributed several miracles to the 'God Clock', their name for the cylinder. In reality, the mild healing it causes is due to a radiation leak and the characters must work out how to steal the cylinder without destroying the fragile faith of the order of St Yvonne of Canary Wharf.

The Fourth War

The fourth cylinder is located in the Van Statten Industries central campus in San Francisco, at the end of the 21st century. But when the characters go to retrieve it, they find they're not the only interested party. Van Statten is using it to power an experimental time window and has been patiently scanning the future, waiting for the exact moment the characters would strike. Trapped in a building that's become a twenty storey boobytrap, they must fight off Autons, Cybermen and the other survivors of the Van Statten collection before they can find the cylinder and escape.

The Fifth Divide

The fifth cylinder was gifted to Christopher Columbus, concealed inside a sextant he took with him on the trip that led to the discovery of America. The characters attempt to sneak aboard but are beaten to the cylinder by a curious, well-dressed Time Lord. He introduces himself as the Folded, his personality changing with every movement he makes, kidnaps Columbus and the cylinder and flees. The characters must stop him and put time right before the new timeline, featuring the United Fiefdoms of Odin, under the rule of Queen Olafsdottir, replace the USA forever.

The Sixth Sense

Having retrieved the fifth cylinder, the TARDIS is en route to the sixth when it materializes in an abandoned mansion house. The characters soon realise something has gone badly wrong and they're only partly corporeal. Even worse, the year is 1917 and the spiritualism movement is at its height. Even worse, Lady Constance Grayling, occult adventuress (and grandmother of Emma Grayling – see ***Hide*** in **The Eleventh Doctor Sourcebook**) is a medium and the only one who can hear or see them. Now, the characters must work with Constance to fix the damage to the TARDIS and find the cylinder before the Folded, at the séance as one of the guests, makes his move.

The Seventh Son

With the second half of the list destroyed, the Doctor and his companions have no idea where to look first. Until, to their amazement, a phone rings in the Adjunct and the call is for them. It's the Master, and he knows exactly where the other six cylinders are. He refuses to tell the Doctor where unless he takes the pair of them back to their early days in Prydon Academy. Desperate not to cross the Doctor's timeline, the characters must assist their old foe in what at first appears to be an attempt to reform.

At the same time, they meet a younger version of the Folded, gaining an insight into their terrifying new foe's past.

The Eightfold Watch

In the wake of the previous adventure, the characters have got their hands on the Folded and his pocket watch. When they study it, they realize the Time Lord has managed to store each one of his personalities to date on the watch and as a result none of them can quite take full possession of his body. The eight personalities are constantly warring with one another and what they have to say will change how the Doctor and the characters view the Matrix Adjunct forever. And when the Folded triggers a booby trap, the personalities on the watch are all forcibly downloaded into the characters. Now they must settle a centuries' old war, get the TARDIS back on track and work out if they need to stop the Folded, help him, or both.

The Ninth Life

The connection between the Folded and Geneva Van Statten is revealed as the Doctor discovers he, a young Time Lord inspired by the Doctor's exploits, went to Earth and tried to help her. Instead, Rassilon caught him and drove him mad. The Ninth Cylinder was hidden by him and the only person who can get to it is Geneva Van Statten. The characters must return to Earth, convince Geneva to help them and travel to a secret UNIT outpost beneath the Swiss Alps where the cylinder, and a pair of Dalek agents are waiting for them.

The Tenth Renegade

The tenth cylinder is hidden in Gallifrey's future on a space station run by the Time Lord Judiciary, and when the characters arrive they're shocked to discover the Sixth Doctor on trial for his life in a nearby courtroom. They're even more shocked when they find the Tenth Doctor quietly snooping around in a different part of the ship. He's here looking for them, because he remembers them warning him when he was them (timey-wimey) that there was something very odd going on with the Watchmaker. At the exact moment he says that, the alarms sound and the ship goes onto full alert. A dangerous prisoner has escaped. The Watchmaker is on the loose...

The Eleventh Hour

The characters have discovered the truth about the Watchmaker, that he's a version of the Valeyard from the far future and he's intent on using the Apocalypse Clock to make the universe a fixed point in space time unlockable only by the Doctor sacrificing his remaining lives to him. The characters confront Rassilon with this news and are horrified to find he knew all along. The Valeyard travelled to the past, helped Rassilon set up the Adjunct and agreed to help build the Apocalypse Clock in return for the Doctor's remaining lives. This personality imprint of Rassilon is the old, tyrannical version of the Time Lord and he will rule over everything, even if he has to freeze it in amber to do so. The characters, separated from their TARDIS, must escape the Adjunct, rescue the Folded and stop Rassilon from activating the Apocalypse Clock.

The Last Time

The Apocalypse Clock has chimed, and the universe is a fixed point in time. The only way to save creation is to agree to the Valeyard's demands but if the Doctor does that, he's doomed. Racing the wave of temporal crystallisation, the TARDIS rushes to warn Gallifrey of the impending disaster whilst the characters fight for their lives in the Adjunct. The answer lies in the Folded's watch, just what personalities are in there and precisely why Rassilon chose 13 lives. The Apocalypse Clock has one hour before it strikes again and if Rassilon still controls it the universe is doomed. If the Doctor controls it, then the clock can be stopped and the universe saved.

THINGS TO DO

Retrieve the 12 cylinders, explore the various time periods, explore the Adjunct, discover the truth about the Folded, stop Rassilon, stop the Valeyard, stop the Apocalypse Clock.

ACTION SCENES

Snowmobile chase with the Van Statten troops, help evacuate Camera Station, fight off the non-individualistic Cybermen, avoid the booby traps in the Van Statten campus, duel with the Master at Prydon Academy, cure or stop the Folded, access the UNIT facility in Switzerland, fight off the Dalek agents, rescue the Tenth Doctor from the Justice Station, recover the TARDIS, stop the Apocalypse Clock, rescue the Folded, and fight Rassilon in the burning remains of the Adjunct.

PROBLEMS

The Valeyard is strong enough to defeat Rassilon and take control of the Apocalypse Clock if he wants. Rassilon, if he gets his hands on the Valeyard's key, will be able to leave the Matrix and become flesh again.

THE MYSTERIOUS PLANET

'You have brought disorder where order once reigned!'

SYNOPSIS

Ravolox, 2 million years in the future

In deep space, a colossal, hexagonal spacecraft moved into position and hauled the TARDIS inside. The Doctor found himself in a courtroom, facing the Inquisitor and the Valeyard, a Time Lord who demanded that he be put on trial for crimes against time. As evidence, the Valeyard offered a recent adventure of the Doctor and Peri, showing the events on screen.

The Doctor and Peri arrived on the planet Ravolox. Peri was miserable that the weather was still so bad and the Doctor was intrigued, because Ravolox was one of the oddest places he'd ever been. The planet was exactly the same size, mass and had the same orbital rotation as Earth. Even stranger, the world had been reported destroyed by a solar flare 500 years previously.

They investigated further and found a tunnel system. Going down what seemed to be a flight of steps, the Doctor became fascinated, talking about spending a year on Ravolox writing a thesis. Peri was crushingly depressed by how sad the world seemed and it was only made worse when they found an old sign on the floor; Marble Arch. Barring a billion to one chance, they were standing on Earth.

At this point, the Doctor on the space station interrupted the narrative to challenge its relevance and ask where Peri was. The Valeyard replied that she was where he had left her and that his disorientation from being pulled from time would soon pass.

Nearby, on Ravolox, Sabalom Glitz and Dibber, a pair of mercenaries, watched the Doctor and Peri make their way into the tunnels. Glitz talked at length about how much he hated competition, so much so that he lost his chance of shooting the Doctor. Frustrated, the two moved on, spying a group of the natives. Glitz got their attention, using a grenade, and asked to be taken to their leader. They obliged and he met Katryca, the Queen of the Free. On the way into her settlement, Glitz and Dibber both noticed the black light mast that they'd been hired to destroy. Glitz attempted to charm Katryca and claimed the mast had drawn the fireball that had devastated the planet to it but she revealed that not only were they not the first offworlders that she'd met, but that they were the ones to give her the weapons she needed to

finally kill someone called the Immortal. Glitz and Dibber were disarmed and locked up and Katryca and her people prepared for war.

Their plans were delayed when Peri was captured by the tribe and told that she would join the Free, and Katryca would gift her many husbands. Locked up with Glitz and Dibber, she found out a version of the truth from Glitz; they had been sent to destroy the black light mast but couldn't because the village viewed it as a totem. Overpowering their guard, the three escaped and set a bomb on the mast.

Down below, the Doctor had found a very modern, very functioning tunnel complex and been captured the moment he picked up a bottle of water. He was interrogated by Balazar, the Reader of the Books, who informed him that water stealing was punishable by stoning and, after interrogating the Doctor, released him to be stoned to death. The Doctor opened an umbrella to defend himself from the worst of the attack but was still knocked unconscious. They were about to beat him to death when Merdeen, the Guard Leader, received a message from the Immortal. The Immortal ordered him to bring the Doctor to him.

When he did, the Doctor discovered the Immortal was a colossal robot aided by Humker and Tandrell, two humans. The robot introduced itself as Drathro and explained there was a problem with its black light systems. The Doctor identified it instantly, and offered to leave to get materials to fix it but Drathro refused. The robot was programmed to keep people underground and couldn't accept anything different. Eventually, the Doctor was forced to electrify Drathro and his assistants and escape.

Elsewhere in the complex, now revealed to be Marb Station, Balazar was troubled by what the Doctor had said. Merdeen took him to one side and revealed that there had been no fire for hundreds of years and he was free to leave. At that moment, the Doctor appeared and Merdeen quickly reassured him he meant no harm and begged him to help Balazar escape. As they did so, Peri, Glitz and Dibber, pursued by tribesmen, entered the complex and the group were reunited just in time to find themselves in a standoff between Drathro's service robot and the tribesmen. All seemed lost until a tribesman called Broken Tooth, who Balazar recognised as a former Marb Station resident, shot the sensors of the Service Robot. The Doctor tried to return to the complex but the tribesmen forced them all to return to the village.

There, the Doctor tried to reason with Katryca but, again, she was unimpressed. She imprisoned them again and Glitz confirmed that the planet was in fact Earth. Peri was still digesting this information when the Service Robot tore the wall down, stunned the Doctor and left with him. In the ensuing chase, the others escaped and the robot was disabled by the tribesmen who, emboldened, finally staged an assault on the complex. Peri rescued the Doctor, so startled by events he vocally regressed to his fourth incarnation for a moment, and they set off to stop Katryca and disable the black light system.

They were too late and Katryca was murdered by Drathro. Desperate to help, the Doctor returned and offered to fix the black light system but soon realised it couldn't be fixed. Even worse, black light generators were so unpredictable he had no way of knowing if the inevitable explosion would kill them, cause a chain reaction that would rip the galaxy apart or cause a dimensional imbalance that would destroy the universe. He pleaded with Drathro but the robot wouldn't change its mind and insisted that no one be allowed to leave.

Elsewhere Glitz and Dibber were discussing their mission when the audio suddenly cut out in the courtroom. The Doctor protested and the Valeyard explained that some of what they had to say was for the Chancellor's ears only. Earlier, the Doctor had asked how the Matrix could record events that he wasn't present for and the Valeyard told him any event happening in proximity to a TARDIS could be recorded by the Matrix.

Balazar and Peri met Merdeen, who was guilt-stricken over having to kill a loyalist who suspected him of being a traitor. They begged him to help get into the sealed chamber where Drathro and the Doctor were and he relented, leading them in through the food processing system. Sensing this, Drathro restarted the fans and defensive lasers and they were only saved when Dibber blew a hole in the wall.

Despite the heavy weaponry he was carrying, Drathro disarmed him easily and he was only saved when Glitz told the robot they had black light on their ship. The robot agreed to join them and Glitz reminded it about the "information". It picked up a data canister and the mercenaries led it out as the Doctor and Peri frantically tried to stop the explosion. The Doctor ordered Peri to flee and she did so, the Doctor not far behind. The black light system exploded and only destroyed Drathro's chambers, killing the robot. The Doctor and Peri left, telling Balazar and Merdeen to head to the surface and be reunited with the Free.

Back in the courtroom, the Doctor declared that he had saved the universe and began to state his case. The Valeyard cut him off and told him that there was much more evidence to come and the Doctor's life would be called for by the end of the case.

CONTINUITY

- The Doctor is no longer Lord President of Gallifrey – he has been deposed for neglecting his duties. He still uses the title from time to time though (see ***Remembrance of the Daleks*** in **The Seventh Doctor Sourcebook**).

- We get a glimpse of those resourceful pockets of the Doctor's – amongst the contents are a torch, a can of oil, a paper mask, a teddy bear and... a bag of jelly babies. Would you like one?

- The Doctor has been on trial before – in ***The War Games*** (see **The Second Doctor Sourcebook**) – and his punishment in that was forced regeneration.

RUNNING THE ADVENTURE

This is the most challenging set of adventures anyone can run with the Sixth Doctor as there are literally two things happening at once all the time. The trial is a constant, overarching plot whilst the four adventures that are cited as evidence happen in isolation. You have to keep two groups of characters moving at the same time, establish the overall plot and resolve the internal plots too. It's very difficult, or it seems to be. But, when you look at it in detail, it turns out to not only be simple, but it very nearly runs itself.

There are three ways you could run this and make it work. The first is the most obvious: ignore the trial. Treat these as a series of standalone adventures and slot them in wherever you see fit. There's plenty of stuff to work with here and you could go for ages without ever touching the trial.

The second possibility is run the adventures as written up to the point where the TARDIS is grabbed by the Justice Station and then have the characters

on trial for their lives. This has a lot to recommend it; it's a perfect big finish to a run of stories, the trial is pretty action packed when you run it as a single piece and it makes your life easier in the short term. In the long term it's anything but easy though. This method requires you, and everyone else, to remember exactly what happened when you played these adventures and unless you have recordings of them (and I'd recommend that you give that a go, as it's always fun listening back to how a session plays out) then everything is open to questioning. Of course, that's also kind of the point, so if you're smart, you can use your version of events and the characters' version to represent the differing viewpoints of the Doctor and the Valeyard.

The third option may seem the hardest but it's actually pretty simple; run the adventures exactly as they are. Open with the characters being arrested, put on trial and shown their past actions then jump into the adventure that's being used as evidence. Play that through normally until you start getting to the sections where things have been censored or altered and have the characters make an Awareness + Knowledge roll (Difficulty 18). Any level of success will get them the knowledge that something isn't right, but they can't figure out quite what, proving that the Valeyard has an agenda.

Also, if you want to limit the amount of 'Objection!' interruptions, have them pay a Story Point to make one, or to frame their own scene as evidence – you can always give them a few more Story Points especially for the trial scenes.

The other thing to remember about this adventure is that it's actually very sad. Earth has become nothing more than a casual plaything for forces the characters can't even comprehend and the Marble Arch sign is an echo of a world they knew that's just not there any more. There's hope here, certainly, but the opening should be a little sombre.

WHEN EXACTLY DOES THE WORLD END? THIS TIME?

The Doctor quotes the apocalyptic fireball that destroyed Earth as having taken place 500 years before their arrival, and that they are currently 2 million years in Peri's future. The interesting thing about both that, and the nature of the fireball is that it all seems a little familiar. Specifically, it all sounds a lot like the events that led to the Doctor and Amy arriving on Spaceship UK in ***The Beast Below*** (see **The Eleventh Doctor Sourcebook**).

Now, there's a very clear date for that adventure: the 29th century. That's way off the two million years that's quoted by the Doctor but given he's suffering from temporal amnesia, and that the Valeyard is messing with what the Matrix is showing us, that may not be accurate. Plus, there's a certain elegance to the Time Lords (who are neat if nothing else) quietly lifting Earth out of its solar system at a time where it's mostly deserted and scheduled to be burnt anyway. Of course you don't have to do this and could just have it exactly as presented; that 1,995,000 years into the future, Earth was dragged out of its solar system by the Time Lord and dumped elsewhere.

THE UNDERGROUND PROJECT

Whilst the Marb Station has far more going on than first appears, there's another way of running it, detailed below. Use whichever works for you.

This was one of the very few times Earth got lucky. There was enough warning of the fireball that extensive underground shelters were created from the transit systems of major cities. New York, Paris, London, San Francisco, Rome and the others extended the tunnels out as far as they could, reinforced and reopened old ones and chose their best and brightest to take shelter. In some countries, mines and other underground facilities were reworked to provide shelter for the general population but, even with the warning, not everyone could be saved. Nonetheless, several thousand people were scattered across London alone in the various stations, waiting for the fires to pass so they could return to the surface and rebuild. But, 500 years on, the citizens of Marb Station at least were told the fires still raged...

DRATHRO

Drathro was one of three highly intelligent robots placed at Marb Station to look after the Sleepers. A maintenance robot, Drathro was a towering presence, standing seven feet tall and with a sweeping, horned head.

Drathro was programmed to use the 500 inhabitants of Marb Station to help maintain the health of the Sleepers, placed in suspended animation beneath the station. He was able to communicate, plan and defend himself with his electrified claws.

For all this, Drathro was never able to move past his programming. When the black light generator he, and the Sleepers, relied on malfunctioned he couldn't let the 500 citizens of Marb Station escape, or try and contain the explosion. Drathro followed orders to the end and, ultimately, it killed him.

DRATHRO

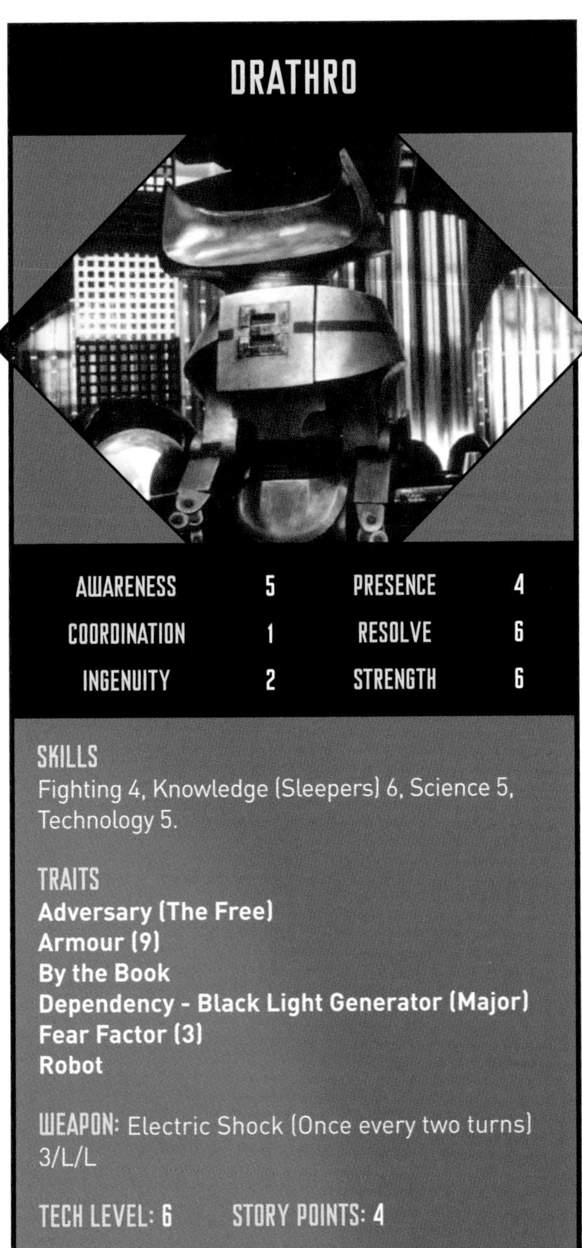

AWARENESS	5	PRESENCE	4
COORDINATION	1	RESOLVE	6
INGENUITY	2	STRENGTH	6

SKILLS
Fighting 4, Knowledge (Sleepers) 6, Science 5, Technology 5.

TRAITS
Adversary (The Free)
Armour (9)
By the Book
Dependency - Black Light Generator (Major)
Fear Factor (3)
Robot

WEAPON: Electric Shock (Once every two turns) 3/L/L

TECH LEVEL: 6 **STORY POINTS:** 4

WHERE'S L2?

We see Drathro, who has a plate on his chest saying L3. We also see the Maintenance Robot, who's the L1. So where's L2? Here are a couple of possibilities:

Big Brother: L2 is actually the Marb Station computer system, once sentient in its own right. Over the centuries it's broken down to the point where it's just a normal computer system. This would make sense as L3, Drathro, is in charge of the system and L1, the maintenance robot, is used by the system.

Guarding the Sleepers: The L2 is a smaller, more mobile version of Drathro that acts as a nurse for the Sleepers. It too is powered by the black light generator and shuts down when it explodes.

L2

AWARENESS	4	PRESENCE	3
COORDINATION	3	RESOLVE	6
INGENUITY	2	STRENGTH	3

SKILLS
Fighting 4, Knowledge (Sleepers) 6, Medicine 6, Science 5, Technology 5.

TRAITS
Armor (6)
By the Book
Dependency - Black Light Generator (Major)
Fear Factor (3)
Robot

WEAPON: Electric Shock (Once every two action rounds) 1/3/L

TECH LEVEL: 6 **STORY POINTS:** 2

THE L1 SERVICE ROBOT

Unlike Drathro (and, maybe, the L2), the L1 is designed to venture into the outside world if needed. It's a rugged, wardrobe sized (and shaped) robot with caterpillar tracks, equipped with metallic tentacles that can be used to manipulate objects or restrain a captive. Silent, implacable and imposing, it's an intimidating opponent and a symbol of Drathro's power.

THE L1 SERVICE ROBOT

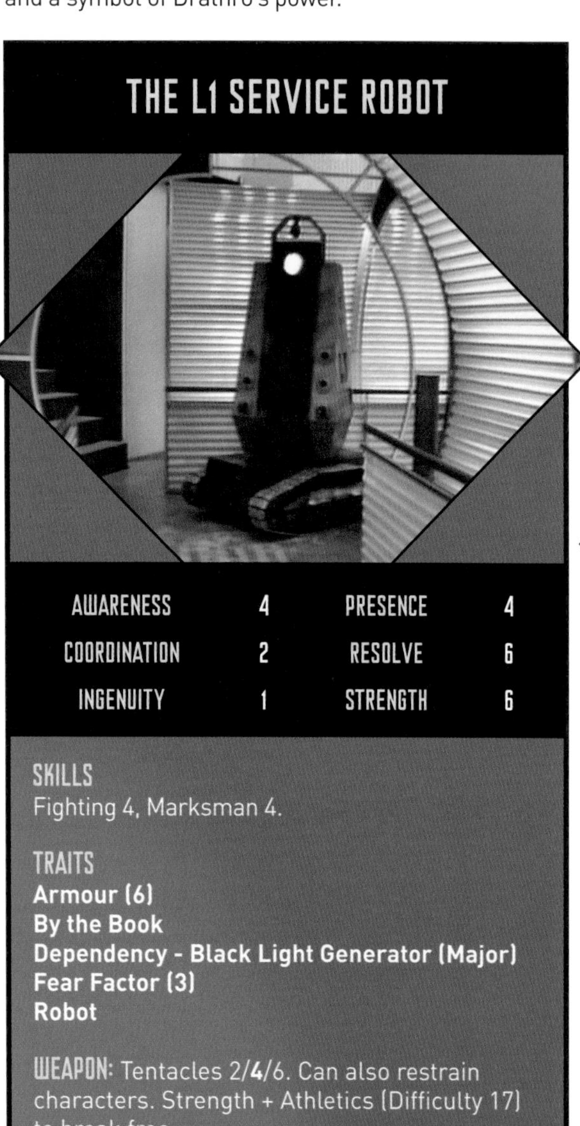

AWARENESS	4	PRESENCE	4
COORDINATION	2	RESOLVE	6
INGENUITY	1	STRENGTH	6

SKILLS
Fighting 4, Marksman 4.

TRAITS
Armour (6)
By the Book
Dependency - Black Light Generator (Major)
Fear Factor (3)
Robot

WEAPON: Tentacles 2/**4**/6. Can also restrain characters. Strength + Athletics (Difficulty 17) to break free.

TECH LEVEL: 6 STORY POINTS: 2

SABALOM GLITZ

Sabalom Glitz never met anything he couldn't steal, or pay someone else to steal for him. An eloquent speaker, and clearly in love with his own voice, Glitz seems an odd man to have chosen mercenary as a career. However, Glitz has enjoyed a long, storied, occasionally violent time in the industry because of three things; his charm, the fact he plans ahead and his willingness to throw anyone else in harm's way to ensure he isn't. Sabalom Glitz may not be a particularly good man, but his heart's in the right place. He's just not in any hurry to tell people where that place is. Charming, erudite, polite, overly verbose and on occasion mildly sociopathic. Sabalom Glitz loves to talk, loves to charm and, despite his hard-edged career choice, loves to avoid a fight. His old fashioned charm and love of language are far more useful armour than anything he's carrying and, married with his cheerful sense of self preservation and Castidillion Mark 7 Life Preserver, have kept Glitz out of many a spot of bother.

SABALOM GLITZ

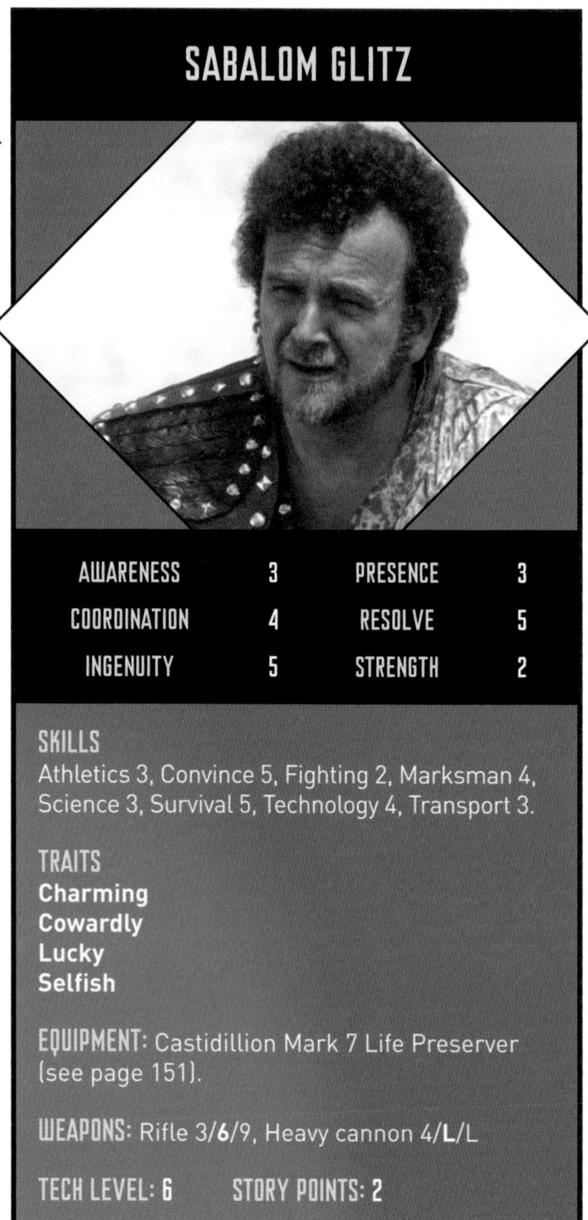

AWARENESS	3	PRESENCE	3
COORDINATION	4	RESOLVE	5
INGENUITY	5	STRENGTH	2

SKILLS
Athletics 3, Convince 5, Fighting 2, Marksman 4, Science 3, Survival 5, Technology 4, Transport 3.

TRAITS
Charming
Cowardly
Lucky
Selfish

EQUIPMENT: Castidillion Mark 7 Life Preserver (see page 151).

WEAPONS: Rifle 3/**6**/9, Heavy cannon 4/**L**/L

TECH LEVEL: 6 STORY POINTS: 2

KATRYCA

The Queen of the Free has spent her life in the shadow of not only the Great Totem, but the Immortal. The stories told to her by those who've made their way up from Marb Station have fascinated and enraged her in equal amounts. For centuries, she and her people have thrived whilst, beneath their feet, the Immortal has kept other survivors in captivity. Katryca knows she needs all the help she can get, knows her enemy is almost indestructible and doesn't care. A war is coming and she aims to win it.

KATRYCA

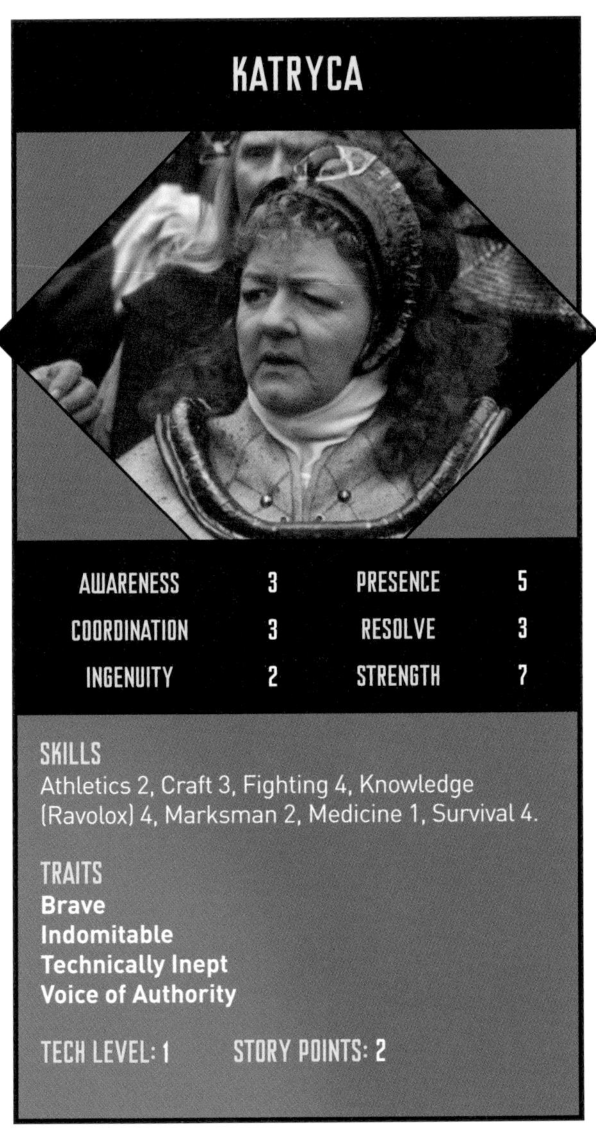

AWARENESS	3	PRESENCE	5
COORDINATION	3	RESOLVE	3
INGENUITY	2	STRENGTH	7

SKILLS
Athletics 2, Craft 3, Fighting 4, Knowledge (Ravolox) 4, Marksman 2, Medicine 1, Survival 4.

TRAITS
Brave
Indomitable
Technically Inept
Voice of Authority

TECH LEVEL: 1 STORY POINTS: 2

DIBBER

Dibber likes violence. He's awfully good at it. He's also far smarter than he lets on, and has fallen into a useful double act with Mr Glitz. Glitz does the talking, Dibber does (all) the heavy lifting and the paydays are normally pretty good. Of course, from time to time Dibber would like to get a little more credit (and credits) for his intelligence but for now he's happy being Mr Glitz's muscle.

DIBBER

AWARENESS	2	PRESENCE	3
COORDINATION	3	RESOLVE	4
INGENUITY	3	STRENGTH	5

SKILLS
Athletics 3, Convince 2, Fighting 5, Marksman 4, Medicine 2, Survival 3, Technology 3, Transport 3.

TRAITS
Fast Healing
Sense of Direction
Technically Adept

WEAPONS: Rifle 3/**6**/9, Heavy cannon 4/**L**/L

TECH LEVEL: 6 STORY POINTS: 2

SEEING THE WORLDS

The Free are a really good place for new characters to jump aboard from, especially in light of this adventure. The best way to play them is completely without front. These are people who only know how to be honest because that's all they've ever been, have minimal social graces and will have a minor panic attack the first time they set foot on an alien world. Perfect companion material in other worlds. Plus, remember most of the Free are escaped Marb Arch residents so know their way around technology even if it, and they, are a bit rusty.

ROSENCRANTZ AND GUILDENSTERN ARE ARMED

Glitz and Dibber aren't just threatening, they're *funny*. Glitz loves the sound of his own voice and Dibber is far smarter than he projects. Remember that and they'll be memorable, if occasional, villains.

MERDEEN

Merdeen is tired. He's tired of the Immortal and his pointless demands. He's tired of water rationing when he knows there's water to spare on the surface. Most of all, he's tired of looking at generations of men and women living and dying in the service of an uncaring master. Merdeen doesn't want out himself, he has too much to do, but he wants to save his people. If he has to do that one at a time, then so be it.

MERDEEN

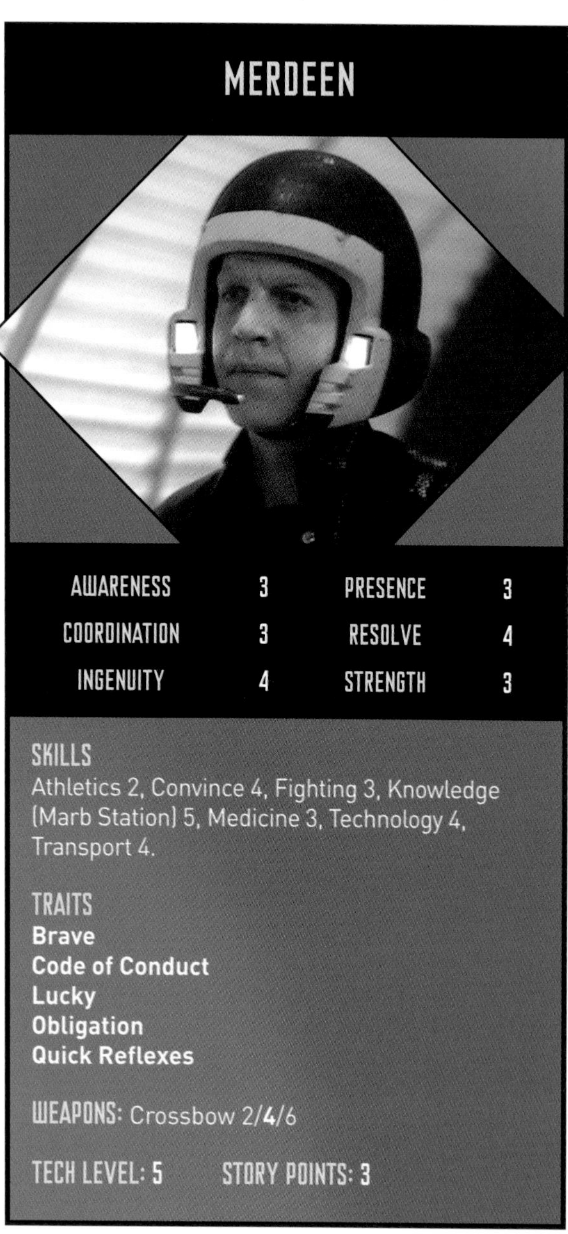

AWARENESS	3	PRESENCE	3
COORDINATION	3	RESOLVE	4
INGENUITY	4	STRENGTH	3

SKILLS
Athletics 2, Convince 4, Fighting 3, Knowledge (Marb Station) 5, Medicine 3, Technology 4, Transport 4.

TRAITS
Brave
Code of Conduct
Lucky
Obligation
Quick Reflexes

WEAPONS: Crossbow 2/**4**/6

TECH LEVEL: 5 STORY POINTS: 3

BALAZAR

Balazar is desperately interested in things. All things, *everywhere*. As the Reader of the Books, Balazar has spent a lot of time poring over the wisdom hidden in the words of HM Post Office and the other Holy Texts and he'd really rather like to find out more. But there are no more holy books, meaning that Balazar has learned everything there is to know in his world.

So he studies hard, tries to forget the questions that keep coming to him and waits for the day when the Immortal will choose him for something great. Hopefully involving more reading...

BALAZAR

AWARENESS	3	PRESENCE	2
COORDINATION	3	RESOLVE	4
INGENUITY	3	STRENGTH	3

SKILLS
Athletics 2, Knowledge (The Holy Books) 6, Knowledge (Marb Station) 5, Science 2, Transport 2.

TRAITS
Adept
By the Book
Lucky
Quick Reflexes
Technically

TECH LEVEL: 5 STORY POINTS: 2

HUMKER AND TRAMDRALL

Drathro's assistants look, act and think alike, especially when they're trying to get credit for each other's achievements. Driven but not dedicated to their work, the pair are all too aware of how fragile their position is.

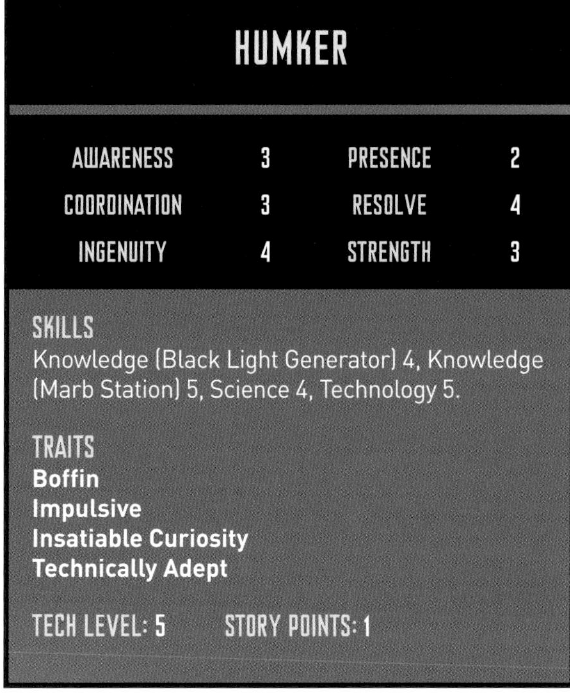

HUMKER

AWARENESS	3	PRESENCE	2
COORDINATION	3	RESOLVE	4
INGENUITY	4	STRENGTH	3

SKILLS
Knowledge (Black Light Generator) 4, Knowledge (Marb Station) 5, Science 4, Technology 5.

TRAITS
Boffin
Impulsive
Insatiable Curiosity
Technically Adept

TECH LEVEL: 5 STORY POINTS: 1

TRAMDRALL

AWARENESS	4	PRESENCE	2
COORDINATION	4	RESOLVE	4
INGENUITY	3	STRENGTH	3

SKILLS
Knowledge (Black Light Generator) 4, Knowledge (Marb Station) 5, Science 4, Technology 5.

TRAITS
Boffin
Impulsive
Insatiable Curiosity
Technically Adept

TECH LEVEL: 5 STORY POINTS: 1

BROKEN TOOTH

Broken Tooth used to be like Balazar, desperate for more. Then Merdeen saved him and suddenly, he had all he could take and more. The sheer weight of information overwhelmed him for a while but before long Broken Tooth had taken his place as one of the Free's fiercest warriors. Now, at long last, he has a chance to save his friends at Marb Station.

BROKEN TOOTH

AWARENESS	3	PRESENCE	3
COORDINATION	3	RESOLVE	4
INGENUITY	3	STRENGTH	4

SKILLS
Athletics 3, Craft (Woodwork) 3, Fighting 4, Knowledge (Marb Station) 4, Marksman 4, Survival 4, Technology 2.

TRAITS
Brave
Forgetful
Tough
Unlucky

TECH LEVEL: 1 STORY POINTS: 2

THE FREE

The survivors of the fireball, joined by the few people Merdeen has been able to get to the surface, the Free are small in number. Living in wattle-and-daub huts, they survive by hunting and gathering what they can from the returning ecosystem of the planet. But even they know it isn't enough, they aren't enough. Something needs to be done, and soon.

FREE TRIBES MEMBER

AWARENESS	3	PRESENCE	4
COORDINATION	2	RESOLVE	3
INGENUITY	3	STRENGTH	4

SKILLS
Athletics 3, Craft 3, Fighting 2, Knowledge (History of the Free) 4, Knowledge (Woodwork) , Medicine 3, Marksman 4, Survival 5.

TRAITS
Argumentative
Indomitable

TECH LEVEL: 1 STORY POINTS: 1

THE STATION GUARDS

The people of Marb Station have led a sheltered existence, never any larger than the confines of their underground home. As far as they're concerned, the world above is an inferno and they are the only people left alive. The Immortal provides for them, educates them and keeps them safe. They want for nothing. Except of course, for the ones that do...

THE STATION GUARDS

AWARENESS	3	PRESENCE	3
COORDINATION	4	RESOLVE	4
INGENUITY	3	STRENGTH	3

SKILLS
Athletics 2, Fighting 2, Knowledge (Marb Station) 5, Marksman 1, Science 4, Technology 4, Transport 3.

TRAITS
Brave
Keen Senses

TECH LEVEL: 4 STORY POINTS: 1

NEW TRAITS

All Too Much (Minor Bad)
For all the wonder and joy of travelling in time, to say nothing of the comfort that comes from knowing your home time will always be there, sometimes the weight of the centuries is too much. Just like Peri felt when she saw the Marble Station sign, the weight of history comes crashing down on the character. Any time an adventure is set on the characters' homeworld or somewhere the character states reminds them of their homeworld, every action is at -1 unless their life is threatened.

Station Guard (Special Good)
With Drathro destroyed, the Station Guard and the Free were finally able to reunite as a species and explore their world. However, for some of the Guard, the world is not enough. Any character wanting to choose Station Guard as a starting background pays 6 Character Points and gets the following attribute bonuses:

+1 Awareness, Athletics 1, Knowledge (Marb Station) 5, Science 2, Technology 2, Sense of Direction, Insatiable Curiosity.

TECHNOLOGY

Black Light Generator
The black light generator converts UV energy into black light, which is in turn used to power Drathro, the Sleepers' suspended animation capsules and the L1. The system is tremendously powerful, durable and insanely complicated. Even worse, it becomes progressively more unstable as time goes by, leading to the scale of the eventual catastrophic damage it causes only ever increasing.

When running this adventure, the black light generator is troubling because it's a ticking bomb that will go off. There's no way to stop it, just mitigate the damage. Even worse, it's so insanely overpowered, as well as overcomplicated, that coming into possession of one will make the characters at least as much of a target as Drathro.

With that in mind, emphasise the experimental nature of the tech, as well as how fiddly it is. An Ingenuity + Technology (Difficulty 28) roll is needed just to minimise the explosion to Drathro's chambers so the chances of them having anything left to work with are fairly minimal. Nonetheless, use the Black Light Generator as scenery rather than an item; it'll make everyone's lives easier.

FURTHER ADVENTURES

- **The Doors of Drathro:** Comparing photos of their homes and home times, the characters spot something unusual. There's a set of identical doors in the back of every single photo. Doors that span centuries, or worlds, yet, somehow, impossibly, are always there. They look further and realise that the doors are in every photo they have, and in each one they are opening more and more. There's something glittering on the other side of them, a huge, imposing figure with a horned head and, just next to him, a flash of garish frock-coat. The Doctor and Drathro, somehow, are everywhere and everywhen in the universe at once and the characters soon discover the truth. The black light generator on Ravolox blew up, and the universe has shifted dimensionally. There are other versions of them out there, other Ravoloxes, other generators. The chain reaction has to be stopped or every universe, everywhere, will shatter...

- **Visitors from Down the Street:** The characters return to Ravolox to help the Free and the Station Guards make the most of their world, to find the camp deserted. Searching around, they find evidence of a battle and large groups of people walking to the nearest coast. When they get there, they find an impossible flotilla of ships at anchor. Everything from tiny wooden rowboats to spacecraft, all combined to make a floating shanty town, which the Free and the Station Guards have joined. But did they do it of their own free will? Why are there sudden, violent attacks all over the shanty town? Why does every policeman wear the same face? The Earth's position in time was damaged by the black light generator and now it's slipping out of phase with the rest of the universe. To make matters worse, the Nestene Consciousness, searching for food planets, has found one and now the last dregs of humanity will be soldiers or food. Unless, of course, the Doctor can persuade it otherwise.

- **The King's Cross:** After leaving Ravolox, the Doctor is surprised to find a large cross-shaped mark on the outside of the TARDIS. When he touches it, the TARDIS spontaneously dematerialises. After a frantic chase across the countryside of whatever planet they're currently on, the Doctor and his companions find the ship safe, sound and occupied. The man inside claims to be the King of Cross, the ruler of Ravolox who has claimed the TARDIS as his own. But how did he get here? How does he know how to fly a TARDIS? And why does he look...familiar? Another Time Lord has been on Ravolox, an old foe who likes to meddle and has been looking for revenge for a long, long time. Now, he has his chance.

MINDWARP

'Well, even a nervous Time Lord must appear to act with confidence at all times.'

SYNOPSIS

Thoros Beta, 2379

The Valeyard continued to present his evidence and showed the Doctor and Peri arriving on the planet Thoros Beta. They had come there having acquired a CD phaser, a beam weapon of incredible power, from a Thordon warlord. The Doctor was troubled that the warlord, from a relatively primitive race, had been sold one from Thoros Beta. Peri asked what they were going to do and the Doctor told her they would stop them. He laughed off her concerns when she asked if anyone else could do it, and proceeded. In the Court the Valeyard pointed out this was an example of the Doctor's callous attitude.

Despite his reassurances, the pair entered a cave and were almost immediately attacked by the Raak, a mysterious creature. The creature was killed by the CD Phaser (the Doctor saying he'd fired accidentally, the Valeyard saying he'd murdered it in cold blood) and the pair stumbled inside. There, they found an advanced water-based power generator and were immediately arrested. Their captor asked if they were part of Crozier's work and they agreed. The pair were taken to a lab, along with the corpse and when it became apparent that they were in serious trouble, the Doctor suggested Peri assist him in the "skedaddle" medical procedure. Which was, of course, a code word for them to run away.

They did so, but weren't pursued as they'd run down a tunnel where Dorf was chained. Part man, part dog, the initially terrifying creature warmed to the Doctor when he was kind to it and the pair fled further on. They hid as a caravan passed by. The caravan consisted of several Mentors, including Sil. Peri was horrified that he was there and again the Doctor brushed her concerns aside, assuming she'd already known Thoros Beta was Sil's homeworld. Despite his protestations in the courtroom, the Valeyard insisted that the Doctor watch the recording as it played out.

In the lab the pair had narrowly avoided Crozier and Matrona Kani, two scientists in the employ of the Mentors, were hard at work. They were working on a machine that could transfer consciousness between bodies, and their current subject, King Yrcanos of the Krontep was resisting their attempts to pacify him. They upped his treatment and, unseen, the Doctor and Peri crept in. The Doctor recognised the machine immediately and began making changes to it, but was interrupted by Sil and his convoy. The equipment was meant for Sil's leader, Lord Kiv and, curious as to why the Doctor was there, Sil had him strapped into the machine.

The Doctor convulsed in agony and Yrcanos woke up, broke free of his restraints, destroyed some of Crozier's instruments and fled. Peri and a barely conscious Doctor followed. Yrcanos stopped and began ranting about how he would extract vengeance, something the Doctor said he would enjoy, and then passed out. In the courtroom the Doctor was becoming worried. He said he had no memory of these events and the Valeyard assured him he was in for a surprise if that was true.

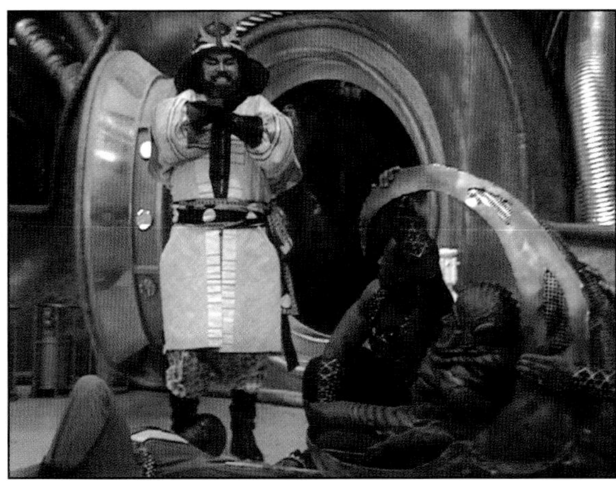

In the lab, Lord Kiv, Crozier and Sil were discussing the situation. Lord Kiv's brain was swelling and he was suffering blinding headaches. To make matters worse, he was suffering them on the eve of vital negotiations and Crozier had been brought there to solve the problem once and for all. However, the machine was proving difficult to perfect and they had yet to find a correct host body to transfer Kiv into. He ordered the pair to keep working and told them they would be killed if they failed.

Elsewhere, Yrcanos planned to steal weapons and acquire troops from where new slaves were bought into the compound and the three snuck there. However, just as Yrcanos was about to attack, the Doctor warned the guards. Yrcanos fled and, as Sil entered the room, Peri held a CD phaser on Sil. She fired blind, narrowly missing him and begged the Doctor for help. He refused, she dropped the weapon and fled. Sil, impressed by the Doctor's opportunism asked what had led to the change of heart and he said it was because the odds of Sil succeeding were far greater. The Doctor was concerned with keeping himself alive, and he had the best chance of doing that with Sil. In the courtroom the Doctor was enraged, convinced that the footage could not be him. The Valeyard pointed out that the Matrix could not lie and they continued.

Alone and terrified, Peri ran into Kani, who recognised her and made her an offer. She could join the Mentors' servants rather than be turned over. Reluctantly, she agreed and was attached to a coterie of servants being sent to the Commerce Room. With a veil over her face, Peri was asked to bring Lord Kiv his medication. The Doctor recognised her straight away but toyed with her for a moment before unmasking Peri in front of Lord Kiv. He told Kiv she was an enemy of Thoros Beta and he would interrogate her. In the courtroom, again, the horrified Doctor told the jurors that this was part of the Valeyard's ploy, to show events that he was remembering in the worst possible light. The Valeyard was scornful of the Doctor's memory returning, but he insisted this was all part of his plan, to lull the Mentors into a fall sense of security so he could talk to Peri alone.

Back on Thoros Beta, the Doctor had tied Peri down on the shore and was interrogating her as the tide came in. He asked her questions, then appeared to reveal that it was a plan. Peri, relieved that his brain hadn't been scrambled, begged him for help and the Doctor revealed it was a trick. He needed information from her because unless he could help them, Crozier would implant Kiv's brain into his body. Peri was terrified as the Doctor continued to threaten her until Crozier told him to bring her back in so other interrogation methods could be used. The Doctor led her back to the complex and Yrcanos attacked them, threatening to kill the Doctor.

Peri stopped Yrcanos from doing it and the Doctor fled. Enraged, the Barbarian King turned on her but she stood her ground, insisting that the Doctor wasn't

always like this. Yrcanos relented and the pair left, heading further into the tunnels. There, they found Dorf, who Yrcanos recognised as an old friend. Dorf begged them to kill him and Yrcanos insisted he use the hatred he felt to power the coming battle, so that he could die well in that. Dorf agreed and Yrcanos entered a trance, saying he was calling on his troops to come to their aid.

Meanwhile, Crozier had found a Mentor corpse that was a near perfect match for Kiv. With the Doctor's help, he carried the operation out and Kiv woke up in his new body. Sil, desperate to be the first thing his master saw, instead caused him to recoil in horror. To make matters even worse, Kiv's brain was rejected by the body and its old habits and memories began to reassert themselves. They needed a new stable body and with Kiv's guards prepared to execute them if they failed, Crozier suggested Peri. The Doctor, still feigning betrayal, tried to distract him from her but Crozier insisted.

Elsewhere, Peri, Yrcanos and Dorf had been captured by the resistance. The slaves were being shipped in from Thoros Alpha and some of the Alphans had escaped. Yrcanos was delighted, believing they would be a fine army and, after some persuasion, they agreed to help him. Yrcanos' first order was to go the arms dump to grab weapons, but they were ambushed and held at gun point. In the courtyard, the Doctor watched in horror as Peri, Yrcanos and Dorf were apparently gunned down.

In reality, they had been stunned and were taken to the cells with the other resistance members. As each was taken out one by one to be experimented on, Peri told Yrcanos of Earth and the people she loved. He couldn't understand the concept and explained that, on Krontep, you welcome a glorious death because each one brought you closer to the life where you were a King.

Peri asked what he would do the next time he died and he said he'd join the other Kings in the afterlife where, again, they'd engage in glorious battle. Despite the horrific ordeal she'd gone through, Peri laughed. Then she was taken to the lab, where Crozier found her a perfect candidate and prepped her for surgery.

The Doctor, desperate to save her, went to Yrcanos' cell and tricked the guard. Yrcanos and Dorf escaped and Yrcanos was about to kill the Doctor when he pointed out that they needed to save Peri. To do this, they had to go to the Control Room, where the mental restraint on the slaves could be switched off. They successfully freed them but Dorf was killed.

The Doctor and Yrcanos both headed for the lab but, halfway there, the Doctor passed the TARDIS. It was suddenly illuminated and he stopped, walked backwards into it and disappeared. In the courtroom, the Doctor flew into a rage at being pulled from time at this exact moment. The Inquisitor told him that it was a direct order from the High Council.

Yrcanos made it to the lab and threw himself into an attack. However, the Time Lords threw a time bubble around him, which meant his attack would be held until the Time Lords could be sure Crozier's work had been completed. In the courtroom, a horrified Doctor demanded to know why the Time Lords were acting like this. The Inquisitor explained that Crozier's work would upset the natural order of evolution and they had to be sure it worked before they stopped it.

On Thoros Beta, the work was a success. As Peri sat up, Yrcanos burst into the room. He watched in horror as Peri spoke with a deep voice as Kiv's conscience took over from her own. Grief-stricken and furious, Yrcanos fired wildly at everyone in the room, killing them, including Peri.

At the courtroom, the Doctor was equally furious and demanded to know the truth about what was going on. He insisted that there was more he wasn't being told and he planned to find out.

CONTINUITY

- The Mentor, Sil, was first encountered in ***Vengeance on Varos***.
- The events at the start of ***The Mysterious Planet*** actually took place, chronologically, mid way through this adventure.
- The Valeyard comments that the Doctor's companions tend to find themselves in danger twice as often as the Doctor himself.

RUNNING THE ADVENTURE

There are two ways to run this adventure, one of which makes the difficult dual narratives used a virtue and one that completely ignores the trial until there's absolutely no way to avoid it. The first is you present the adventure exactly as it is here, and intercut between the characters in the courtroom and the events on Thoros Beta. This has a lot to recommend it, if nothing else that it's how the story plays out and provides a welcome structure to events. It's also worth considering playing with the effects of Temporal Amnesia, as detailed below, and having the characters slowly remember what happened. In doing so, of course, they remember things differently to how the Matrix is presenting them which further clues everyone in to the Valeyard's evil motives.

The second method works along very similar lines, but you move this adventure to the very start of the campaign. Play it absolutely as a normal adventure, with no indication of the trial. Then, as the Doctor is racing to the control room to save Peri, have him suddenly drawn into the TARDIS. This opens up some fun possibilities, detailed below:

- **Along for the Ride:** The characters frantically try and reason with the Doctor, rushing into the TARDIS to try and get him back. It dematerialises and they find themselves on trial with him. This is also a great way to introduce new characters, as they're swept up in events.
- **Marooned:** Another way to play the trial is to only have the Doctor there and have his companions marooned on Thoros Beta. That gives the trial a lot of dramatic urgency and leaves the fate of everyone there nicely ambiguous for a follow up adventure. Alternatively, this is an opportunity to swap the cast round and retire some characters, as we eventually see Peri has been.

- **Not on the List:** If you were feeling very sneaky, have this adventure reveal that someone who claims to have been with the Doctor on Thoros Beta in fact wasn't and simply stood with him in the courtroom. Who is this new character? What do they have to gain? Why do they know the Doctor and the other characters but not vice versa?

- **Separated:** Some of the characters made it to the TARDIS whilst others were left behind. What did they have to do to survive? Did they? Use the Matrix here to cut between the two groups, perhaps with the Valeyard using the ongoing struggles of the abandoned group as proof of how the Doctor lets his friends down over and over.

Regardless, there's a central challenge you need to face head on here: this is a story where a companion dies. If you have a character who fits this role, and is either happy to find themselves in the circumstances, then that's great, but you may very well not be so lucky. If you don't, but the transference is still carried out, then you need to be aware of the repercussions. No one likes getting killed, especially due to the capricious nature of the Time Lords, so go easy on characters when you have to, but keep the atmosphere and horror building when you don't. Or, you could have an NPC put through the process which gives you all the fallout but in a far cleaner package. After all, the only thing scarier than Yrcanos would be Kiv's business brain in Yrcanos' body.

Then, of course, there's the issue of the Time Lords themselves. This adventure gives you a perfect opportunity to contrast the Doctor with his own people. Yes he's arrogant and condescending, but he's passionately concerned with saving lives. The Time Lords think on an entirely different scale, with the loss of live on Thoros Beta, especially the horrifying manner of Peri's death, completely acceptable as long as conscience transferral is stopped. After all, we can't have everyone regenerating, can we? It's a nasty, desperate ploy and they know it and it's the perfect opportunity for you to show the cracks starting to appear in their resolve.

Aside from these two major points, this is arguably the fastest paced adventure the Sixth Doctor has. It's a mad sprint from the Raak all the way down to Lord Kiv's final body. Keep it going flat out, but slow the pace down enough to let the horror of just what Crozier's doing sink in.

KING YRCANOS

Yrcanos of the Krontep is a man of massive stature, massive actions and massive volume. A warlord with a glorious, bloody history behind him, he was pulled from the fields of battle because Crozier thought he'd be a good candidate for Lord Kiv's new body.

Yrcanos exists in a constant state of barely contained rage and Crozier has had to work constantly to keep the massive warrior down. Even that may not be enough. Because Yrcanos wants his glorious death and if he ever gets the opportunity, he's going to take as many of his transgressors with him when he goes.

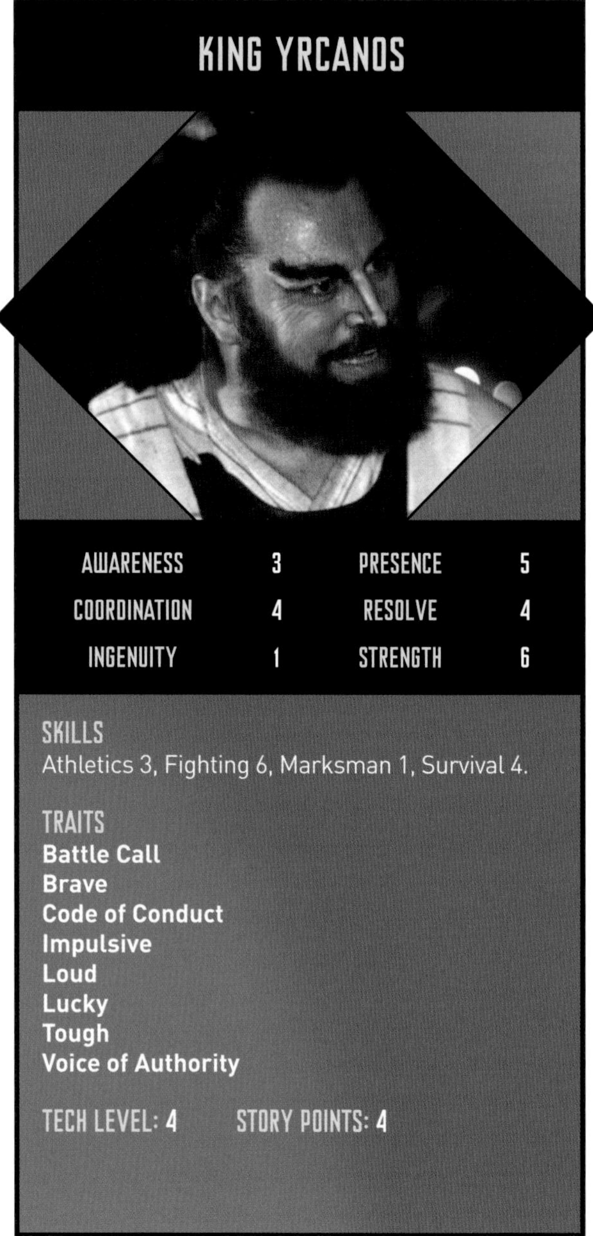

KING YRCANOS

AWARENESS	3	PRESENCE	5
COORDINATION	4	RESOLVE	4
INGENUITY	1	STRENGTH	6

SKILLS
Athletics 3, Fighting 6, Marksman 1, Survival 4.

TRAITS
Battle Call
Brave
Code of Conduct
Impulsive
Loud
Lucky
Tough
Voice of Authority

TECH LEVEL: 4 STORY POINTS: 4

THE KRONTEP

The Krontep aren't just a warlike species, their entire culture revolves around it. The Krontep believe that they exist to fight and the manner in which they fight, and die, is all part of a continual evolution of their souls. When a Krontep has a powerful enough, good enough soul they die and are reborn as a King. When that King dies, they are reborn in the Krontep afterlife with the Kings that have proceeded them, where, of course, they fight a never ending war with one another. It's an unusual belief and yet, for the Krontep, a comforting one. For all their cheery brutality though, the Krontep are a moderately advanced race. They're comfortable with beam weaponry, have some degree of space travel, can speak other languages and enjoy a valued reputation amongst the Third Zone governments as a fighting force more socially acceptable than the Androgums.

THE KRONTEP

AWARENESS	2	PRESENCE	3
COORDINATION	4	RESOLVE	4
INGENUITY	1	STRENGTH	5

SKILLS
Athletics 4, Fighting 4, Marksman 2, Survival 2, Technology 1.

TRAITS
Brave
Impulsive
Indomitable
Tough

TECH LEVEL: 4 STORY POINTS: 1-2

NEW TRAIT: BATTLE CALL (SPECIAL GOOD)

Battle Call is a Special Good Trait that costs 2 Character Points. Krontep all believe that their dead ancestors are with them at all times. Krontep Monarchs believe they can communicate with these ancestors and, even better, use them to pass word to their followers.

By spending a Story Point, the Krontep Monarch can enter a trance where he summons Fortuna, the Krontep Goddess of Battlefield Communication. She finds their relative and passes the message on. Most commonly this is a call for support in a coming battle and, a surprising amount of the time, it works. Scientists have yet to prove that the Krontep have any psychic powers, but their belief in their ancestors seems to be all the support they need.

Characters with this trait gain a +2 to all Resolve rolls when entering combat. As an option, if they spend 2 Story Points, they can summon reinforcements.

"Brom Brom!" and "Brom Brom Savuda!" are two other phrases Yrcanos uses an awful lot. Whilst tranlsations are unclear "Brom Brom!" seems to be an expression of excitement and "Brom Brom Savuda!" "I am excited! Battle is NEAR!"

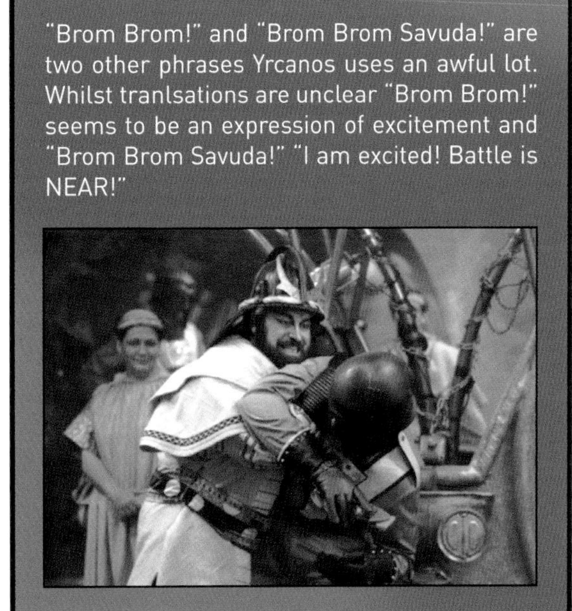

LORD KIV

Lord Kiv is a genius and it's killing him. The constantly swelling and expanding brain of a financial genius like him is no longer being contained by the frame he was born with. Kiv suffers regular, horrifying headaches and, as his brain grows, they get worse. Soon they'll kill him, but Kiv has other ideas, because growth markets are something he knows all too well and there are no shortage of candidates for his replacement body. He has the money, all he needs is the time.

LORD KIV

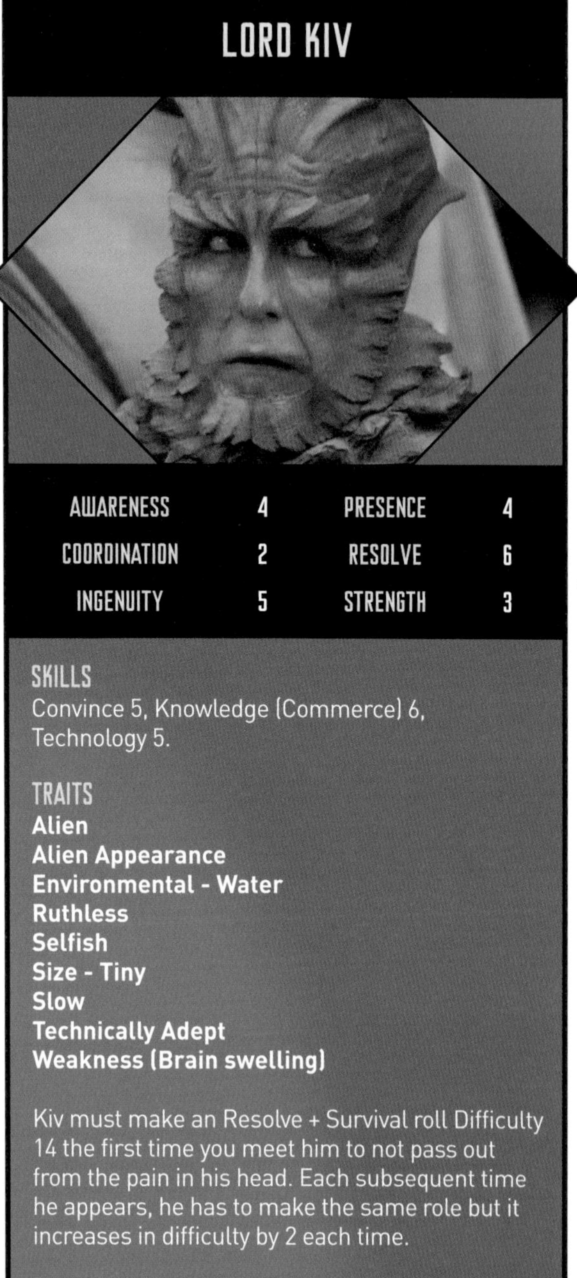

AWARENESS	4	PRESENCE	4
COORDINATION	2	RESOLVE	6
INGENUITY	5	STRENGTH	3

SKILLS

Convince 5, Knowledge (Commerce) 6, Technology 5.

TRAITS

Alien
Alien Appearance
Environmental - Water
Ruthless
Selfish
Size - Tiny
Slow
Technically Adept
Weakness (Brain swelling)

Kiv must make an Resolve + Survival roll Difficulty 14 the first time you meet him to not pass out from the pain in his head. Each subsequent time he appears, he has to make the same role but it increases in difficulty by 2 each time.

TECH LEVEL: 6 STORY POINTS: 3

SIL

Sil has changed since the last time the Sixth Doctor met him, and not for the better. Instead of humbling him, his experience on Varos only drove him to greater heights of success to the point where he was noticed by Lord Kiv. Kiv, the ruler of the Mentors, promoted Sil to Senior Business Advisor, meaning Sil was to accompany him constantly and offer business advice. This being Sil, he proceeded to offer the most fawning, worthless advice he could at every opportunity.

Unfortunately, that's exactly what Kiv was expecting. Having promoted Sil to keep him on side and not at the head of a hostile takeover, Kiv now has to put up with his obsequious aide's worthless opinions on a daily basis. Sil, on the other hand, has never been happier. He has a promotion and the ear of a sickly, ailing Lord. If he can save him, the credit will be Sil's. If he can't, then the position will be. Either way, he wins and that's just how Sil likes it.

SIL

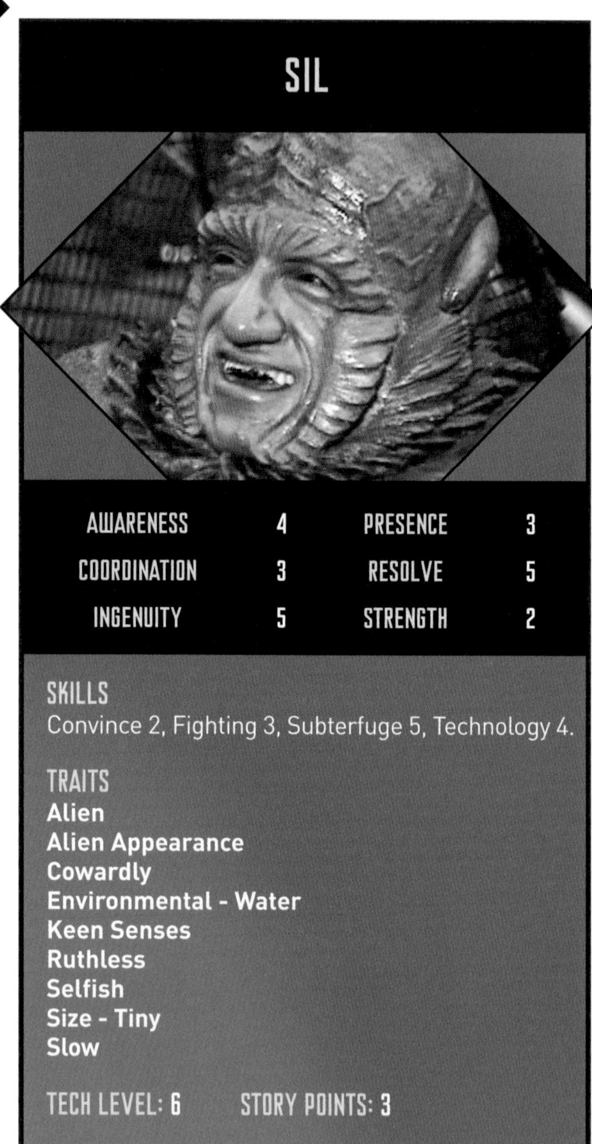

AWARENESS	4	PRESENCE	3
COORDINATION	3	RESOLVE	5
INGENUITY	5	STRENGTH	2

SKILLS

Convince 2, Fighting 3, Subterfuge 5, Technology 4.

TRAITS

Alien
Alien Appearance
Cowardly
Environmental - Water
Keen Senses
Ruthless
Selfish
Size - Tiny
Slow

TECH LEVEL: 6 STORY POINTS: 3

CROZIER

Crozier is the best geneticist in the galaxy. He's also one of the most wanted. To Crozier, a brain is a musical instrument and the songs he plays with it will change the universe. He knows some will die along the way but as long as the work isn't affected, neither is he. When he gets bored, which he does, he experiments and things like Dorf the Lukoser happen. They're happening more and more, often too. Because Kiv's time is running out and Crozier doesn't have a suitable candidate yet. If he can't find one, his life will be forfeit and, if that's the case, then who will finish his greatest composition?

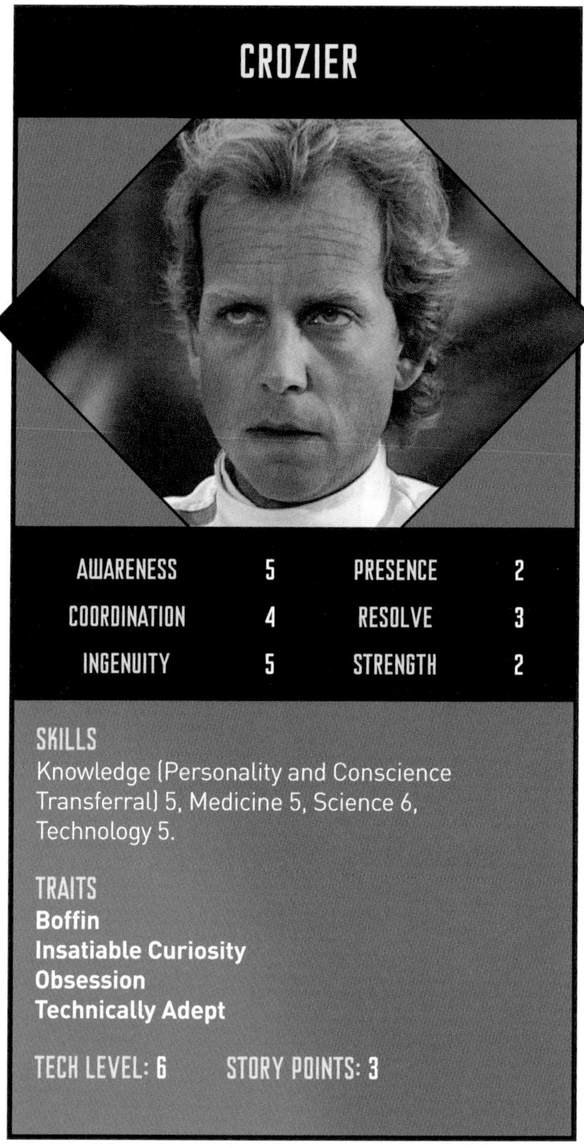

CROZIER

AWARENESS	5	PRESENCE	2
COORDINATION	4	RESOLVE	3
INGENUITY	5	STRENGTH	2

SKILLS
Knowledge (Personality and Conscience Transferral) 5, Medicine 5, Science 6, Technology 5.

TRAITS
Boffin
Insatiable Curiosity
Obsession
Technically Adept

TECH LEVEL: 6 STORY POINTS: 3

MATRONA KANI

Matrona Kani works with Crozier, not for him, despite what he thinks. She's a brilliant scientist in her own right, a woman who should be at the forefront of her field. Instead, she's been relegated to running servants for a dying old Mentor and a demented scientist with a vastly over-inflated sense of his own self-importance. Kani is better than this, she knows she is. Which is why, when it comes down to it, she'll take any chance she can get to stab Crozier in the back.

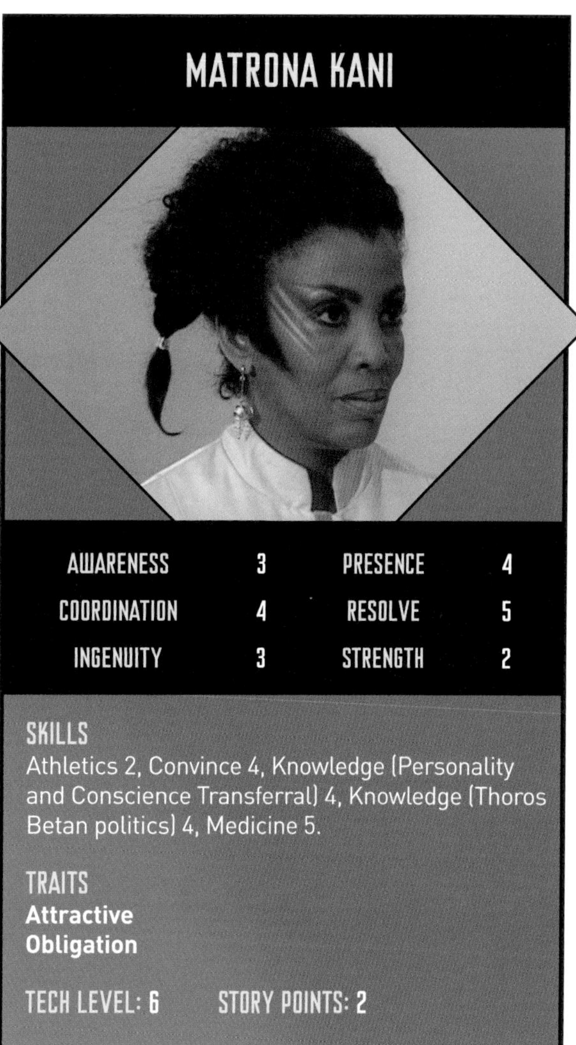

MATRONA KANI

AWARENESS	3	PRESENCE	4
COORDINATION	4	RESOLVE	5
INGENUITY	3	STRENGTH	2

SKILLS
Athletics 2, Convince 4, Knowledge (Personality and Conscience Transferral) 4, Knowledge (Thoros Betan politics) 4, Medicine 5.

TRAITS
Attractive
Obligation

TECH LEVEL: 6 STORY POINTS: 2

FRAX

Frax serves Crozier. He enjoys his work because he's told to. He knows to stay away from the Raak and the Lukoser and he knows trouble when he sees it. The Doctor and Peri are clearly trouble, but Frax doesn't mind. Because whilst he enjoys his work, it does bore him, and chasing the pair of them around will at least give him something to do.

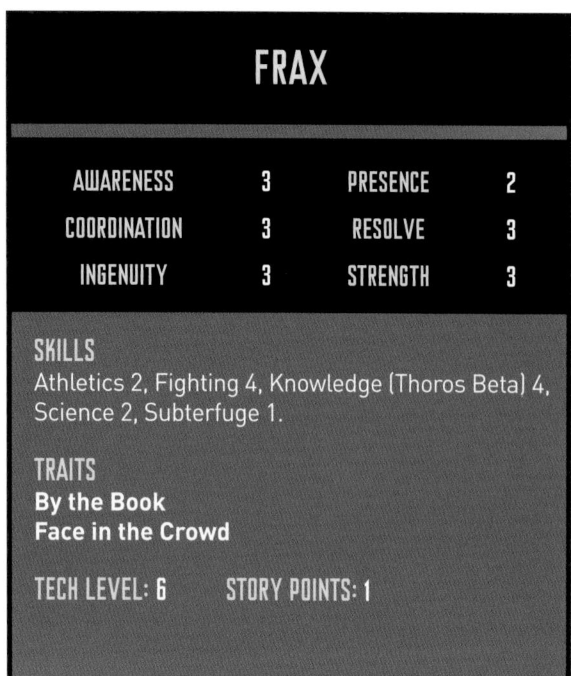

FRAX

AWARENESS	3	PRESENCE	2
COORDINATION	3	RESOLVE	3
INGENUITY	3	STRENGTH	3

SKILLS
Athletics 2, Fighting 4, Knowledge (Thoros Beta) 4, Science 2, Subterfuge 1.

TRAITS
By the Book
Face in the Crowd

TECH LEVEL: 6 STORY POINTS: 1

ALPHAN RESISTANCE MEMBER

Desperate to avoid slavery at the hands of the Mentors, a small group of Alphans have broken out and hide in the tunnels, surviving where they can and waiting for their chance to strike.

ALPHAN RESISTANCE MEMBER

AWARENESS	3	PRESENCE	2
COORDINATION	3	RESOLVE	4
INGENUITY	3	STRENGTH	4

SKILLS
Athletics 2, Fighting 3, Marksman 2, Medicine 3, Technology 2.

TRAITS
Brave
Face in the Crowd
Fast Healing
Impulsive

TECH LEVEL: 6 STORY POINTS: 1

DORF THE LUKOSER

Dorf used to be one of Yrcanos' trusted advisors, sitting at the right hand of the mighty warlord. Now, Dorf lies at his feet. A twisted abomination, half man and half wolf, Dorf lives his life in agony. He was an amusement for Crozier, a way of relieving the tension before returning to his great work. Now, he's chained in a tunnel, fed scraps and begging for death. This is no life for a Krontep warrior. He deserves a glorious death. He deserves to die knowing his foe has died. He deserves glory. And now, with his King released, he may finally have his chance.

DORF THE LUKOSER

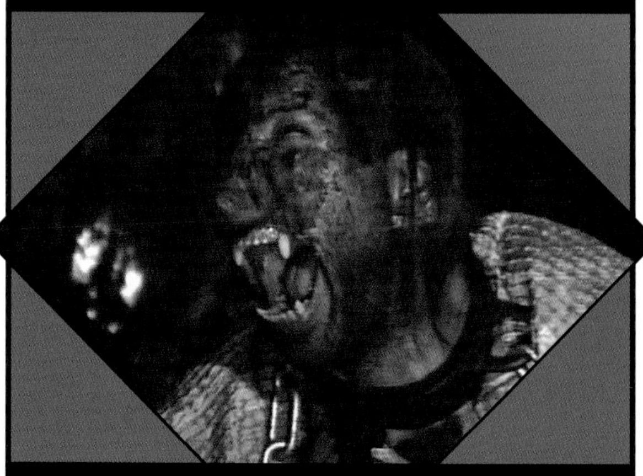

AWARENESS	5	PRESENCE	3
COORDINATION	4	RESOLVE	3
INGENUITY	2	STRENGTH	5

SKILLS
Athletics 5, Fighting 5, Survival 3.

TRAITS
Brave
Clumsy
Distinctive
Fear Factor 1
Keen Senses

Dorf must make a Resolve + Survival (Difficulty 12) roll once every scene to deal with the horror of what's been done to him, or else he spends the rest of the scene catatonic with abject revulsion.

WEAPONS: Teeth 2/**4**/6, Claws 1/**2**/4

TECH LEVEL: 4 STORY POINTS: 1

TUZA

The head of the Alphan slave resistance, Tuza has no idea what he's doing. He knows these men need a leader and he wants desperately to be that man. He also knows they have no weapons and precious little hope. For now all he can do is keep them safe and out of sight and wait for his chance. Tuza wants to strike back but without a plan, there's no hope.

TUZA

AWARENESS	3	PRESENCE	4
COORDINATION	3	RESOLVE	4
INGENUITY	3	STRENGTH	4

SKILLS
Athletics 3, Convince 2, Fighting 3, Knowledge (Thoros Beta) 3, Marksman 1, Subterfuge 2, Survival 2, Technology 2, Transport 2.

TRAITS
Brave
Code of Conduct
Lucky
Obligation
Quick Reflexes

TECH LEVEL: 6 **STORY POINTS:** 1

THE RAAK

Another one of Crozier's 'Distractions', the Raak used to be a simple, herbivorous sea creature. Now, it's a hulking monstrosity, in constant agony and perpetually enraged. Coralled in the tunnels around the ocean generator, it's used as little more than a guard dog.

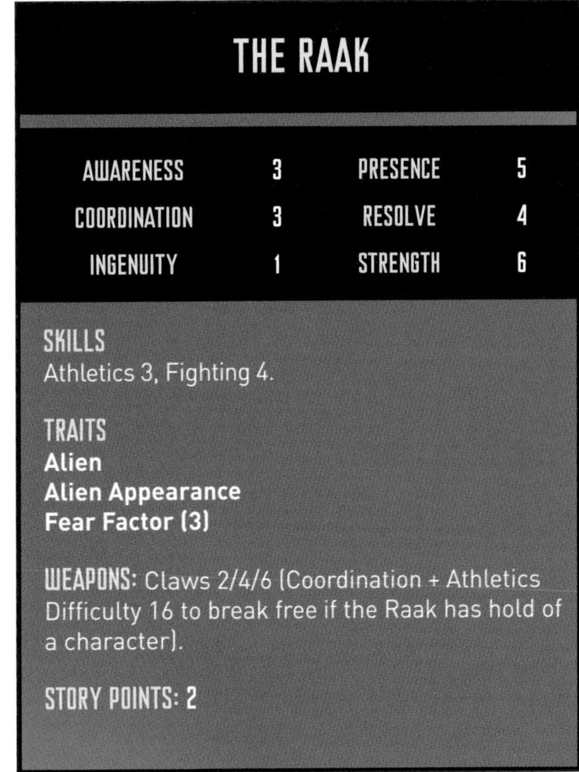

THE RAAK

AWARENESS	3	PRESENCE	5
COORDINATION	3	RESOLVE	4
INGENUITY	1	STRENGTH	6

SKILLS
Athletics 3, Fighting 4.

TRAITS
Alien
Alien Appearance
Fear Factor (3)

WEAPONS: Claws 2/4/6 (Coordination + Athletics Difficulty 16 to break free if the Raak has hold of a character).

STORY POINTS: 2

THOROS ALPHAN SLAVE

The Thoros Alphans are just one of the races enslaved by the Mentors. They favour physically capable men to carry them from place to place, and protect them when needed.

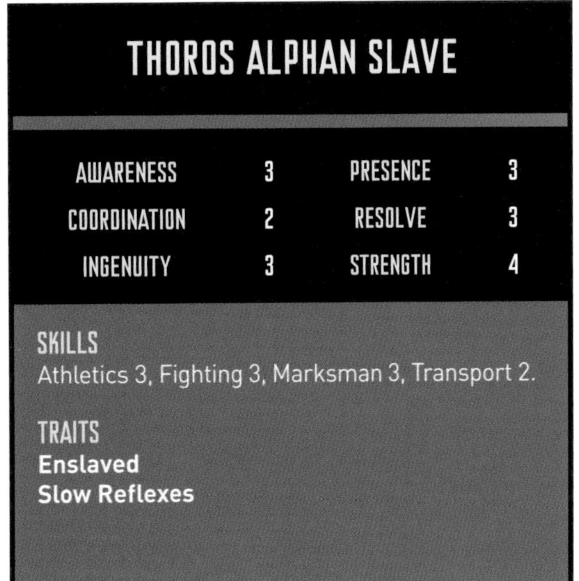

THOROS ALPHAN SLAVE

AWARENESS	3	PRESENCE	3
COORDINATION	2	RESOLVE	3
INGENUITY	3	STRENGTH	4

SKILLS
Athletics 3, Fighting 3, Marksman 3, Transport 2.

TRAITS
Enslaved
Slow Reflexes

TECHNOLOGY

The Conscience Transference Machine

The Conscience Transference Machine is the most important piece of technology developed anywhere in the universe for centuries. The reason is simple: it can transfer the living memories and personality of someone into an entirely new body, giving them a new lease on life. The only restrictions are that the body must be perfectly preserved and as close as possible in cerebral complexity to the original subject. A more developed brain is preferable. Think of it as more room to move your stuff into.

The machine is, unsurprisingly given it's the first non-Gallifreyan one of its kind, huge. Occupying most of a room, it combines a cerebral scanner and mapping computer with surgical equipment enabling the two subjects to be prepared and the process carried out.

The system is also surprisingly adaptable and can be used to detect whether someone is telling the truth. This is done via the same mapping process that conscience transferral requires, but at five times the speed. The agony caused by the scan is almost unbearable and any character undergoing it must make an Resolve + Survival (Difficulty 20) roll to not pass out. An Awareness + Fighting roll (Difficulty 20) can be used to resist it with the difficulty increasing by 1 each action round. The Psychic Training Trait can be used to fight the process as well.

The agony endured by a subject being scanned has some surprising side effects. Whilst fast and brutal, the scan is also very detailed and after one scan a user will know if someone is a candidate for transferral. More worryingly, if another candidate is connected to the machine at the same time, there will be some crossover between their personality traits – this is why the Doctor developed a sudden, brief love of weapons and battle after being connected to the machine at the same time as Yrcanos.

Transferral is a nightmarish process both for the staff and the 'vessel'. If they're unlucky enough to still be alive and have a personality of their own when the process begins, they must make an Awareness + Survival Roll (Difficulty 18), escalating by 2 each round, to not let the invading personality overwrite them. If they fail more than three times on the run, then their personality is erased from their body and the invading one 'moves in'.

Once successfully in the body, the new personality's Attributes and Skills are all reduced by -3 for the first turn they're conscious. This penalty then drops to -2 for the first week in their body and -1 for the month following until they're used to things like being taller, their new voice and, in Kiv's case, feet. Once that first month is over, backed up by regular doses of anti-rejection drugs (and regular backups on the machine's hard drives, just to be sure), the subject is officially the proud owner of a brand new body.

Except, of course, it's not as easy as that. Or as grim, which, let's face it, is a relief.

The most obvious way to play with the Conscience Transferral machine is easy. Don't. It's a galactic hot potato the likes of which not even the Doctor encounters very often, a machine so powerful and that changes the evolutionary structure of every sentient species so completely that the Time Lords do the one thing they hate – intervene – to make sure it's destroyed. Treat it the same way as Drathro's black light generator; hideously complex, amazingly dangerous and almost completely unknowable. Then throw Yrcanos at it.

Of course there's still the problem of the machine being a success, and the possible, singularly horrible death of Peri or another character. That's where the second option comes in. One of the characters has been successfully put through the process? Have their personality stored on a buffer in the machine. There's huge scope for an adventure that sees the characters fighting one of their own and trying to get them subdued long enough to be put through the machine again. Or, have the character's conscience transferred into a robot or a computer. Better still, have them swap consciences.

Think about the dramatic potential of having Peri in Kiv's old body, Kiv in Peri's body, neither one of which is accepting the new conscience inside it as Sil makes a hostile takeover. They'd have to work together, as well as with Yrcanos and the resistance, to stop him and somehow end up back in the right bodies (or a different new one in Kiv's case). There's no such thing as a definitive end here, not unless you want there to be one.

That also leads to the possibility of some real fun and games for the character fighting off the invasive personality. From their point of view, that would look like everything they've ever known crumbling or being subverted and every roll or decision they made would throw more walls up between them and the enemy. It'd be a tough situation to run, especially as they'd be separated from the rest of the group, but it'd be an epic situation for them to be in. Plus, the machine could always be modified so their friends could join in and help out... If you want to try this out, use the Matrix combat rules later in this chapter as they're both mental-based environments.

The third option is the most controversial (and, arguably, the most fun). Have it work. Have it work and be usable by your characters. The Time Bubble fails (or perhaps Yrcanos picked up enough of the Sixth Doctor's intellect to know the machine was the only chance of saving Peri) and suddenly the characters find themselves in possession of the most precious item in the universe. Which also renders death meaningless and one of the oldest, most powerful races in history will do everything they can to stop it being used or, worse, mass manufactured.

Suddenly, the characters have to deal with making sure each consciousness is in the right body, the countless groups wanting the machine and the Time Lords doing everything they can to stop them.

The Time Bubble

When the Time Lords threw a Time Bubble around Yrcanos and everyone near the transference machine, they created something very similar to a Time Spur. The only difference is that instead of being built around a paradox, the Time Bubble is built around a specific event that the characters are either not meant to achieve, or must do.

The Time Bubble isn't lifted until this event is resolved and everyone inside it has no idea of what's taking place, unless, of course, they have Feel the Turn of the Universe. If they do and successfully sense the boundaries of the time bubble (Difficulty 19) they must decide whether to act against it or not. After all, that may just what the Time Lords are waiting for.

See pg. 200 of **The Time Traveller's Companion** for more on Time Spurs.

NEW TRAIT: TEMPORAL AMNESIA (MINOR BAD)

The character has been plucked out of the time stream. This has wreaked havoc on their short term memory (-3 to all Awareness rolls) and almost as much damage on their long-term (-2 to all Knowledge). The character will regain the memories the longer they stay in one place but do so in a fractured, incomplete way. On returning to their time, their memories will reappear instantly.

FURTHER ADVENTURES

- **The Forevers:** The Doctor and companions return to Thoros Beta to find the entire planet has become a resort. The weather has been altered, the planet has been moved out of its orbit and the dingy caves are long gone. The Mentors are now the servants, and the people they serve are the Forevers. It's the 52nd century, and the Forevers have gathered to celebrate the anniversary of St Crozier and the Burning Cerebellum, the miraculous technological breakthrough that allowed them to live forever. From the shores of the Champagne Sea to the depths of the Body Mine, the Doctor and companions are about to discover the horrific truth about Thoros Beta, the machine and why the Time Lords didn't act when the machine was first turned on. Now, their only hope is Peri, a Forever herself. If they can help her remember her first life, she'll help them. If not, the next bodies the Forevers download into will be the characters' own...

- **On the Bubble:** The TARDIS is marooned, stuck to the side of a Time Bubble orbiting Pluto in the year 2011. And it's not alone. There is life on the bubble, creatures that have evolved to feed off time and, in one case, evolved to escape from a temporal prison. The Daleks weren't the only things the Time Lords fought and now, one of them is clawing its way through the last prison that could hold it, less than a mile from a working time machine. The Couldhavebeen King is building himself from the fragments of lost seconds, and he's hungry for more.

- **Yrcanos Returns:** The TARDIS arrives on Krontep during the festival of Sacred Violence, when the wars fought all year round long are combined for one, brief night into one glorious battle. Making their way through a planet-sized bar room brawl, the Doctor and his companions run into the last person they expected to see; Yrcanos. He survived, returned home and demands their help with his last great battle. He intends to sail (using the machine) into the mind of Lord Kiv and rescue Peri once and for all. All he needs is a time machine, some luck and the aide of Fortuna, Goddess of Battle. The odd thing is, he seems to have all of them. Yrcanos has had a run of very good luck since the last time they met and it may have more to do with the Rani, on Krontep in disguise, than he thinks. Is she acting for the Time Lords? For herself? And can Peri truly be saved?

TERROR OF THE VERVOIDS

'The crew is aboard. The last passengers are reporting in. Many will never complete the journey, for, in order to protect a secret hidden on the space liner, one will become a murderer.'

SYNOPSIS

The spaceship *Hyperion III*, 2986

Still grief-stricken over Peri's death, the Doctor asked for a recess so he could build a case for the defence. He was allowed to and returned to the courtroom with evidence from an adventure that had yet to occur. The Matrix showed the starliner *Hyperion III*, in orbit around the planet Mogar. With a hold full of the rare metals Mogar was known for, the ship had almost finished taking on passengers. The Doctor warned the court that many of the people aboard wouldn't survive as, on the screen, an elderly passenger called Kimber introduced himself to another passenger. He thought the man was a mineralogist called Hallett but was told he was mistaken. At the same time, Professor Sarah Lasky, under tremendous stress, met with her colleagues Bruchner and Doland. All three were worried that Grenville may be an investigator. The liner pulled away and their voyage began.

In the communications suite, Edwardes, the ship's communications officer picked up an odd craft close to the ship. He attempted to raise it on comms but was knocked out by an unseen figure, who then used the comms equipment to send an urgent message to the TARDIS.

The Doctor picked the message up in the middle of a rigorous exercise regime set for him by his new companion, Melanie Bush. Mel insisted he drink carrot juice to help with his vitamin intake and the Doctor reluctantly did so, until the arrival of the message. It read;

"...perative traitor be identified before landing on Earth."

They materialised in the ship's hold and the Doctor felt uncomfortable, saying he could sense evil. He attempted to go but Mel argued with him long enough that they were captured by ship security. When they were taken to the bridge, the Doctor was delighted to find an old friend – Commodore 'Tonka' Travers – in command. Travers was less pleased to see the Doctor and confined his two stowaways to the passenger quarters. When they left, Travers confided in Security Officer Rudge that if the Doctor was given enough room, he'd solve their problem for them.

The Doctor was still trying to figure out who had sent the message and Mel suggested he ask for a passenger manifest. He agreed whilst she wandered the ship, looking for any clues. When Rudge found her she asked to be taken to the gym and he showed her the various machines and headphones, with a built-in microphone, that could be used to listen to the workout instructions. Lasky was also in the gym and as Mel watched, she saw Doland come in and tell her that their lab had been broken into. The two scientists rushed out and as soon as they did, a voice on Mel's headphones told her to take the Doctor to Cabin 6.

In the lab, Lasky and her two assistants found the huge pods they were transporting intact but the demeter seeds had been stolen. As they tried to work out who could have done this, the Doctor was trying to get the passenger manifest. After a friendly, if slightly threatening, chat with Mr Rudge, Mel arrived to drag him away. The Doctor refused saying he felt like he'd just be walking into a trap and Mel went without him.

In the courtroom, the Doctor again claimed the scenes had been changed.On screen, Mel entered Cabin 6 to find signs of a huge struggle and a single shoe left on the bed. She heard someone in there and was about to hide when the Doctor appeared. He explained that his refusal was a ruse and they discussed the boot, as well as the demeter seeds.

At the waste disposal unit, Rudge contacted Travers. The Commodore reluctantly came down to discover evidence that someone had been thrown into the unit and from there out into space. Rudge had found a boot and as the Doctor and Mel arrived, they explained it was the twin of the one they'd found in the cabin. They discovered that the cabin had belonged to Grenville, a name the Doctor didn't recognise, declaring there was nothing that could be done. Mel, refusing to believe this, went to the cargo hold. She ran into Edwardes who showed her the hydroponics centre that had been set up for Lasky and co. He opened the door to give her a guided tour but was electrocuted. Unseen by Mel, a hand punched out of one of the seed pods.

Two guards arrived, confirmed Edwardes was dead and one led Mel away. As soon as she was out of the room, the guard left inside was killed. On the bridge, Rudge brought the Doctor to help question Mel and it became clear she had no idea what had happened. Rudge received a message from the medical team sent to retrieve Edwardes' body, saying there was no sign of it or the guard that had been left there. Travers asked the Doctor what was going on and Mel said a killer must be aboard. Travers decided to accelerate the trip, and changed course so they passed near the Black Hole of Tartarus, shaving 72 hours off their arrival time. One of the Mogarians aboard, a race who needed sealed tanks to breathe, asked if this would be a risk but Travers assured the passengers everything would be perfectly safe.

Time on the ship passed and in the courtroom the Doctor pointed out that a scene showing the Passenger Lounge included someone who was about to die.

One of the Mogarians took a drink and began to convulse. The Doctor rushed forward, demanding the man be given oxygen even though Mogarians found it toxic. He removed the dying figure's face plate to reveal...Grenville. Or Hallett, as the Doctor knew

him. He explained that Hallett was an investigator, specialising in undercover work and that, when Mr Kimber had recognised him before, Hallett had faked his own death to avoid being discovered.

In the court, the Valeyard asked the Doctor how he'd been able to tell Hallett wasn't a Mogarian. The Doctor rewound the Matrix to the point where the Mogarians had all spoken to Travers about the black hole. Two of them had touched their translator circuits to speak English, one hadn't. That was Hallett.

Vowing to no longer be passive in the situation, the Doctor and Mel talked things over and realised that the seeds were given to them so they would investigate the hydroponics centre. They didn't find anything new but when they came back up the Doctor saw Lasky leaving an isolation room wearing a face mask. The Doctor distracted the guard and they grabbed masks and snuck in. Inside they found a half-human, half-plant woman secured to a table pleading for help.

Lasky, Bruchner and Doland rushed in and sedated her and Doland told them the truth. The woman is Ruth Baxter, Doland's assistant. During the cross-fertilisation experiments some pollen entered a tiny scratch in Ruth's thumb. The plant maturation process used her body as a foundation and she mutated. They were keeping her heavily sedated in the hopes that someone on Earth could cure her or reverse the infection.

Later, Mel heard a noise in the ducting by the gym. Thinking quickly, she stuck a pair of headphones over one of the vents and the microphone picked up voices planning to kill all animal-kind on the ship. She was so intent on listening that she didn't hear someone sneak in behind her. They knocked her out using anaesthetic and dumped her in a waste disposal bin. She was only saved when the Doctor came into the gym, heard the tape and raced to the waste disposal unit. However, by the time they got back to the gym, the killer had removed the tape.

Nearby, Mr Kimber disappeared and when he hadn't touched the drink a stewardess had brought him, the alarm was raised. Bruchner was pushed to breaking point and he decided to burn the project notes for the work he, Lasky and Doland had been working on. Lasky tried to reason with him but he knocked her out, stole a gun and hijacked the ship, vowing to send it into the nearby Black Hole of Tartarus.

The Doctor, Lasky and Travers tried to break into the bridge but discovered it had been filled with marsh gas, secreted by one of the creatures. Bruchner was killed but the ship was still heading into the black hole and the passengers were panicking as it started to shake apart. Rudge brought the two Mogarians to the bridge and they were able to steer the ship thanks to their enclosed environment suits.

However, the celebrations were short lived when Rudge revealed he and the Mogarians were working together and were hijacking the ship. The Mogarians

considered the metals taken from Mogar to be theft whilst Rudge, on his last voyage, was sick of taking orders from men like Travers and wanted a nice big payout to retire on. Unknown to him, on the bridge someone killed the Mogarians by throwing liquid oxygen on them.

Mel had been able to get to the passenger lounge ahead of Rudge and warned Doland and Janet, one of the stewardesses, about the hijacking. They hid whilst Rudge secured the lounge and alerted the guards. Mel snuck into the ducts and warned the Doctor. The Doctor, still unaware of what had happened on the bridge, told Mel to attack there instead. She did so, and found the Mogarians dead. Realising that showing he was outnumbered was the only way to get Mr Rudge to stand down, she and the others took the faceplates of the aliens' suits to Rudge. With his accomplices dead, Rudge was overpowered and ran into the corridors of the vessel where the creatures in the hold found and killed him.

The Doctor got Commodore Travers' permission to search the passenger cabins for the missing tape and sent Mel to check Lasky's gym locker in case it was there. The Doctor was met by Doland who suggested the cabinet in the hydroponics work centre as a possible hiding place. The Doctor followed him down there and Doland handed him the tape; he was the killer.

He told the Doctor everything; the creatures that had been killing people were Vervoids, plant-based lifeforms that would run on sunlight and replace every robot in every factory and farm. The Doctor claimed it was slave labour and Doland fired at him. Nothing happened and the Doctor revealed he'd disarmed the gun. Doland fled and was arrested only for both he and the guard to be killed by the Vervoids.

With the situation deteriorating, the Doctor, Mel, Travers and Lasky met on the bridge to discuss what to do. Lasky thought the DNA of the Vervoids was faulty but the Doctor pointed out that they had referred to "animal-kind" in the recording. Every animal ate plants and that meant the Vervoids hated all animal life. Lasky finally realised this was why Bruchner had been so hysterical and agreed to help destroy them. Travers asked the Doctor to do anything he could to stop the creatures.

In the Court, the Doctor pointed out that this proved he was not meddling and was asked to help. The Inquisitor agreed but the Valeyard asked for further evidence.

On the *Hyperion III*, Lasky had reached her lab hoping to make herbicide to fight the Vervoids. The creatures had got there ahead of her and taken all the chemicals meaning they were powerless. The Vervoids appeared and despite the Doctor's pleas, Lasky tried to reason with them. They killed her and left, taking her back to their lair in the ship's ducting, Following them, the Doctor and Mel saw the collection of their victims' bodies, a grotesque version of a compost heap.

The Doctor comforted a horrified Mel and had an idea, inspired by his last conversation with Lasky. Returning to the bridge, he asked if there was any vionesium onboard. vionesium released light and carbon dioxide in huge quantities when exposed to air. He planned to expose the Vervoids to the vionesium, forcibly ageing them to death. Travers lowered the temperature across the ship, forcing them to return to the ducting where the Doctor and Mel were waiting. They activated the vionesium and the Vervoids grew, withered and died, turning into nothing but dead leaves. Tired and shocked, but alive, the time travellers bid farewell to Travers and Janet and left.

In the courtroom, the Valeyard asked a triumphant Doctor if any of the Vervoids had survived. He replied that if even a single leaf had reached Earth the planet would have been doomed. The Valeyard then changed the accusations, saying that if the Doctor had killed all the Vervoids, that meant he had committed genocide, a crime the Time Lords could not forgive.

CONTINUITY

- The Matrix contains future knowledge but is regarded as predictive rather than accurate (see ***The Deadly Assassin***, in **The Fourth Doctor Sourcebook**).

- Since this adventure is from the Doctor's own future, technically he has not met Mel yet. We never do see how they first met.
- The TARDIS can receive mayday messages.
- Travers and Hallett have met the Doctor before.
- Things the Doctor keeps in that garish coat of his: magician's flowers, an electronic lockpick.
- The Doctor has had to make a similar judgement call about the genocide of a species before – he chose differently that time (see ***Genesis of the Daleks*** in **The Fourth Doctor Sourcebook**).

RUNNING THE ADVENTURE

There are two ways to run this adventure. The first is as an absolutely classic 'Base Under Siege'. You have all the right ingredients: the implacable alien threat, the enclosed space and the ticking clock of trying to survive long enough to either get to Earth or to stop the Vervoids getting to Earth. If you go down this route then the setting of the *Hyperion III* makes it all the easier. The ship's huge and eminently defensible in a lot of places so encourage the characters to get creative in their ways of dealing with the Vervoids. Maybe the dehumidifiers in the gym dry them out? Maybe the bridge is the only secure place and the only place the Vervoids actually want to get to? Maybe the Vervoids take hostages as a means of forcing the characters' hands? This way, this is an adventure where they're locked on a speeding ship with a group of killers and it needs to be played for all the atmosphere and tension you can wring from it.

The other way to run it is to take the human agendas on display and go even further with them. Have the Vervoids function as a background threat but have the characters constantly trying to deal with human crises. Maybe Edwardes survives but is obsessed with rescuing a friend of his he last saw on the cargo deck, or Rudge kills Hallett, convinced he knows about the plan? Maybe Commodore Travers isn't pleased to see the Doctor because he has something of his own going on? Make the Vervoids the danger the characters can see, but surround them with a more insidious danger they have to find out and keep the clock ticking.

PROFESSOR SARAH LASKY

Professor Lasky has made it her life's work to cure hunger. She did this by focusing not on the boundless waves of cold technology that attracted her colleagues, but on plants and vegetables. Lasky's work, aided by her assistants Doland, Bruchner and Baxter, proved hugely successful and she developed the demeter seeds that would end world famine forever. However, that wasn't enough, Lasky wanted to make a change to the whole galaxy and to do that she needed to think bigger. The Vervoids were born from that idea, a creature that could do the work of a robot with none of the environmental damage. The price was most of her career and any sense of self outside her work. Sarah Lasky knows she's relentless, driven and difficult to work with. She also knows that she gets results no one else can and that her mark will soon be made. It's worth every moment.

PROFESSOR SARAH LASKY

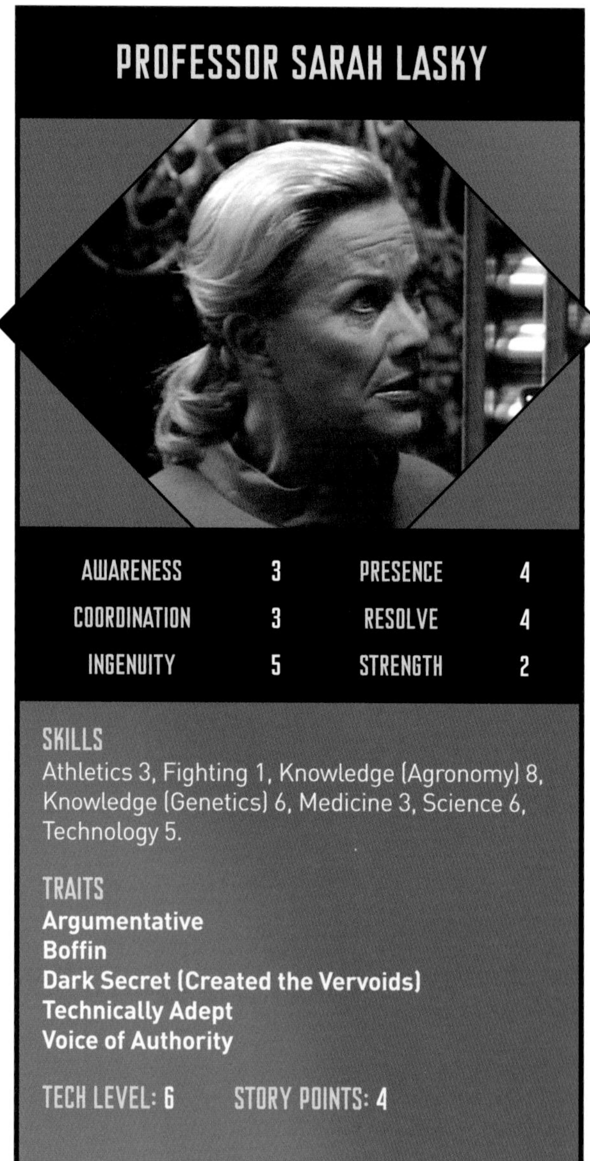

AWARENESS	3	PRESENCE	4
COORDINATION	3	RESOLVE	4
INGENUITY	5	STRENGTH	2

SKILLS
Athletics 3, Fighting 1, Knowledge (Agronomy) 8, Knowledge (Genetics) 6, Medicine 3, Science 6, Technology 5.

TRAITS
Argumentative
Boffin
Dark Secret (Created the Vervoids)
Technically Adept
Voice of Authority

TECH LEVEL: 6 STORY POINTS: 4

DOLAND

Doland used to know what he wanted; the same thing as Lasky. But the last few weeks have been too much. First Ruth's accident and then... success, and everything that came with it. The Vervoids are too perfect, too intelligent. Doland knows what they're capable of, he's heard them dreaming in their seed pods. The only thing that terrifies Doland more than being caught for what they did is the Vervoids escaping and, now, it seems both have come true.

DOLAND

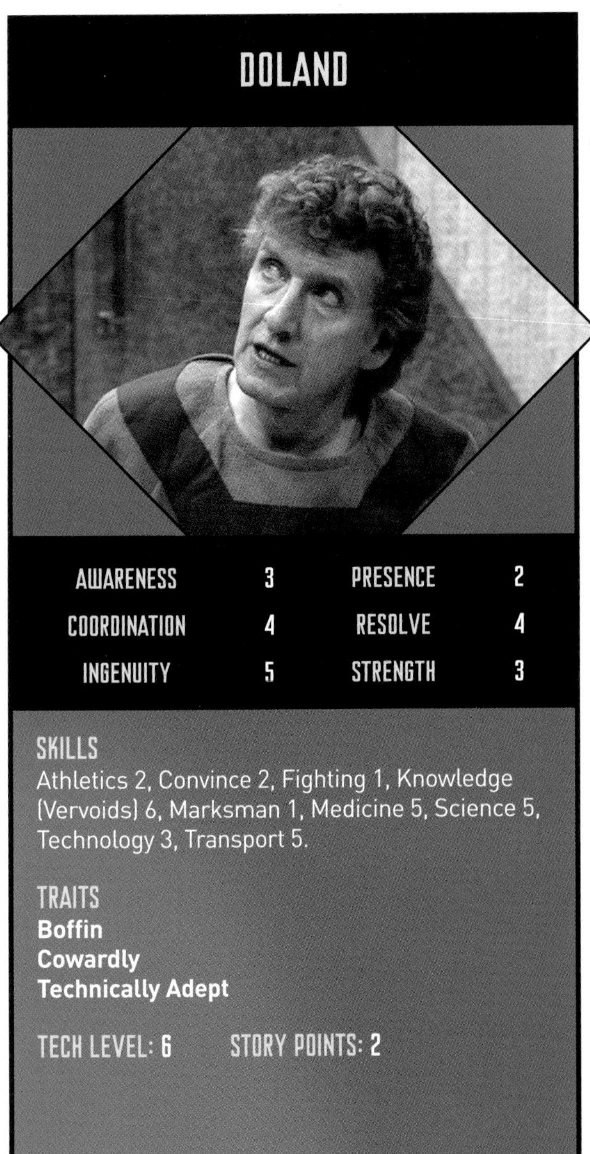

AWARENESS	3	PRESENCE	2
COORDINATION	4	RESOLVE	4
INGENUITY	5	STRENGTH	3

SKILLS
Athletics 2, Convince 2, Fighting 1, Knowledge (Vervoids) 6, Marksman 1, Medicine 5, Science 5, Technology 3, Transport 5.

TRAITS
Boffin
Cowardly
Technically Adept

TECH LEVEL: 6 STORY POINTS: 2

BRUCHNER

Bruchner likes success. Bruchner likes money. Lasky's work gives him both those and the fun of having his overly large brain stimulated by something other than working out how to break people for once. The Vervoids will be the thing that puts him over the top, the success story that will finally let him write his name across history. If he has to write it in the blood of the people they've killed, then so be it.

BRUCHNER

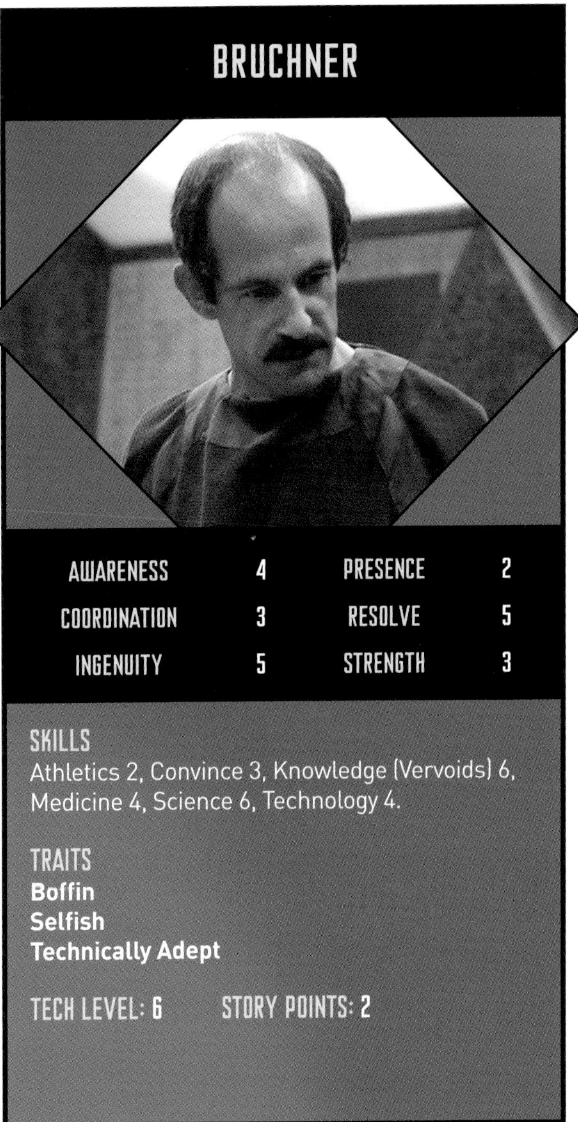

AWARENESS	4	PRESENCE	2
COORDINATION	3	RESOLVE	5
INGENUITY	5	STRENGTH	3

SKILLS
Athletics 2, Convince 3, Knowledge (Vervoids) 6, Medicine 4, Science 6, Technology 4.

TRAITS
Boffin
Selfish
Technically Adept

TECH LEVEL: 6 STORY POINTS: 2

SECURITY OFFICER RUDGE

Rudge is tired. He's tired of smiling and waving at these idiots. He's tired of people too stupid to find a room on a ship with a dedicated passenger deck and most of all he's tired of men like Commodore Travers. Men who pick at his every word, check his shoes, whether he's standing to attention. Petty tinpot dictators and not one of them an ounce of the character he has. Rudge is done, Rudge is out and he's going to sort himself out before he goes. After all, it's the least he deserves for putting up with these people so long.

SECURITY OFFICER RUDGE

AWARENESS	3	PRESENCE	2
COORDINATION	3	RESOLVE	4
INGENUITY	4	STRENGTH	4

SKILLS
Athletics 3, Convince 2, Fighting 2, Knowledge (*Hyperion III*) 6, Marksman 2, Subterfuge 4.

TRAITS
Charming
Dark Secret
Face in the Crowd
Ruthless

WEAPON: Sidearm 2/**4**/L

TECH LEVEL: 6 STORY POINTS: 2

RUTH BAXTER

All Ruth knows is she isn't herself. Her body is mutating, her senses shifting until she feels the pulse of UV light, smells carbon dioxide, is nourished by sunlight. It's beautiful and frightening and agonising, all at once. It has to stop and she just wants to be normal again.

RUTH BAXTER

AWARENESS	2	PRESENCE	4
COORDINATION	2	RESOLVE	2
INGENUITY	2	STRENGTH	5

SKILLS
Athletics 1, Fighting 1, Knowledge (Vervoids) 5, Medicine 4, Science 4, Technology 4.

TRAITS
Distinctive
Fast Healing
Outcast

TECH LEVEL: 6 STORY POINTS: 1

COMMODORE TRAVERS

Travers is unflappable. A lifetime of service in space has meant he's seen almost everything and knows that the two things you need to make sure you come home in one piece are a tight ship and a little luck.

He has the ship, although Rudge is clearly free-wheeling on his last voyage and now, he has the Doctor. Which means his luck may have changed. The only problem is, Travers doesn't know if it's for better or worse.

COMMODORE TRAVERS

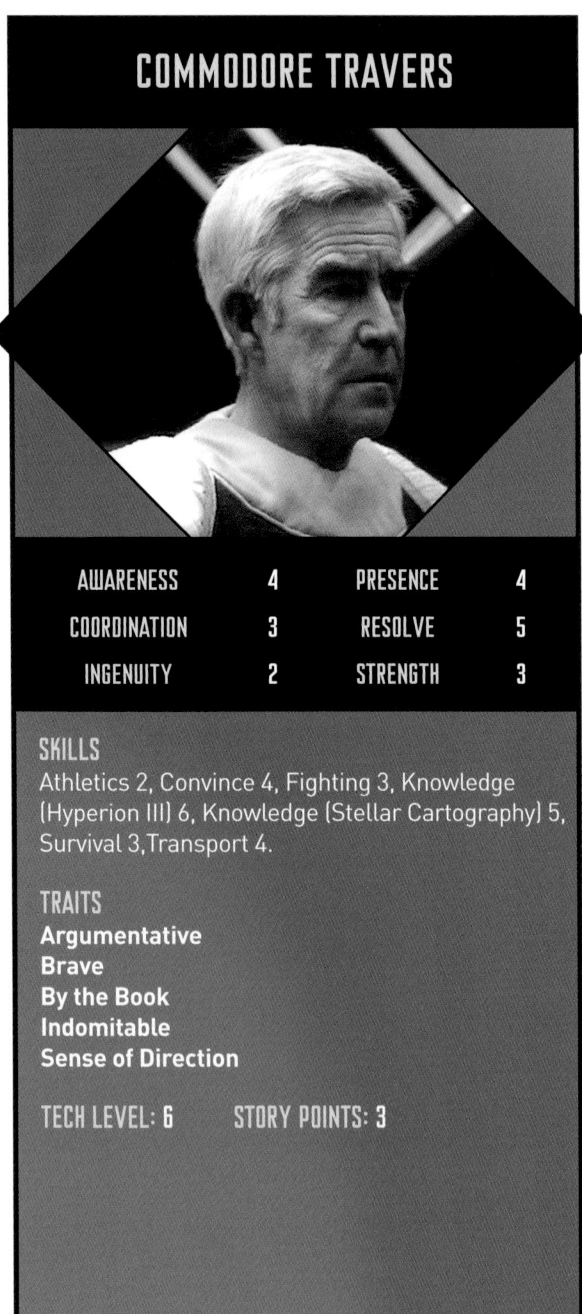

AWARENESS	4	PRESENCE	4
COORDINATION	3	RESOLVE	5
INGENUITY	2	STRENGTH	3

SKILLS
Athletics 2, Convince 4, Fighting 3, Knowledge (Hyperion III) 6, Knowledge (Stellar Cartography) 5, Survival 3,Transport 4.

TRAITS
Argumentative
Brave
By the Book
Indomitable
Sense of Direction

TECH LEVEL: 6 STORY POINTS: 3

THE VERVOIDS

The Vervoids are a genetically engineered plant race created by the team led by Professor Sarah Lasky. They are bipedal, standing six and a half feet tall and have a distinctive, orchid-like crest which their head, resembling the centre of a flower, sits within.

The Vervoids were intended to be an ecologically sound, far cheaper, replacement for robots and menial labour. Their bodies are made out of reinforced plant fibre and wood and as a result they gain nourishment from sunlight rather than food. However, the level of cognisance they needed to be able to function effectively was too high for them to not realise the true nature of their lives. The Vervoids are slaves of all animal-kind and for the sake of them and the countless trillions of their plant ancestors, they must wage an impossible war against all mammalian life, starting with Earth.

Vervoids are tremendously intimidating creatures face to face, and deadly in close combat. However, they're not fast, meaning that provided you're clever, or lucky, you'll escape. But any Vervoid leaf contains the ability to bud into a full Vervoid and only one is needed to restore the species.

AWARENESS	3	PRESENCE	4
COORDINATION	2	RESOLVE	4
INGENUITY	3	STRENGTH	5

SKILLS
Athletics 1, Fighting 3, Survival 2.

TRAITS
Alien
Alien Appearance
Alien Senses
Environmental
Fear Factor
Natural Weapons
Slow Reflexes
Special – Spores
Technically Inept
Weakness (Vionesium)

WEAPON: Claws 1/**2**/4

MARSH GAS: The Vervoids can release marsh gas which, in an enclosed area requires any characters to make a Strength + Survival roll (Difficulty 12). Failure means they take 1 level of damage. In addition, the gas reduces visibility, inflicting a -1 Awareness and -1 Coordination penalty on any creature that relies on sight.

SPORES: The Vervoids are covered in spores. These will, if they enter a cut on an opponent, cause one level of damage per day. Once three of a victim's attributes have been reduced to 0, they are converted into a Vervoid. Similarly, unless a Vervoid is completely destroyed, any green leaf will sprout a new Vervoid seed pod in one day, which will hatch as a fully grown Vervoid a day later.

TECH LEVEL: 1 STORY POINTS: **4-6**

JANET

Janet's OK, and that's a pleasant surprise. She's trained for disasters, knows where the exits are, knows what to do and she's ready. What's really pleasing her is she's dealing with it even after things go from bad to worse, again. In fact, when they get home, Janet's thinking of enlisting. She's good in a crisis.

JANET

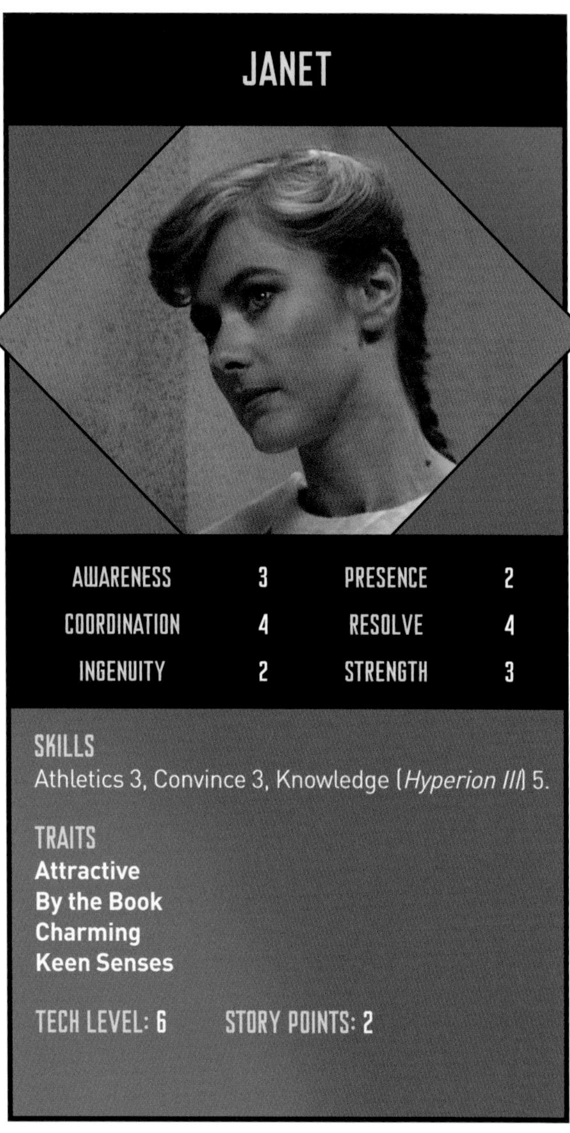

AWARENESS	3	PRESENCE	2
COORDINATION	4	RESOLVE	4
INGENUITY	2	STRENGTH	3

SKILLS
Athletics 3, Convince 3, Knowledge (*Hyperion III*) 5.

TRAITS
Attractive
By the Book
Charming
Keen Senses

TECH LEVEL: 6 STORY POINTS: 2

MR KIMBER

Mr Kimber is absolutely convinced that there's a man he knows on this flight. Grenville is the spitting image of an investigator who helped him out years ago, a Mr Hallett. Mr Kimber feels terrible for having blurted out Hallett's name, because if it is him then he must be undercover. So, Mr Kimber has decided to stay quiet and calm and keep his eyes open. Because if it is Mr Hallett, he may need some extra help.

MR KIMBER

AWARENESS	2	PRESENCE	2
COORDINATION	2	RESOLVE	3
INGENUITY	3	STRENGTH	2

SKILLS
Athletics 1, Convince 3, Knowledge (Mogar) 5.

TRAITS
Charming
Forgetful
Slow Reflexes

TECH LEVEL: 6 STORY POINTS: 1

GRENVILLE/HALLETT

Hallett is going to have to improvise. It's bad enough being dropped on Mogar after the last job but now, with Mr Kimble recognising him, he's going to have to get creative. It's a shame too, Kimble was a charming old sort but Hallett can't stop and chat.

If he's right, someone on Lasky's team is bringing something impossibly dangerous to Earth and he can't stand by and let that happen. But, in order to protect everyone, first, he's going to have to be dead. Then he can get things done.

GRENVILLE/HALLETT

AWARENESS	4	PRESENCE	4
COORDINATION	4	RESOLVE	5
INGENUITY	4	STRENGTH	4

SKILLS
Athletics 4, Convince 3, Fighting 4, Knowledge (Law Enforcement) 5, Marksman 4, Medicine 3, Science 2, Subterfuge 5, Survival 4, Technology 3, Transport 3.

TRAITS
Brave
Face in the Crowd
Indomitable
Keen Senses
Unlucky

TECH LEVEL: 6 STORY POINTS: 2

EDWARDES

Edwardes knows what he saw. He saw a small ship, just off the Hyperion III, refusing hails. Then he was unconscious. He's a good officer, a hard working member of the crew. He'll make this up to the Commodore and he knows just where to start. That hydroponics bay set up in the hold...

EDWARDES

AWARENESS	3	PRESENCE	2
COORDINATION	3	RESOLVE	3
INGENUITY	4	STRENGTH	3

SKILLS
Athletics 2, Fighting 2, Knowledge (Communications Systems) 5, Marksman 2, Survival 1, Technology 4.

TRAITS
Attractive
Face in the Crowd
Unlucky

TECH LEVEL: 6 STORY POINTS: 1

THE MOGARIANS

Native to the airless world of Mogar, the Mogarians are a testament to life's perseverance. They've adapted to breathe the trace gases trapped in the caves that cover the surface of their world, using pressure suits with masks based on their own natural breathing baleen.

Tall, thin and precise to the point of being belligerent, Mogarians have a deserved reputation for being amongst the most driven races in the galaxy as well as one of the most cautious. The reason for this is simple: a single mistake on Mogar can mean death. Their precision is a survival tool, but it, and Mogar's vast wealth of rare metals have made them a major player on the galactic stage.

THE MOGARIANS

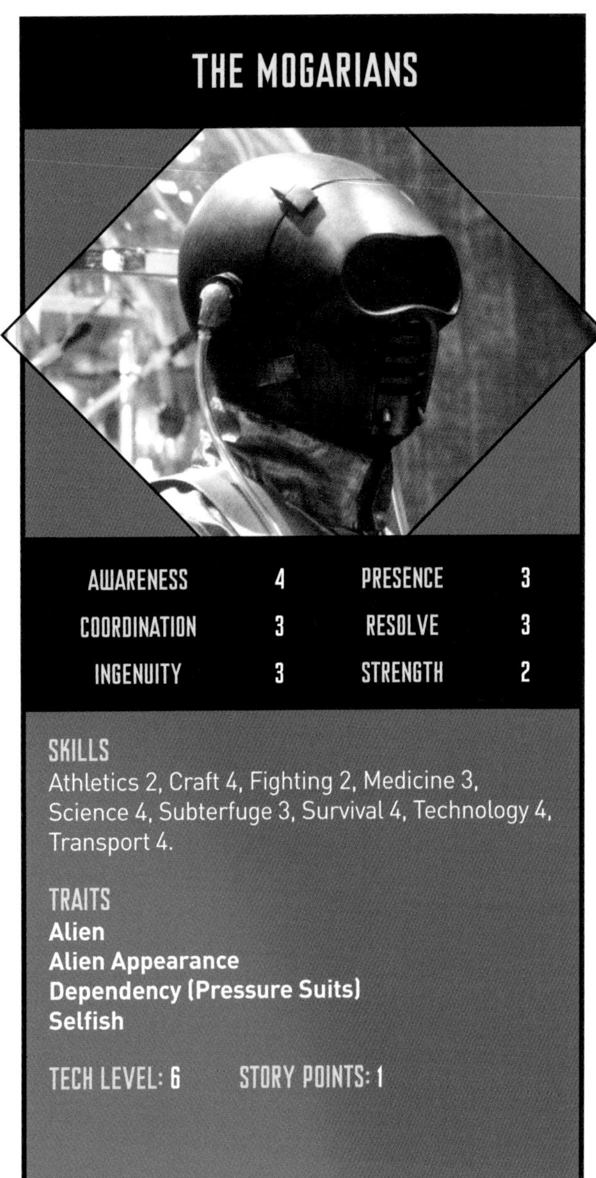

AWARENESS	4	PRESENCE	3
COORDINATION	3	RESOLVE	3
INGENUITY	3	STRENGTH	2

SKILLS
Athletics 2, Craft 4, Fighting 2, Medicine 3, Science 4, Subterfuge 3, Survival 4, Technology 4, Transport 4.

TRAITS
Alien
Alien Appearance
Dependency (Pressure Suits)
Selfish

TECH LEVEL: 6 STORY POINTS: 1

TECHNOLOGY

Demeter Seeds

Demeter seeds can grow in any circumstances, at all. They are genetically engineered, with the size and type of the plant customisable by the buyer, to gain sustenance from whatever's around them, whether that's soil, sunlight or the trace gases of the surface of Mogar. The moment they germinate they begin to grow and will continue to do so until they reach the factory pre-sets. They can then be harvested. Needless to say, the demeter seeds have had a revolutionary effect and the few areas of the galaxy where people were still hungry have long since been fed. The only problem is, the seeds are too good, too durable; they can be harvested but they can never be successfully uprooted. Pesticide becomes nutrients for the demeter seed so the only way to get rid of them is by burning them out. Doing this, of course, renders the land they're in all but barren. To make matters worse, several governments have expressed concern (and several others have expressed interest) in using the demeter seeds as a weapon. The plants provided to clients are incapable of releasing seeds themselves but just one demeter seed-bearing plant would be enough to render an entire city block into urban forest in very little time.

Vionesium

A rare metal found on Mogar, vionesium is similar to Magnesium. Both react incredibly strongly but where Magnesium reacts to heat, vionesium reacts to oxygen. When vionesium is exposed to Oxygen, the metal burns fiercely brightly, delivering the equivalent of a year of sunlight all at once. This has a devastating effect on plant life exposed to the reacting vionesium, as its cells effectively overload from the sheer quantity of energy being absorbed. The Doctor and Mel used vionesium 'grenades' to destroy the Vervoids on the Hyperion III and, ironically, the devices have found a use across the galaxy as a risk-free defoliant. Anyone looking directly at a vionesium grenade when it goes off must spend a Story Point or make an Awareness + Survival (Difficulty 16) roll to look away. If they don't, they take a -3 penalty to Awareness for the rest of the scene due to being blinded by the light.

Damage: 4/8/L
Traits: Restriction (Plants only)

Laser Lance

An emergency cutting tool used to open dropped bulkheads, the laser lance is a large weapon requiring two handlers. This enables the powerful cutting beam to be precisely controlled.

Damage: 2/4/8

FURTHER ADVENTURES

- **Spring of the Vervoids:** The TARDIS arrives on Mogar, five years after the events of this adventure. They find it covered in sweeping fields of silver grass. The grass is converting the trace gases trapped in the planet's crust into an atmosphere, but one that is oxygen-based. Trying to find out why the Mogarians are terraforming their world in a way that could kill them, the Doctor and his companions discover Sil has bought the planet outright and is having it changed into his retirement home. The Doctor and his companions must work out how to drive the Mentors off world, perhaps with the aid of the Vervoids.

- **Summer of the Vervoids:** 15 years after the events of this adventure, the TARDIS arrives on Mogar and is greeted by something unthinkable; the Vervoids have returned. The plants cover the planet, which also now has a breathable atmosphere thanks to a crop of demeter seeds and, to their surprise, welcome them. The Vervoids explain that they reappeared five years after the events on the *Hyperion III* and found sanctuary here because the Mogarians, due to the lack of atmosphere on their planet, don't consume plant life. The two races live side by side peacefully and the Mogarians have used the Vervoids' hard-won status as a sentient race to help control mining on their world. All seems well, until a Vervoid is killed during the welcome banquet, silver seeds suddenly appearing all over its skin. As the Vervoid becomes a demeter seed grenade and infects dozens of others around it, the characters find themselves trapped beneath the surface of Mogar and caught between two warring vegetation hive-minds; The Mogarian Vervoids want peace, but the sole survivor of the *Hyperion III* disaster wants to murder every member of animal-kind.

- **Autumn of the Vervoids**: Arriving on Mogar, the Doctor and his companions are horrified to find the planet in quarantine. The Vervoids and the Mogarians are both being killed by a trans-species virus and the TARDIS crew are trapped on world with them. Now they must find a cure for the disease, talk down the Earth navy intent on attacking the planet to keep it contained and discover who was responsible. In doing so, they'll end up being present at the birth of a new species, as the Vervoids and Mogarians combine, the plants acting as symbiotic lungs for a race who've spent their entire lives unable to breathe on their own world.

THE ULTIMATE FOE

'In all my travelling throughout the universe, I have battled against evil, against power-mad conspirators. I should have stayed here. The oldest civilisation: decadent, degenerate, and rotten to the core. Power-mad conspirators, Daleks, Sontarans, Cybermen - they're still in the nursery compared to us. Ten million years of absolute power. That's what it takes to be really corrupt.'

SYNOPSIS

The Justice Station, the Future

The Doctor was still insisting that the Matrix evidence had been tampered with. Trying to settle the argument once and for all, the Inquisitor brought in the Keeper of the Matrix, who testified that the only way to enter the Matrix was with the Key of Rassilon, which only senior Time Lords had access to. The Doctor accused him of allowing forgeries and the Keeper retorted that the key never left his side. The Doctor insisted that a copy had been made and the Valeyard closed the case, refusing to hear any more.

Outside, two travel pods were drawn onto the ship. They were carrying Sabalom Glitz and Mel who arrived to testify in the Doctor's favour. They explained that they were sent there by an unknown benefactor and the Doctor was speculating as to who this could be when he appeared on the Matrix screen: the Master.

The Master explained that he was speaking from inside the Matrix, thus proving the Doctor was right and that the Valeyard could have falsified the evidence. He had enjoyed the courtroom battle but was intervening because the thought of the Valeyard winning was too much for him.

Glitz mentioned that he and the Master had done business before and the Doctor questioned him about the secrets he'd been trying to steal back on Ravolox. Glitz revealed that the secrets were actually from the Matrix, stolen by a group of Andromedan astronauts. Nicknamed the Sleepers, the Andromedans had travelled in cryogenic suspension from their home constellation, stolen the secrets and then hidden on Earth. Their plan was to build the Marble Arch shelter and hide there in suspended animation for the centuries it would take their robotic rescue mission to find them. The Time Lords found them and used a device called a Magnetron to haul the entirety of Earth's solar system light years away from where it should be. This meant the robotic mission couldn't find the Sleepers and also caused the fireball that devastated Earth.

The Doctor was enraged that his own species could be so callous. The Master went further, explaining that the Valeyard was an amalgamation of all the Doctor's evil, a gestalt regeneration that existed somewhere between his twelfth and final life.

The High Council were aware of the Valeyard's existence even though the Doctor wasn't and had offered him all the Doctor's remaining lives if he could successfully frame the Doctor for the council's own actions. The Doctor demanded the trial be thrown out and, in the confusion, the Valeyard fled.

Following him out of the courtroom, the Doctor and the Keeper recognised the Seventh Door into the Matrix, just outside. Using the Keeper's key, the Doctor and Glitz followed the Valeyard inside and found themselves in a recreation of Victorian London. The Doctor appeared first and followed the distant echo of the Valeyard's maniacal laughter to a nearby building. Hands reached out from a water barrel outside to try and drown him but Glitz arrived just in time to stop them. He handed the Doctor a note from the Master saying exactly where the Valeyard was hiding and, as the Doctor read the building's name aloud, it appeared behind them. As they approached, Glitz was shot in the chest with a harpoon and apparently killed.

Back in the courtroom, the Master explained that the Valeyard had only tweaked small sections of the evidence to convict the Doctor, and that Peri had in fact survived. He also admitted that the Valeyard was a more powerful enemy than the Doctor and he hoped the pair would destroy each other. He also revealed, to the horror of the people watching, that he had ensured that the court proceedings were shown on Gallifrey and now, every Time Lord knew the truth.

Back in the Matrix, Glitz had been saved by his Mark 7 Positidion Life Preserver. He and the Doctor entered the Fantasy Factory where the Valeyard was based and were confronted by Mr Popplewick, an officious bureaucrat. The Doctor and Glitz tried to reason with him but eventually barged past to discover... an exact duplicate of Mr Popplewick. The Duplicate explained that the 'Very Junior Mr Popplewick' was programmed not to expect visitors and had the Doctor sign a form agreeing that should he die the Valeyard would receive all his future lives. The Doctor and Glitz were told to wait for the Valeyard to see them but instead pushed on through the next door. Instead of an office, the Doctor found himself alone on a beach. He called for Glitz but suddenly hands appeared from beneath the sand and dragged him down. A horrified Glitz arrived and tried to save the Doctor but was too late.

A few seconds later, the Doctor rose out of the sand nearby, completely unharmed. He explained that reality was so mutable in the Matrix that he could deny the Valeyard's traps with enough effort. Suddenly, the Valeyard appeared, popping in out of existence and taunting the Doctor. He explained that if he killed the Doctor he'd be whole, not only receiving all his remaining lives but finally be freed from all the Doctor's good qualities. He disappeared and a cloud of nerve gas blew in, forcing the Doctor and Glitz to take refuge inside a nearby beach hut.

The hut turned out to be the Master's TARDIS who explained that the Valeyard lacked all the Doctor's morality. This meant he was more evil than the Master, and the Master couldn't accept the idea of a rival. He had to be stopped. The Master lied to the Doctor, saying he and Glitz needed to retrieve his Tissue Compression Eliminator from elsewhere in the TARDIS and left the control room. As they did so, the Master triggered a massive burst of sensory information that rendered the Doctor catatonic. Explaining that this way he could use the hypnotised Doctor to draw the Valeyard out, the Master shifted his TARDIS to the Glitz Factory and ordered the

Doctor out into the courtyard. The hypnotised Time Lord obeyed and the Master and Glitz hid as the Valeyard came out to see what was going on. The Master ambushed him but the TCE had no effect and the Valeyard fired back with explosive quills that knocked Glitz out and forced the Master to flee.

The Doctor stood completely still in the middle of the courtyard. Mel's voice finally broke him from the trance. She explained that the Valeyard had fled and took him back to the station to clear his name. However, when the Inquisitor repeated the clip showing the murder of the Vervoids and asked Mel if that was what had happened, she had to agree. The Inquisitor found the Doctor guilty of genocide and ordered his remaining lives forfeit. He accepted the sentence.

In the real courtroom, Mel and the Inquisitor watched as the Doctor was apparently led to his own execution. Unable to stand by, Mel stole the Keeper's key and entered the Matrix. She reached the Doctor in time to save him, but was amazed to find out he knew the truth. He explained that the Mel who'd 'rescued' him knew things she couldn't possibly know and he was using the execution to force a confrontation with the Valeyard. Together, they set off for the Fantasy Factory.

Back in the Master's TARDIS, he tried to hypnotise Glitz into helping him but, when it failed, used bribery. The Master persuaded Glitz to return to the Doctor and 'help' him and Glitz did so. On the way, he found the master copy of the Matrix Secrets he'd seen destroyed on Ravolox. Mr Popplewick confronted him and Glitz forced the servant to take the Doctor and himself to 'Mr Chambers'. Glitz returned to the Master's TARDIS and the Doctor and Mel confronted Popplewick. The Doctor peeled off Popplewick's mask to reveal the Valeyard. They discovered that, concealed in the room was a particle disseminator that would fire through the Matrix screen and murder everyone in the courtroom. The Doctor sent Mel back to warn the Time Lords and frantically tried to defuse the device as his evil self looked on.

Back in the courtroom, the Inquisitor learned that the High Council had stood down and there was anarchy on the streets of Gallifrey. The Master offered to help, in return for absolute rule. As he made this offer, he put the tape carrying the Matrix secrets into his TARDIS console. However, the Valeyard hid the real tape, and the fake locked the Master and Glitz in place as it distorted time inside his TARDIS.

Mel got back to the courtroom and warned them but they were unable to turn off the screen. They began to evacuate as the Doctor sabotaged the Valeyard's weapon and fled, causing a massive feedback loop that encompassed his enemy and destroyed the Fantasy Factory. The effect also lashed the courtroom through the screen as the people still in there took cover.

The Doctor made it back to the courtroom and found everyone was alright. The Inquisitor gratefully dropped all the charges and told the Doctor that Peri had lived after all. The Doctor was relieved and also surprised when the Inquisitor asked him to stand for President. With the High Council gone, the Doctor was now a senior Time Lord and a strong candidate. He declined and endorsed the Inquisitor instead. On his way out of the courtroom, he asked that the Time Lords be lenient with Glitz. He and Mel left, and she began, once again, talking to him about his exercise regime.

In the courtroom, the Inquisitor ordered the Keeper of the Matrix to begin helping with the clean-up. He agreed, but, unseen by her, was now the Valeyard...

RUNNING THE ADVENTURE

This is far and away the hardest of these adventures to run, because it's where the two plotlines meet and resolve. If the timing in the previous has gone wrong, it will become apparent here. Likewise, any changes you've made to the trial mean there's a good chance some of this adventure hasn't, or won't, happen. From the outside, it looks daunting, but when you break it down there are three events and a problem in this adventure that need to be addressed if you're going to run it successfully.

The first is the Master's intervention, which in this case involves sending Mel and Glitz to provide new evidence. Firstly there's a lot of fun to be had with exactly how and when he finds them and gets them to the travel capsules (in fact, this is a perfect way to bring any characters marooned on Thoros Beta back into the fold). Secondly, this is the moment that forces the hand of the Valeyard, sets up the Matrix as a legitimately threatening environment and finally shows the treachery of the High Council.

All of which are ideas that can be expressed earlier and in different formats or adventures. You don't even need to have people sent to the station, as long as all the other characters are already there. In fact, the Master's presence in the Matrix could pose such a huge threat that the Doctor's trial is suspended whilst it's dealt with, or he and the other characters are forced to work with the Valeyard to defeat the Master. This is a mutable event, one you can put where you need to and use in any way you see fit.

The second event is trickier. The revelation that the Valeyard is the Doctor's dark side is so climactic it has to come at the end of the campaign. That means it has to come in this final adventure, whatever form you choose to run it in. One way would be to have the characters or Doctor realise it thanks to a clue he's left on the forged Matrix evidence or a slip up in mannerism or turn of phrase. Another would be to have the Master working more insidiously, using an agent in the courtroom to slip the Doctor clues or to trick the Valeyard. If you wanted to you could have the Doctor make an Awareness + Knowledge roll (Difficulty 30) the first time they appear in the courtroom, then again at 25 every time the Matrix has been tampered with. Drop it between 2 and 5 points every time this takes place until the Doctor realises the only person who could successfully frame him... is him. This relies on a dice roll, which isn't going to work for some people, but does give the agency in the adventure back to the characters instead of simply having them react. Regardless of how you get it, bear in mind this fact is the one that accelerates the entire campaign towards its end so make sure you're ready when it is revealed.

This in turn leads to the question of what exactly you do with the Valeyard. The Doctor left him, presumed dead, in the Matrix in the adventure, but he clearly got out. Again, any changes you made to the campaign along the way may dictate changes to the fate of the Valeyard, but even without those there are some interesting places you can go.

The most obvious one is the Valeyard lives, and escapes to fight another day as he does here. There's a lot to recommend that, after all Time Lords love the long game and he's a fantastic recurring villain. However, after such an intense few adventures your characters may want a little more closure.

The Valeyard being imprisoned on Gallifrey offers a lot of possibilities. He's the Doctor and, crucially, he's the Doctor from towards the end of his life meaning that he's vastly more experienced. The idea of the Valeyard being an early warning system of sorts for the Time Lords has a lot of potential.

DOES THE VALEYARD KNOW ABOUT THE TIME WAR?

That's unclear, so it's up to you. If he does, and he survives the campaign, you could either paint him as a tragic hero trying to save Gallifrey from the man who will ultimately burn it or a traitor who wants to see his people destroyed and manipulates both them and the Daleks into war. Either way, once the Valeyard gets wind of the Time War, and the Doctor's actions within it, no power in the universe will stop him trying to use that to gain the advantage over his rival.

If the Valeyard remains at liberty then you could always have him insinuate his way further into Gallifreyan society, either to control it, prepare it or manipulate it towards the coming war. He has the potential to be as fun a renegade Time Lord as the Master, the Rani or the Monk just with an added... personal touch.

One interesting way of playing things would be to have the Valeyard try and manifest earlier in the Doctor's life, perhaps by going back and altering some of his decisions. After all, he does have unlimited access to the Matrix, so he knows where and when to strike.

DOES THE VALEYARD HAVE A TARDIS?

We never see it, but probably, and given his origin, it might well be the Doctor's own TARDIS, just from a different time in his life. This is another way the Valeyard can strike back at the Doctor, by overwriting his era's TARDIS with the Valeyard's own. Think of ***Journey to the Centre of the TARDIS*** (see **The Eleventh Doctor Sourcebook**) but with a raging, evil TARDIS instead of an angry, hurt one.

If the Valeyard's truly dead then that also opens up some interesting possibilities. The Doctor, fascinated, and horrified, by the absence he now feels could begin to skew towards the darker, grimmer behaviour his future self showed. He could be haunted by visions of his future self and driven to try and save him somehow. Alternatively, the Valeyard could manipulate the Doctor into fanning the flames of the Time War, knowing from his own position further up the time stream just how much damage it will do the Doctor.

Then of course there's the possibility that the Valeyard wins. If this happens, then the Doctor's remaining lives are gifted to the Valeyard and the Doctor is executed.

Except, of course, the Doctor and the Valeyard are the same person so how can that be? The easiest solution here is simply to swap their personalities. Having the Valeyard at the centre of the group has a lot of potential for drama, especially if it becomes apparent the Doctor is still there, desperate to get his body back. Perhaps an unscheduled trip to Thoros Beta and the Consciousness Transference Machine is in order?

Finally, there's the resignation of the entire High Council. This is the one that has the least immediate impact on your characters but the largest possible impact on future adventures. The Time Lords are one of the oldest, most powerful societies in the universe and this adventure reveals that not only are they engaged in a cold war with the Andromedans but that they are prepared to do anything to protect themselves. Even worse, with the Doctor refusing the Presidency, the Time Lords are leaderless until the Inquisitor can be voted in.

Again there are a couple of ways this can be played. The most obvious is that the Inquisitor is made Madame President and the Time Lords get things back on track. This opens up the possibility of a closer relationship with the Time Lords, with the Inquisitor calling on the Doctor for his expertise and as exactly the sort of 'deniable' agent he's been numerous times in the past. Who knows, maybe she's the one who has him install the phone that's in the TARDIS console from the Ninth Doctor onwards...

Similarly, you could have the Inquisitor elected but with the Valeyard's influence growing ever stronger, leading to her sending the Doctor on ever more dangerous missions or keeping him on Gallifrey more and more until the Valeyard has the chance to strike.

Another, far more radical option would be to have the Doctor agree to become President once again. The entire focus of the campaign could shift to Gallifrey with the other characters adjusting to life as part of the President's staff, living in the middle of one of the oldest cultures in the universe and running into the various other companions that end up there. Or, you could have the Doctor as a hands-on President, still doing what he normally does but being directed to places by the Time Lords. Essentially exactly the same set up as them using him as an agent, they're just much more up front about it.

This adventure offers countless opportunities to take your characters in new directions. Be bold, seize the opportunities and see where, and when you end up. Who knows, if the Doctor sticks around on Gallifrey they may finally fix the TARDIS' Chameleon Circuit.

MR POPPLEWICK

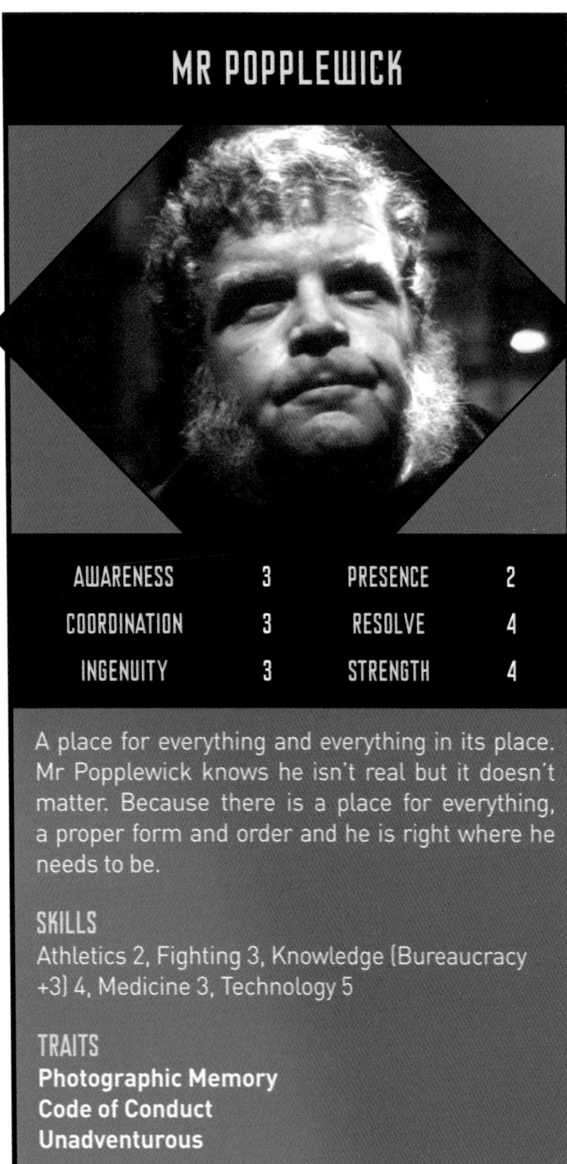

AWARENESS	3	PRESENCE	2
COORDINATION	3	RESOLVE	4
INGENUITY	3	STRENGTH	4

A place for everything and everything in its place. Mr Popplewick knows he isn't real but it doesn't matter. Because there is a place for everything, a proper form and order and he is right where he needs to be.

SKILLS

Athletics 2, Fighting 3, Knowledge (Bureaucracy +3) 4, Medicine 3, Technology 5

TRAITS

Photographic Memory
Code of Conduct
Unadventurous

THE ANDROMEDANS

Here's what the Doctor knows about the Andromedans by the end of this adventure:

- They're from the Andromedan galaxy.
- Getting from there to this galaxy takes so long they have to enter suspended animation to survive the trip.
- The Andromedans broke into the Matrix and stole some of the Time Lords' secrets. Then, they hid out on Earth and waited for the robotic recovery vessel that had been sent to get them.
- The Time Lords used the Magnetron to move Earth and in doing so made certain the recovery vessel would miss the Sleepers. They then arranged to have the secrets retrieved in such a way that they couldn't be traced.

This is interesting, certainly, but when running this adventure it boils down to 'These mysterious people you never met stole a thing you didn't know about and hid on Earth causing all this bother.' There's no context as to why the Andromedans did this or how they did, making this part of the adventure somewhat incomplete. So, here are a few things you can do with the Andromedans that makes them a more tangible threat both here and in future adventures:

- In ***The Mysterious Planet***, replace Drathro and the L2 with the Sleepers, giving them a face and a presence and dropping some early hints that they're interested in Time Lord secrets. Don't explain them, but make them feel like a real threat.
- In ***Mindwarp***, drop hints that Crozier is working for the Andromedans or that Sil has recently bought into an 'off-galaxy' futures company interested in consciousness transferral.
- In ***Terror of the Vervoids***, have the Andromedans back one of the hijacking attempts and change the ship's course so it's heading towards one of their own robotic vessels.

THE MATRIX

The Matrix is arguably the most incredible thing the Time Lords ever created; a micro-universe designed like a brain and filled with countless intelligences and a complete back up of all the Time Lords who had reached the end of their lives. A constantly evolving history of the universe, the Matrix was added to every second of every day and monitored by Time Lords of the highest rank and stature. It was often used as a sandbox, the Time Lords simulating events within the Matrix so they could react accordingly when those events The constantly mutable nature of reality within the Matrix means that anyone with the strength of will can shape it how they see fit and also means deadly force is always in the hands of those who want it. However, this element of its makeup had been lost to history and was only rediscovered when the Four Doctor was forced to engage then Chancellor Goth in a mental duel that took place on a landscape Goth had created. Since then, the Time Lords' ability to shape reality within the Matrix has been commonplace and, as this adventure shows, that's not a good thing.

ENTERING THE MATRIX

Entering the Matrix normally requires a physical connection to one of the linking machines, enabling the Time Lord to connect their mind with the countless numbers already in there. However, the Seventh Door into the Matrix can also be used to enter it physically. The first difference is immediacy; using the Door is instantaneous, using the machine takes a couple of Action Rounds. In each case, the sheer density of information causes a level of damage to the Time Lord that carries over to their presence in the Matrix. The second is that whilst Deny Reality can still be used, any damage caused in the Matrix is carried back to the real world.

BUILDING A WORLD IN THE MATRIX

To create a virtual world like the one the Valeyard used, the character must spend sufficient time building it. This costs 3 Story Points and allows the character to build the world they want to interact with. This could be anything from the Dickensian offices that the Valeyard favours to a stag night boat cruising down the Thames in 2013 or a tropical island in the 52nd century. If the character doesn't have something specific in mind, their subconscious will and you can establish the base reality.

WAR IN THE MATRIX

War in the Matrix is a complex thing, based on nuance and will more than strength. The two minds at war clash with each other using four basic abilities, all of which cost Story Points.

Enforce Reality (1SP)

Whenever another character attempts to Deny Reality, the creator of the virtual world they're in can cancel that action by spending a Story Point themselves and winning an Opposed Resolve + Convince roll. Think of the Nerve Gas that forces Glitz and the Doctor up the beach.

Create Reality(1SP)

The creator can pull whatever object they need out of thin air. Anything from a backpack to an Androgum can be conjured up by making a Resolve + Convince roll at Difficulty 12. However, anything, or anyone, created disappears at the end of the scene. They can be added to the world permanently by spending an additional Story Point. Unless you're already thinking of dialling up a previous incarnation of the Doctor. Those don't come as cheap, with a Difficulty of 14 and a Story Point cost of 2. The explosive quills the Valeyard throws at Glitz and the Master are a good example of this.

Deny Reality (1SP)

The character flat out refuses to believe something has happened, undoing it through sheer force of will and by making a Resolve + Convince (Difficulty 15) roll. The Doctor rising back up out of the beach, completely unharmed, would be the same effect.

Augment Reality (2SP)

The character makes a small change to the environment of the Matrix, such as finding a passage, or successfully unlocking a door. The Valeyard used this ability to make the screen into the Matrix both visible to him and two way, allowing him to murder the council.

ENDING THE CONFLICT

Once two minds are engaged in a Matrix conflict, both are locked into the dream world until the 'creator' mind withdraws, is rendered unconscious or is killed. Once this has occurred, any remaining characters must make a Resolve + Convince roll at Difficulty 15 to escape. Being killed in the Matrix results in the brain death of the physical body that inhabits the real world. Damage to Strength and Coordination does not carry over into the real world, but all other damage does. Having the Matrix disconnected while the character's mind is still inside will cause 2D6 damage to the character from the shock of the sudden disconnection.

TRAVEL CAPSULES/EXTRACTION TARDISES

For a Time Lord to go anywhere quickly, something has to have gone badly wrong. However, when you live for millennia, things often do go badly wrong and if a Time Lord is luckless enough to lose their TARDIS, they still need to make their way home. Travel Capsules were created for these dire situations, a TARDIS within a TARDIS, which the Time Lord could flee to when their main vessel broke down. The capsules are programmed with one destination – Gallifrey – and lack the scale of a standard TARDIS. Instead, they have mission-adaptable interiors, wrapping their charge up in inertia dampening foam for take-off and landing and expanding into a comfortable, spacious set of rooms for travel. A modified version was also used during the Time War to extract Time Lords from dangerous situations.

An Extraction TARDIS would be placed within a few miles of the Time Lords' location, programmed to look like a building or a vehicle and to wait. In many cases they were used by Time Lords fleeing a Dalek assault or bringing vital intelligence back. Some, though, still remain unused, quietly sitting in their assigned locations, waiting for a passenger who will never come.

AWARENESS	1	PRESENCE	1
COORDINATION	4	RESOLVE	4
INGENUITY	5	STRENGTH	5

SKILLS
Knowledge 8, Medicine 1, Science (Temporal Physics +2) 6, Technology 6, Transport 2.

TRAITS
Chameleon Circuit
Code of Conduct
Face in the Crowd
Fast Healing
Feel the Turn of the Universe
Forcefield (Minor)
Hostile Action Displacement System
Isomorphic Controls
Life Support
Lucky
Psychic
Scan (x2)
Sense of Direction
Telepathy
Tough
Transmit
Vortex
Unadventurous

ISOMORPHIC CONTROLS (MINOR): These lock the TARDIS so it can only be used by the passenger Time Lord. The controls can be reset once the TARDIS arrives at its destination, but prior to that anyone other than the passenger trying to modify them will receiving an electric shock (1 level of damage per round of contact after the first). Disabling the system requires a TL7 or higher species to make an Ingenuity+ Technology Roll (Difficulty 18).

LIFE SUPPORT (MAJOR): The TARDIS Life Support systems are designed to give the operator the ability to tailor their environment however they see fit. This appears to be a luxury but in many cases, the Time Lord piloting the Extraction TARDIS has either been altered to suit the environment of their mission or is evacuating the area with assistants. The Life Support controls allow the environment to be tailored to all their needs.

ARMOUR: 20

SPEED: 19 (MATERIALISED)

STARTING DAMAGE: D6 +2 POINTS

COST: 3

TECH LEVEL: 10 **STORY POINTS:** 3-5

MAGNETRON

During the Dark Times, when the Time Lords warred with the Great Vampires, difficult decisions had to be made. Time Lord criminals were offered new regeneration cycles in return for deniable missions, Time Lords went deep into the primordial past of the universe to try and cut the vampires off at the root and when they couldn't, they went to war. The Bow Ships of the Time Lords are the stuff of nightmare, and legend, the universe over but there are two devices more powerful, and terrifying, even than them: the Cruciform and the Magnetron.

The Magnetron remains preserved on Gallifrey as a reminder of what the Time Lords were once capable of. It's a planetary scoop, using black hole energy to manipulate the fabric of space to near breaking point. This effectively 'yanks' the target, be it a planet or solar system, light years away from where it had previously been located. The effect is horrific, massive atmospheric fires and seismic activity killing most of the population. As a result, it was used as a last ditch weapon, either to save worlds from being consumed by the Great Vampires or, in the bad, middle stages of the war, to deny them of food planets they'd already taken over.

The Magnetron is one of the most powerful weapons ever created, and even using it requires a unanimous vote of the Gallifreyan High Council. The only time this has happened post war was the decision to move Earth and its solar system in order to prevent the Andromedan Sleepers from acquiring Gallifreyan secrets.

> The Magnetron is a weapon of absolute last resort that does near total damage. It's not something the characters should ever get their hands on. Besides, the consequences of it being used are much more interesting, as Ravolox demonstrates.

MARK 7 COSTIDILLION LIFE PRESERVER (MAJOR GADGET)

The danger faced by a traveller, in space, time or both can change in seconds and sometimes armour just isn't enough. Costidillion Industries (a subsidiary of GMC, of course) have developed the answer to this problem with the Costidillion Mark 7 Life Preserver. A small unit worn on the belt or shoulder pad of any enterprising traveller, freelance security consultant or retrieval specialist, it monitors radiation, motion and the heart and adrenal rates of its wearer. As long as they remain stable, the Mark 7 does nothing.

Should any of those change across a 5 second period, the Mark 7 analyses the change, comes up with the best fit response to it and acts. This takes the form of either a full body force field in the event of explosive decompression, fire or cold or a localised force field facing any attack. This field is extremely strong, removing -4 from a successful to hit roll.

The Mark 7 has proved highly successful although it does have problems in sustained emergencies. After the initial attack, the wearer must make an Ingenuity + Technology roll (Difficulty 14) to ensure the unit has time to cool down. The second time it's used the difficulty raises to 16, and so on by increments of 2. Once the preserver fails, the next damage done it is all transferred to the wearer.

Cost: 2 Story Points

FURTHER ADVENTURES

- **The Sleeper Wakes:** The Doctor and his companions are contacted by an Andromedan envoy who wishes to negotiate a non-aggression treaty. He requests a meeting on Titan III and the TARDIS sets off, carrying a group of demanding Gallifreyan dignitaries to carry out the talks. When they arrive on Titan III, the crew are shocked to find that the Andromedans share a single, galaxy-wide consciousness and are curious as to why everyone in our galaxy isn't networked together. As the talks continue, they come to understand why and relations between the Time Lords and the Andromedans are going well.

  Until, with the sound of a thousand TARDIS engines, Titan III dematerialises and reappears hanging high above the galactic plain.

The asteroid is a Time Lord relic, left over from the Dark Times. It's been programmed to act as a final quarantine post for Time Lords too ill or insane to return home and, when the characters reach the central computer, they find its convinced that everyone on the asteroid is infected. Then the Doctor hears the Andromedan Singularity whispering in his head. A nano-technological plague has been released by the Andromedans. It's harmless, designed to connect each mind present but Titan III has reacted to it and unless the characters can cure it, the asteroid will never let any of them return home.

- **The Other Doctors:** The First Doctor appears on every Matrix screen on Gallifrey, irritably tapping on the glass before disappearing. A few seconds later, the Second and Third, in mid-argument, appear. Then the Fourth and the Fifth. All of them seem trapped and all of them have one message: "SEND FOR A DOCTOR"

The Doctor and his companions are summoned to a Gallifrey starting to grind to a halt. Something is infecting the minds of everyone in the Matrix and they're starting to die. But how do you cure a disease that only exists in a pocket universe? Why is it affecting so many Time Lords but none of the other brains in there? And who is the mysterious, bonneted figure, holding a night light, tending to the sick who disappears whenever someone approaches? As the Matrix begins to fade, the Doctor and his companions find the answer lies on Ravolox in the days after the fireball. But when they get there, they find they're far from alone. A Sontaran raiding party is scouring the burning remains of London and, hiding out from them are three men who also claim to be the Doctor and they have the answer to what's infecting the Matrix. If they can just get off Ravolox alive to deliver it...

- **The Ghosts of Justice:** Decommissioned after the controversy surrounding the Doctor's trial, the Justice Station has been moved into orbit around Gallifrey and is set to be decommissioned. On the night of the ceremony, though, the station reactivates, grabs the Doctor, his companions, the Inquisitor and the Master and vanishes. Inside, the crew have been hypnotised and when the Doctor finally breaks the conditioning, they tell him the truth. The station contains a small adjunct to the Matrix and every Time Lord sentenced in its court has their brain patterns stored there. Now, one has led a revolt and is heading for Dalek space, looking to barter Gallifreyan secrets for new, Dalek bodies. Now, the characters must work together with the Valeyard, inside the Matrix, to stop the Station before the Daleks get their hands on it.

APPENDIX
THE SIXTH DOCTOR AND THE TIME WAR

APPENDIX: THE SIXTH DOCTOR AND THE TIME WAR

INTRODUCTION

The first shots of the Time War have already been fired (see **The Fourth Doctor Sourcebook**), and while there is not yet open conflict in this era, there very well may soon be.

The Sixth Doctor's adventures can be read one of two ways. The first is exactly as it's presented here, with each adventure taking place in a separate place and time and almost no consequences carrying over, aside from the trial. The second way to look at these adventures, is that they're shaped and in some cases defined by the Time War. Looked at this way, the Sixth Doctor, the Rani, the Master and even the Valeyard were all intricately connected to the war, even though they had no knowledge of it yet. It's a different perspective and one you don't have to use by any means. However, if you're running a Time War or post-Time War campaign, then there are ideas here that may be of use to you.

THE TWIN DILEMMA

It's entirely possible that either the Valeyard or the Great Intelligence drove the Doctor to his fatal actions on Androzani. More importantly, the very odd nature of Mestor and the origin story of the 'Sun God' sending the Gastropods to plague Jaconda fits the conflict perfectly. Look at it this way: the Sun God was a Time Lord (Azmael perhaps) who, faced with the strategically vital world of Jaconda falling to the Daleks or simply being wiped out, created a new species that could hold the line. The damage to the world was incalculable, but the Gastropods were hugely physically tough creatures that even the Daleks would struggle to kill. Jaconda would be laid waste, but the line would be held. This would also explain why Azmael, a Time Lord, is Master of Jaconda and also his extreme age. Perhaps he was in charge of the Jacondan Front and, seeing the havoc wreaked on the world by his orders, decided to stay and help as best he could. He didn't tell the Doctor either because he knew it wasn't time for him to know yet or because he too couldn't perceive the conflict despite his part in it.

Adventure Seed

Midnight Sun: With the Daleks massing a fleet on the outskirts of the Jaconda Sector, the Doctor and his companions must travel into the far future of the system to find the Forge, an ancient piece of technology that modifies and enhances any living matter placed within it. When they find it, it's in the hands of a seemingly perfect humanoid man who claims to be Ja'Co, God of the Sun. He refuses to release the Forge to them and the characters must pass a series of tests before sending it back. However, the Daleks track them, enter the Forge and emerge as perfect, serene beings of peace. Now, the Doctor and his companions must work out how to protect this new strain of Dalek and decide whether they can change history and end the war early.

ATTACK OF THE CYBERMEN

The Sixth Doctor runs into far too many experimental time machines for it to be a coincidence. Perhaps the human-designed ship here originated in the 52nd century and was a Time Agency vessel initially sent out to explore the increasingly violent anomalies in the Vortex. Thrown off course by the constant changes caused by the war, it was captured by the Cybermen, who brought it to Telos to try and reverse engineer it, or to use it as a trap to lure in a Time Lord such as the Doctor. It's clear some other races were aware of what was going on and perhaps the Cybermen were amongst those who wanted to take advantage of the temporal chaos.

Adventure Seed

The First:The time machine is discovered, adrift in the Vortex. The TARDIS materializes around it and as the characters explore they find things which seem familiar. The ship is flown from a three sided central console, the time rotor, whilst actually a rotor, rises and falls at the centre of the control room and even the ship's layout seems oddly familiar. They realise that it's more than just an attempt to replicate a TARDIS, it's a direct ancestor of the original TARDISes. Somehow, the time machine made its way to Gallifrey in the distant past and inspired the construction of everything that follows. Now, the ship is unstuck in time, echoes of its past and future walking its corridors and the characters must save it, and hide it from the Daleks, to protect every TARDIS that's to come.

VENGEANCE ON VAROS

The Mentors are entirely too similar in name and appearance to the Gastropods to be a coincidence. Elsewhere in the book, the idea that Mestor is a hyper-evolved Mentor is put forward but it could just as easily be the other way, with Sil and his race the result of massively accelerated or tampered with evolution in the war. Whoever has Sil in their pocket has Varos, whoever has Varos has the Zeitan-7 and whoever has the Zeitan-7 has time travel, making it a vital world and one that Sil and the Mentors could not just hold but exploit in exactly the needed way.

Adventure Seed

Time Rush: A new source of Zeitan-7 has been found on an asteroid called Nostrum Alpha, and all over Varos and the surrounding systems, miners are racing to get their share. The TARDIS lands on the Bad Gamble, one such prospecting vessel and finds things have already started to go wrong. The ship's engines have been sabotaged, the other ships aren't responding to hails and one of the crew comes back from a spacewalk several decades older than when she went out. Time is breaking down around Nostrum Alpha, and the characters must work out whether the trap has been set for the Time Lords, or by them.

MARK OF THE RANI

The Rani isn't, in fact, a Renegade. She's a deep cover Time Lord agent, a woman who volunteered to be ostracised forever in order to carry out the work that needed to be done to win the war. Her experiments on Earth aren't just an effort to save her people, they're also an attempt to work out how to weaponise humanity in the coming war. The Time Lords know that the Doctor favours Earth and crucially, so do the Daleks. The war is coming to Earth, soon, and the Rani is the advance party dedicated to making humanity battle-ready, whether it wants to be or not.

Similarly, you could have the Master, who we know was recruited by the Time Lords to fight at some point in the Time War, sent there to trigger the Industrial Revolution in an early, more focused fashion that would allow Earth to become a weapons hub for the Time Lords.

Adventure Seed

Deniable Operations: The Rani is on the run, her TARDIS is gone and the Daleks are closing in. She pleads with the Doctor to help her return to Gallifrey, but in her past rather than the present. She reveals that she's been acting under orders from the High Council for centuries, but now she's been discovered and has only one option left: cross her own timeline, talk to her younger self and persuade her not to become the woman the Rani is. The characters must decide whether to allow this, stop her or help in a different way, even, as suspicions grow that the Rani's true objective may be delivering the Doctor to her real employer: Davros.

THE TWO DOCTORS

The Third Zone governments clearly have some inkling of the Time War, hence their desperation to not only get the Time Lords to assist in the construction of the KR module, but to perfect it. They can sense the war raging around them and

want some acknowledgement of it. Similarly, the Sontarans can tell the conflict is raging and are desperate to take part in it. Their plan is simple; steal the KR module, take it to Sontar and perfect it, then send countless thousands of clones out across time to engage with Time Lord and Dalek wherever they encounter them.

Or maybe, the entire thing is an elaborate Time Lord ruse designed to spread the Androgum genetic propensity for strength, tenacity and aggression across the universe by sending 'failed' experiments into the time stream. These Androgums are in fact sent to vital points in the history of strategic worlds, becoming heroes (Alexander the Great on Earth perhaps) and instilling both the mindset of the warrior and their genetic traits into the populace. This way, humanity and the other Androgum-seeded races becomes a natural 'firebreak' for the Daleks, fighting them wherever they encounter them and giving the Time Lords much-needed time to regroup.

Adventure Seed

The Last Battle: The KR module has been stolen from the hacienda in Spain and the characters must retrieve it before the damage to the time line is irreparable. They track it to the far future and are amazed to discover that the Sontarans eventually become a spiritual race who have no use for war. Stoll, the Sontaran that stole the module, is disgusted and attempts to take control of the planet, diving back into Sontar's past to find the exact moment the "affliction" began. The characters must find him, stop him and then return the module to the hacienda.

TIMELASH

The Borad is a Time Lord, placed, like Azmael, on Karfel at a strategically vital time in its life. However, where Azmael was interested in work that would let the Time Lords hold the line, The Borad's work was focused on the worst case scenario. If the Daleks won, the Time Lords would need to change massively to survive and the Borad, along with his colleague, the Rani, argued passionately in favour of genetic diversification. However, the Rani argued that the existing Time Lord form could be enhanced but kept intact whilst the Borad became convinced they had to change altogether. He engineered the hideous accident with the Morlox to prove this and became completely obsessed with using Karfelons as a test case for how the Time Lords could not only survive, but improve.

Adventure Seed

The People of the Loch: The TARDIS arrives in the year 1910 on the shores of Loch Fyne. A funeral is being carried out but it's one unlike anything the characters have ever seen before.

The body is treated as though it's just been born, gifts and presents surrounding the casket which is placed on a quay on the loch shore. Suddenly, there's a disturbance out in the water, a burst of regeneration energy from the coffin and the 'corpse' stands up and admires its new body. No one has truly died in Loch Fyne for 700 years, thanks to the Borad and his research. Now, the characters must work out if the Borad has reformed, how he's given the people of the loch the ability to regenerate and what will happen when the Daleks, hot on the heels of the TARDIS, arrive.

REVELATION OF THE DALEKS

Davros set up on Necros having seen the way the Time War was starting to go. He viewed the human Daleks as a logical extension of the Time Lords' own experiments with humanity and carefully split his test population away from the rest of the galaxy who he quietly began to poison using the protein extract. That way he got the best of both worlds, a new supply of Daleks and a galaxy-wide assault on the races he knew he would have to conquer without having to sacrifice a single Dalek to do it.

You could also work this so a version of the Time War has already been fought, and Orcini and his fellow Knights were on the front lines, explaining his special desire to kill Davros. Or, given the amount of wars the Daleks have been involved in, perhaps Orcini's experience comes from them.

Adventure Seed

The Knights of Davros: Famed throughout the galaxy for their courage and dedication to defending the weak, the Knights of Davros and their leader, Orcini are beloved wherever they go. They saved the galaxy from the Gallifreyan tyrants and now, with Davros Station opening, will unify the galaxy once and for all under the single, benevolent mind of their patron, St Davros.

Something is horribly wrong. The Daleks have won and now, in a time line where TARDISes are hunted through the vortex by modified Dalek 'Timehounds', the Doctor and his companions must travel to the near future, and a secret battle on Earth's moon, to stop this time line becoming fixed.

THE MYSTERIOUS PLANET

This is an event intricately tied up in the Time War already, but there are other ways to approach it. Firstly, Earth could be moved as much because the Time Lords want to hide it from the Daleks as from the Andromedans. After all, the Matrix Secrets stolen by the Andromedans could be as much use to the Daleks as themselves. Or you could have the Andromedans working for the Daleks meaning the Time Lords use the Magnetron to not only hide Earth but burn any remaining Dalek sympathisers from its surface.

Adventure Seed

Mind of the Daleks: Whether the Andromedans were working for the Daleks or not, it doesn't matter, they're all dead now. The Daleks have landed on Ravolox and intercepted the Matrix Secrets from the Andromedans. There goal: to enter the Matrix itself and exterminate the greatest treasure trove of the Time Lords. The characters must enter the Matrix themselves and do battle with some of the most twisted minds ever to have lived.

MINDWARP

Crozier is working for the Time Lords on a means of transferring consciences into new bodies. This is being done for two reasons: to help Time Lord spies go undetected and to provide a final escape for the Time Lords in the event they lose the war, much like the Borad's research. The discovery of this project by the Doctor also explains his removal at the exact moment it takes place and the Council's eagerness to destroy any trace of the project or their involvement with it.

Or maybe, Crozier is working for the Daleks in an effort to perfect conscience transferral so each Dalek can be immediately transferred into a new body, retaining their memories and experiences.

Adventure Seed

Timewarp: The success of Crozier's research comes as no surprise to the Time Lords. He is their last best hope to survive the end of the Time War. At the instance that the Doctor uses the Moment, the most powerful of the Time Lords transfer their consciousnesses back in time to specially prepared clone batches beneath Thoros Beta. As the Sixth Doctor returns from the Justice Station to find Yrcanos and Peri, he also finds future incarnations of the Time Lords – more terrible and vengeful than those he has just escaped – waking up, and not one, not two but three future incarnations of himself hot on their heels.

TERROR OF THE VERVOIDS

The Daleks steer Professor Lasky's research so the demeter seeds and Vervoids are both ready at the same time. They plan to release them over Earth, turning the planet into one huge demeter plant and establishing the Vervoids as the new dominant race. The Daleks will then conquer them, a much easier proposition than dealing with humanity.

Or maybe the Time Lords, desperate for Zeitan-7, try and mine it from Mogar. The Daleks also arrive and the ensuing battle strips the planet of its atmosphere and renders the Zeitan-7 unusuable for thousands of years. The Time Lords manipulate Professor Lasky's research so the demeter seeds will grow into plants that refine the Zeitan-7 and in doing so force her down the route that leads to the creations of the Vervoids.

Adventure Seed

Winter of the Vervoids: Earth is a planet-sized jungle and the Vervoids live there in peace. Time has been changed so humanity simply never existed and soon, when the demeter seeds extract the trace hints of Zeitan-7 from Earth's crust, the planet will burn when the Dalek fleet descends. The TARDIS, barely surviving the massive change to the timeline, arrives on Earth and is faced not only with helping the Vervoids stop the Daleks but repairing the time line so humanity can be saved.

THE ULTIMATE FOE

Possible motivations for the Valeyard were discussed earlier, but the Justice Station, and the interest in the Doctor, could have a real bearing on the Time War. Perhaps the Matrix has shown the Time Lords how the Doctor ends the war and they're desperate to stop their future deaths at his hands.

Adventure Seed

War Without End: The Time War rages in the open, worlds and people popping in and out of existence at random. The characters are veterans, sent deep into Dalek-held territory to retrieve a prisoner who cannot be allowed to stay in the Daleks' hands. He's a highly experienced soldier with detailed knowledge of the Time Lords' plans and if the Daleks break him then all is lost. He's being held on Earth, their most feared prison planet and his name is the Valeyard. The characters must break him out and help change history so everything is restored.

INDEX

(The) 1980s 8

A
Acidic Plants 79
Adventure Seeds 10
Darkness at the Edge of Time 11
Everything, Or Nearest Offer 10
Vault of the Daleks 10
Alphan Resistance Member 128
Amnesia Discs 25
(The) Androgums 64
(The) Andromedans 148
Android 76
Appendix: The Sixth Doctor and the Time War 153
Arak and Etta 46-47
(The) Archivists 104
Areta 46
Attack of the Cybermen **26**
Continuity 28
Further Adventures 36
Running the Adventure 28
Synopsis 26
Technology 36
Telos and Beyond 33
Timey-What Now? 35
Tomorrow, when the War Began 35
Why Totter's Lane? 34

B
Balazar 116
(The) Bandrils 76
Bates and Stratton 32-33
(Ruth) Baxter 138
Bendalypse 79
Black Light Generator 118
(The) Borad 73
Bostock 91
Broken Tooth 117
(Perpugilliam 'Peri') Brown 15
Bruchner 137
(Melanie) Bush 15

C
(The) Calm before the Storm 10
Campaign Seed 105
Action Scenes 108
Adventures 106
(The) Enemies of Time 105
Notable Characters 106
Problems 108
Things to Do 108
Chapter Four: The Trial of a Time Lord 94
Chapter One: And Not a Moment Too Soon 5
Chapter Three: The Sixth Doctor's Adventures 19
Chapter Two: The Sixth Doctor and Companions 13
Chessene 65
(The) Chief Officer 45
Circular logic will only make you dizzy, Doctor 8
(The) Conscience Transference Machine 130
Crozier 126-127
(The) Cryons 28-29
Cyber Controller 30
CyberLeader 31
(Black) Cybermen 31
(The) Cybermen 29-30

D
Dalek 86
(Glass) Dalek 86
Dastari 65
Davros 85
Demeter Seeds 142
Deep Healing Ray 24
Dibber 115
(The) DJ 88
Doland 137
Dorf the Lukoser 128
Drathro 113

E
(Professor) Edgeworth/Azmael 24
Edwardes 141
Excellent? 30

F
Flast 29
Frax 127-128
Free Tribes Member 117

G
GA Process 67
(New) Gadget Trait: Huge (Minor Bad) 68
(The) Gastropods 22
Gazak 77
(Sabalom) Glitz 114
(The) Governor 44
Grenville/Hallett 141
Griffiths 32
Grigory 89
Guardolier 77

H
Holo Generator 67-68
How To Use This Book 4
Humker and Tramdrall 116-117

I
Interface Layer 67
(The) Inquisitor 100
Introduction 4

J
(The) Jacondans 21-22
Janet 140
(Mr) Jobel 87
Jondar 46
(The) Justice Station 97, 98
(Using the) Justice Station 97
Justice Station Guard 101-102

K
(Matrona) Kani 127
(Madame) Kara 88
Kartz-Reimer Module 68
Katryca 115
(The) Keeper of the Matrix 101
(Lord) Kiv 125-126
(Mr) Kimber 140
Kontron Crystals 78
Kontron Crystal Gadgets 78
Deflection Ray 79
Timebreak 78
Time Visor 79
(The) Krontep 125

L
(The) L1 Service Robot 114
(Commander Hugo) Lang 23
Laser Lance 142
(Professor Sarah) Lasky 136
Lilt 90
Luke 52
(Gustave) Lytton 31

M
Magnetron 151
Maldak 45
Mark 7 Costidillion Life Preserver 151
(The) Mark of the Rani **48**
Continuity 50
Further Adventures 56
(The) Luddites 51
(The) Parasites 54
Running the Adventure 50
Synopsis 48
(The) Master 56, 57
(The) Master's Pocket Watch 53
(The) Matrix 148
Building A World In The Matrix 149
Ending the Conflict 149
Entering the Matrix 149
War in the Matrix 149
(The) Mentors 43
Merdeen 116
Mindwarp **120**
Continuity 123
Further Adventures 131
Running the Adventure 123
Synopsis 120
Technology 130
Miners 52
(The) Mogarians 141
Morlox 77
Mustakozene-80 80
Mutant 91
Mykros 75
(The) Mysterious Planet **109**
Continuity 111

Further Adventures 118-119
Rosencrantz and Guildenstern are Armed 115
Running the Adventure 111
Seeing the Worlds 115
Synopsis 109
Technology 118
When Exactly Does The World End? This Time? 112
Where's L2? 113

O
Orcini 90

P
Payne 33
(Mr) Popplewick 148

Q
Quillam 45

R
(The) Raak 129
(The) Rani 53-55
(The) Rani in History 56
(The) Rani's TARDIS 54
(Lord) Ravensworth 51-52
(The) Renegades 95
(Maylin) Renis 75
"Rest is for the weary, sleep is for the dead. I feel like a hungry man eager for the feast!" 6
Revelation of the Daleks **82**
Continuity 84
Further Adventures 93
Running the Adventure 85
Synopsis 82
Technology 92
Tranquil Repose Residents 87
Who are the Grand Order of Oberon? 91
'Rock and Roll' Cannon 92
(Security Officer) Rudge 137-138
Russell 32
Russell's Other Boss 32

S
Sezon 76
Shockeye 65-66
Sil 44, 126
(The) Sixth Doctor 14
Sonic Lance 36
Sontaran Battle Cruiser 68
(The) Station Guards 117
(Natasha) Stengos 89
(George) Stephenson 51
(Marshal) Stike 66
Suspension Technology 92

T
TA Process 67
Takis 89
(The Sixth Doctor's) TARDIS 16
(Why does the) TARDIS revert to looking like a Police Box? 17
Tasambeker 87
Tekker 75-76
Terror of the Vervoids **132**
Continuity 135
Further Adventures 142
Running the Adventure 136
Synopsis 132
Technology 142
(The) Theft 96
Thoros Alphan Slave 129
Time Acceleration Beam 77
(The) Time Bubble 131
Timelash **69**
(The) Borad's (Many) Evil Plans 72-73
But What Is The Timelash Actually For? 78
Continuity 72
Further Adventures 80
Mustakozene-80 Exposure Table 81
Mutation Table 81
Running the Adventure 72
Synopsis 69
Technology 77
(The) Timelash 77
(New) Time Lord Tricks 18
Close Respiratory Passages 18
Completely Impossible Escape 18
Mental Cage 18
Trance 18
Time Lords, Symbiotic Nuclei and the Rassilon Imprimatur 18
Time Scanner 53
Tissue Revitaliser 24
(New) Traits 17
All Too Much 118
Battle Call 125
Clone 74
Dark Echo 105
Dead TARDIS 17
Failed Cyber Conversion 31
Have I Been Here Before? 17
Hostile Action Displacement System 98
Justice Machine 98
Mail In Knight 92
Matrix Interface 99
No Imprimatur 17
Positive Outlook 17
Real World Interface 98
Sensor Preset Controls 99
SIR Officer 24
Slime Trail 23
Station Guard 118
Symbiotic Nuclei 17
TARDIS Sensors 99
Temporal Amnesia 131
Time Lord Mentor 17
Time Scoop 100
Tractor Beam 100
Travel Capsules/Extraction TARDISes 150
(Commodore) Travers 138
(The) Trial of a Time Lord **95**
Introduction 95
(The) Valeyard and the Justice Station 95
Tuza 129
(The) Twin Dilemma **20**
Continuity 21
Further Adventures 25
Running the Adventure 21
(The) Special Incident Room 23
Synopsis 20
Technology 24
(The) Two Doctors **58**
Continuity 62
Further Adventures 68
Running the Adventure 62
Synopsis 58
Technology 67
Third Zone Governments 63
Vehicles 68
Who are Kartz and Reimer? 63

U
The Ultimate Foe **143**
Further Adventures 151
Running the Adventure 146
Synopsis 143
(The) Underground Project 112

V
(Does the) Valeyard have a TARDIS? 147
(Does the) Valeyard know about the Time War? 146
(Does the) Valeyard show them the Time War? 96
(The Many Origins of the) Valeyard 102
(Playing the) Valeyard 102
(The) Valeyard 96, 103
Varl 66
Varosian Guard Buggy 47
Vastial 36
Vena 74
Vengeance on Varos **37**
Continuity 39
Further Adventures 47
(The) Galatron Mining Corporation (GMC) and the Age of the Time-Space Ships 42
Running the Adventure 39
Synopsis 37
Torture as Television 41
(The) Cell Mutator 41
(The) Human Cell Disintegration Bombardment 41
Varos 40
History of Varos 40
(The) Punishment Dome 40
(The) Vervoids 139
Vionesium 142
Vogel 88

W
(HG) Wells 73

Y
(King) Yrcanos 124